ROUTLEDGE LIBRARY EDITIONS: FINANCIAL MARKETS

Volume 15

CAPITAL CITY

CAPITAL CITY

London as a Financial Centre

HAMISH MCRAE AND FRANCES CAIRNCROSS

Routledge
Taylor & Francis Group

LONDON AND NEW YORK

Originally published in 1973 by Methuen
New and fully revised edition published 1984

This edition first published in 2018
by Routledge
2 Park Square, Milton Park, Abingdon, Oxon OX14 4RN

and by Routledge
711 Third Avenue, New York, NY 10017

Routledge is an imprint of the Taylor & Francis Group, an informa business

British Library Cataloguing in Publication Data
A catalogue record for this book is available from the British Library

ISBN: 978-1-138-56537-1 (Set)
ISBN: 978-0-203-70248-2 (Set) (ebk)
ISBN: 978-1-138-56932-4 (Volume 15) (hbk)
ISBN: 978-1-138-56934-8 (Volume 15) (pbk)
ISBN: 978-0-203-70429-5 (Volume 15) (ebk)

Publisher's Note
The publisher has gone to great lengths to ensure the quality of this reprint but
points out that some imperfections in the original copies may be apparent.

Disclaimer
The publisher has made every effort to trace copyright holders and would welcome
correspondence from those they have been unable to trace.

Capital City

LONDON AS A FINANCIAL CENTRE

Hamish McRae
and
Frances Cairncross

METHUEN

A METHUEN PAPERBACK

First edition published 1973
First paperback (revised) edition published 1974
New and fully revised edition published 1984
This (revised) paperback edition published 1985
by Methuen London Ltd
11 New Fetter Lane, London EC4P 4EE
Copyright © 1973, 1974, 1984 and 1985
by Hamish McRae and Frances Cairncross

Reproduced, printed and bound in Great Britain by
Hazell Watson & Viney Limited,
Member of the BPCC Group,
Aylesbury, Bucks

British Library Cataloguing in Publication Data

McRae, Hamish
    Capital city: London as a financial centre. —
    [Rev.]
    1. Financial institutions — England — London
    I. Title   II. Cairncross, Frances
    332.1'09421'2   HG186.G7

    ISBN 0-413-57900-x

Contents

Acknowledgements

The authors and publishers would like to thank the following for
permission to reproduce extracts from the books listed below:
Dent and Sons Ltd and Little, Brown and Company
for *Collected Verse from 1929 On* by Ogden Nash;
The Institute of Bankers for *A Day in the Life of a Banker*.

Introduction

When we wrote the first edition of *Capital City*, in the years between 1969 and 1973, the chapters fell quite naturally under headings such as 'Branch banking' or 'Money market banking'. The functions which these headings described were, by and large, carried out by separate institutions: so under 'Branch banking' we could comfortably dispose of the clearing banks and under 'Money market banking' of the merchant banks.

When we began to rewrite the book for this edition, it soon became apparent that these neat divisions no longer worked. It was not just that in the intervening decade institutions which we had regarded as beyond the City's pale (or relatively unimportant to its business) had grown large enough to justify a section of their own. This had indeed happened to the building societies and to the pension funds. More remarkable, the functions carried out by different types of institution had blurred and overlapped to such an extent that it was extremely difficult to confine them to broadly the same chapter headings as we had done in the 1971 edition.

But confine them we did. People outside the City still tend to think of it in terms of insurance companies, clearing banks, unit trust groups – even if these increasingly offer rival versions of the same services. And, interestingly, we noticed as we progressed that although the functions carried out by the various City institutions had altered, the nameplates on the doors had changed less.

This is more true in the City than in industry. BP still pumps oil and British Leyland makes cars. But other companies have gone to the wall, and been succeeded by a whole new generation of firms, mainly in the electronics, communications and leisure industries – companies such as Racal, Saatchi and

Saatchi, Habitat. In the City, too, the 1970s saw the rise and dramatic collapse of a generation of firms – but the companies which rose and fell were mainly the same ones: the property investors and fringe banks which crashed so spectacularly in 1973. With their demise, there have been few other newcomers. The names of the City firms round a discount houses's lunch table in 1984 would all have been familiar to a guest eating there fifteen years earlier.

The principal companies in the City in the early 1980s are still by and large the ones which dominated it in the late 1960s. But the balance of activities within many of these firms has changed dramatically. For example, far and away the most important task of the clearing banks in the late 1960s was sterling retail banking – mainly through their myriad little branches. By the early 1980s, more than half their deposits and loans were in foreign currencies, and branches had a dwindling importance.

This change in the functions of City firms is reflected in the balance of activities carried out in the City as a whole. Thus in the late 1960s, insurance was the most important source of invisible earnings, accounting for more than the rest of the City put together. By 1982 it had been overtaken by banking, and whilst the earnings of commodity trading, general merchanting and the Baltic Exchange had grown at least as fast as inflation, the invisible earnings of the Stock Exchange were less in real terms than they had been a decade before.

When we wrote the first edition, we were preoccupied by the changes which were beginning to take place in the structure of banking. As it has turned out, the 1970s were a boom period for banking throughout the world. The British banks, rather late in the day, restructured themselves and benefited from this boom. As we were finishing this edition, it became increasingly clear that the major changes facing the City in the next decade – and indeed, facing the world's financial community – would be in securities trading. If international trade in securities takes over, in the late 1980s, from international banking as the main growth area in the world's financial markets, then it will be essential for the City to have built up companies capable of competing with the giant securities houses of the United States and Japan. Just as London's success in the 1970s depended largely on the way the clearing banks transformed themselves into international banks, so in the 1980s it will depend on whether Stock Exchange firms and merchant banks adapt themselves successfully to a new international role.

Within the City, some kinds of firms have become relatively less important – the discount houses, for instance. Others (such as the money brokers, two of which are now larger than any merchant bank) have grown. But the main group which has become more prominent consists of the various institutional investors – the pension funds, life funds, investment trusts and unit trusts. With their growth has come a more widespread concern about the way the City handles its relations with the private investor.

Private individuals put their money into the City in three main ways. First, they may have insurance policies. After the collapse of Vehicle and General in 1971, the policing of insurance companies was tightened up with new legislation in 1973 and put more firmly in the hands of the Department of Trade. Second, they may have bank accounts. With the collapse of the fringe banks in 1973–4, the number of shady banks was thinned out, and the Banking Act of 1979 gave the Bank of England specific powers and responsibility for the regulation of banking. Third, the individual may have money invested in securities, either directly or through contractual savings. Here there is still, as of 1984, very little legislation to define the responsibilities of either the securities trader or the contractual savings institutions.

This may change in the course of the late 1980s. Since the Wilson Committee on Financial Institutions reported in May 1980, there has been growing recognition of the need for a clearer definition of the responsibilities of pensions funds. And a report on investor protection by Professor Gower early in 1984 argued that the self-regulation of the securities market, as then organised, offered the investor less protection than the more formal arrangements of some other financial centres. In the case of insurance companies and banks (and indeed Lloyd's) it has taken financial collapse and scandal to force the City to accept supervision from outside. It would be depressing if it took scandal and collapse to push through the changes needed in the pensions funds and in investor protection. The government has plans to put the control of the City into a legal framework but not until the 1985/6 session.

The City's resistance to control imposed from the outside is increased by its sense of community. The City is a village – or indeed several villages. Almost all the firms and markets described in this book are clustered within a few hundred yards of each other, some down small lanes and alleyways, others in tower blocks along the bigger streets radiating out from the Bank of England. Most of the top people in the City – or at least within the central community of the money markets, banks and stock market – know and usually like each other. They probably bump into each other at various committees, see each other from time to time over lunch, and greet each other when they pass in the street. Meetings are easy in a place where most offices are no more than ten minutes' walk – not taxi ride – apart. Lunch is the epitome of the City's seductive blend of work and social life. It is the occasion on which cautious hints are dropped, delicate information traded and lucrative acquaintances sealed.

It is principally over lunch that financial journalists catch sight of what is happening in the City. One of the pleasures of writing this book has been the sense of being entertained and informed at the same time. One of the least-known qualities of City people is their generosity: their willingness to explain what they are doing well and what they are doing badly. As seen from a newspaper office, the City is much more open and anxious to communicate than most British industrial companies.

This edition of *Capital City* has benefited from this quality even more than the first version. The original book was the product of long hours of discussion and interviews with a great many people in the City who patiently explained mechanisms whose workings were, to them, self-evident. For that we remain grateful. This book has built on that foundation, but it has been constructed more out of the day-to-day flow of information through the *Guardian* City Office and with a great deal of help from the *Guardian's* financial staff. Three of them have read drafts of some chapters and saved us from howlers: Peter

Rodgers, David Simpson and Margareta Pagano. A number of people in the City have also read specific chapters. They include John Atkin, Ian Morrison, Robin Packshaw, Richard Sleight, Stuart Valentine and Brian Williamson, and staff of the Bank of England. The errors which remain are, of course, our own.

Our publishers have been even more patient this time than they were last time: our experience amply bears out the publishers' nostrum that no one misses deadlines on books as regularly as journalists. Ann Mansbridge has been a model of patience. The book has been typed and retyped by Kate Nash and the index compiled by Anne Coles.

Writing a book takes longer than one could believe possible. Rewriting takes longer still. This version of *Capital City* was begun just before our second daughter was born. It was finished just before she went to primary school. So it is to our children, without whom *Capital City* would have been rewritten much sooner, that we dedicate this new edition.

H.M.D McR
F.A.C

London, 1984

ONE

How it all happened

The world's financial centre

On almost any measure you care to take, the City of London is
the world's leading international financial centre. More
international insurance passes through London than anywhere
else. There are more foreign banks in London than in any other
city. More international security business is done in London
than any other centre. If anything, in the 1960s and 1970s
London's dominance increased. The City established itself as
the centre first of the new eurodollar market; and then of
banking's greatest growth area, international medium-term
lending.

To try to explain why the City's institutions work as well as
they do – and to point out where they are failing – is the main
purpose of this book. For part of the explanation one must
naturally look at the way the various City institutions and
markets operate today. But another part of the answer lies in
the City's past: in how, over some three centuries, it evolved
first as a centre for international trade and then for
international finance.

The common explanation for the City's current international
success is that it is an inheritance of the nineteenth century, of
the years when sterling was the centre of the world money
system, and when Britain was the world's major colonial power
and first industrial nation. The City itself used to believe this.
Before the 1967 devaluation of sterling it was widely argued
that the prosperity of the City depended on world confidence in
the pound. The truth was the reverse: it was the very controls
used to prop up sterling that encouraged London banks to
nurture the eurodollar market and thus lay the base for the
City's post-war revival.

I

In fact the direction which the City's development was to take was discernible long before sterling was a world currency or Britain built up her Victorian empire. As for the industrial revolution, the City was involved only at one remove; indeed, it took place almost independently of the City. The prime influences on the early City were none of these. They were rather the peculiar economic and geographical position of London itself, and the enormous volume of government borrowing in the eighteenth century to pay for Britain's foreign wars. In the twentieth century the City has seen a return to the conditions of the eighteenth, in the sense that it has once again had to live on its financial skills.

The impact of London's commerce

The most remarkable thing about London in 1700 was its size. It was already the largest city in the world, with a population of some 600,000 and growing fast. This alone had far-reaching economic effects. Londoners had to buy their food from the rest of the country, thus putting cash into the hands of the farming population and allowing them to build up savings. It also meant that London developed as a market centre. Today Smithfield is still the largest wholesale meat market in the world. But how was it that well over half a million people found their living in London? London was not and never has been important primarily as an industrial centre. The answer lies in the international orientation of the City, and its trade: for an estimated quarter of the capital's working population depended for their livelihood directly on port work.

The port of London dominated the country's foreign trade. At the beginning of the eighteenth century some 80 per cent of England's imports and 70 per cent of her exports passed through London. London's traders needed ancillary financial services – and at the same time generated the capital which financed them.

They required commodity auctions to market their goods, ship auctions to buy and sell vessels. From the quayside and coffee-house auctions of the eighteenth century were to evolve the commodity futures markets and the Baltic Exchange of today. They needed to insure their ships and cargoes. English merchants had been able to insure their ships since Tudor days but there was no formal mechanism for introducing clients to underwriters. By the early eighteenth century a specialized profession of insurance brokers was emerging which collected the signatures of rich merchants prepared to underwrite marine insurance policies. By the middle of the century the brokers were meeting in Edward Lloyd's coffee house; by the end Lloyd's had its own premises and was operating very much as it does now.

Above all, these traders needed to finance their activities – and here is the origin of London's money market. The instrument used to finance both domestic and international trade, the bill of exchange, had been employed by Italian bankers centuries before.* The important development in the City in the eighteenth century was the system of discounting these bills – or exchanging them for cash at a discount – which greatly increased their attraction as a means of providing credit. To start with it was domestic bill finance that grew most quickly. But it in turn provided the mechanism which in the years following the Napoleonic Wars was to make the City the main centre for financing world trade: the international bill on London.

Bill finance developed largely as a result of Britain's peculiar eighteenth-century banking legislation. In 1708 the Bank of England had been granted a monopoly in joint-stock banking, which meant that other banks could only be partnerships. The number of partners in any bank was limited to six. This restriction made branch banking on any scale out of the question and in practice split English banks into two groups – a host of 'country banks' in the provinces, and a smaller number of 'private banks' mainly in London. Traces of both survive today: Barclays was formed out of a group of country banks, while Coutts and C. Hoare are directly descended from the London private banks.

The small size of the country banks precluded their granting large-scale loans, for they did not have the deposit base to carry them. But they could make funds available to traders and industrialists by discounting their bills of exchange, for these

*It is still in common use today, as explained in chapter 3, pp.57-8.

3

bills could, if necessary, be rediscounted – or exchanged for cash again – in London. Through the same mechanism country banks in surplus areas could employ their spare funds. Thus rich farmers and wealthy Londoners lent their cash to provide the emerging industrial areas with working capital. After 1800 there grew up a specialist group of 'bill brokers', who put the holders of bills of exchange in touch with people with sufficient cash to discount them. To start with they merely received a commission for this service. But by the mid-1820s some had developed into discount houses, carrying bill portfolios themselves and borrowing short-term funds from the London banks. In the late 1820s the Bank of England was resigning itself to the role of lender of last resort to these discount houses, and the money market structure that exists today was, in its essentials, complete.

By discounting bills of exchange the banks provided industry with working capital. They did not supply long-term funds on any substantial scale. Yet these funds were available. To see who borrowed them one has to look at the second feature that shaped the City in the eighteenth century – the continual calls from the government for money with which to fight Britain's foreign wars.

The effects of government debt

The sheer weight of the government's borrowing needs ensured that its debt dominated the capital market. By 1721, public debt already stood at over £50 million. From then until 1739 it declined slightly as the country enjoyed the last long period of peace of the century. Between that year and 1815 the country was at war for two out of every three years. By 1816 the debt had risen to £709 million. As Professor Morgan pointed out in a scholarly history of the Stock Exchange, 'The debt, in relation to the national income and to the total value of property, must have been as great as that left by either the First or the Second World War.'*

*E. Victor Morgan and W. A. Thomas, *The Stock Exchange* (London, Elek Books, 1962), p.43.

It was the government's need for funds that had led in 1694 to the foundation of the Bank of England, a chartered company, set up by a group of wealthy London merchants and financiers to lend money to the government. It was the country's first joint-stock bank and, thanks to the Act of 1708, the only one for over a century.

The Bank of England went on to become the government's banker. Before the government found its feet in the stock market, the Bank's major business was lending to the government. Later it handled the issue of government stock and subscriptions for Treasury bills. Loans to the government were paid in the form of Bank of England notes which were convertible into cash on demand (except for a period during the Napoleonic Wars) and soon comprised the bulk of London's note circulation.

However, the Bank's main preoccupation throughout the eighteenth century was making profits for its own shareholders. Besides its government business, the Bank of England acted as private banker to some of the larger London trading companies and merchants. True, in the second half of the eighteenth century, the Governors of the Bank first began to appreciate how much influence the Bank's policy could have on the economy. For a while, it began to act in effect as lender of last resort, running down its holdings of cash at times when money was tight. However, when the Bank's notes were temporarily not convertible during the Napoleonic Wars, the Bank found it could relinquish the responsibility for monetary policy which it had reluctantly assumed. It did not take it up again until the 1820s.

As the Stock Exchange developed in the eighteenth century, it was dominated by government debt. Even at the end of the Napoleonic Wars, it still dealt in very little else.

Government issues in the eighteenth century were floated by contractors, syndicates of merchants who drew up lists of would-be subscribers. The contractors would then bid competitively for the loan, for which the successful contractor would be liable even if some of the subscribers on his list defaulted. From this primitive form of underwriting developed the technique used in the earlier part of the nineteenth century

5

for foreign loans. Some contractors for government loans such as Sir Francis Baring were merchants who turned later to raising funds for foreign governments.

By 1800 stock-broking had emerged as a specialized profession, the distinction between broker and jobber was recognized, and most present-day dealing techniques were already in use. The Exchange had been formally constituted and had acquired managers and trustees, the Official List and regular settling days. In 1802 it moved to permanent premises on its present site by Chapel Court.

Nineteenth-century international dominance

At the end of the eighteenth century it was still Amsterdam and not London which was the world's main financial centre. But London had already developed a number of sophisticated financial institutions – Lloyd's, the Stock Exchange and a money market through which savings and the demand for funds across the country were matched up. Substantial sums could be channelled into government debt. And thanks to the rapid growth of foreign trade passing through the port, London's international orientation had been firmly established.

In the nineteenth century the City was to become more than a purveyor of financial services. It acquired an international money market which attracted short-term funds from all over the world and invested them in finance for trade; and it developed a long-term capital market on which a large part of the funds for the industrialization of the rest of the world were raised. By the eve of the First World War the City had become the focus of the world's international financial system. Sterling, the currency in which both short- and long-term lending was denominated, was deemed as good as gold. And the Bank of England found itself the guardian of a truly international money system, the gold standard.

This was as much a result of the peculiar pattern of British trade and overseas investment as of the City's financial expertise. As Britain emerged as a major international trading power, the City's money market learnt to finance first Britain's own overseas trade, and then a growing volume of trade between third countries, which frequently never touched British shores. Britain's initial industrial leadership meant that the City's capital market found a demand for long-term funds in countries wanting to finance imports of British industrial products and to build up their own export sectors.

The international money market which emerged in the City during the nineteenth century revolved round three institutions: the merchant banks, the discount houses and the Bank of England. The merchant banks' role in providing trade finance grew out of their own early trading activities. The instrument they developed, the 'bill on London', was merely an adaptation of the inland bill of exchange used by the country banks in the previous century. To make the bill of an overseas merchant, whose credit standing would not be known in the City, discountable on the London money market, a London merchant bank would put its signature on it, thus 'accepting' (i.e. guaranteeing) it. Once accepted by a merchant bank, a bill of exchange would qualify for the 'finest' rate of discount (or lowest interest charge) at a London discount house.

In 1832, Nathan Rothschild could already claim* that drafts on London were widely used to finance trade that never touched the UK and add, 'this country in general is the Bank for the whole world ... all transactions in India, in China, in Germany, in Russia, and in the whole world, are all guided here and settled through this country'. The discount houses, descendants of the earlier firms of bill brokers, continued well into the nineteenth century to discount inland bills passed to them by the country banks. But by the middle of the century the volume of inland bills was declining and the discount houses were becoming more dependent on overseas bills. To start with, the discount houses' funds were provided by British lenders. But since London had the only money market where massive sums of

*Before the 1832 Committee of Secrecy on the Bank of England Charter (Minutes, Question 4799), quoted by Wilfred King, *History of the London Discount Market* (London, Routledge and Sons, 1936), p.264.

money could be profitably invested for very short periods, by the middle of the century it was attracting funds from all over the world.

The Bank of England's prime role in this international money market was as lender of last resort. From the late 1820s onwards it stood behind the discount houses prepared *in extremis* to re-discount the houses' better-quality bills. Because the Bank was prepared to do this the houses were able to finance their massive bill portfolios with money that could be withdrawn virtually at a moment's notice.

The Bank of England was initially prepared to rediscount the houses' best-quality bills (the ones on which default was least likely) because it was profitable. Slowly and painfully the Bank learnt that it could, through its function as lender of last resort, control the stability of the money market. It did so only after the City and the entire banking system had been shaken by a number of serious crises. The one which has seared itself most deeply in the City's memory occurred in 1866 when Overend, Gurney and Co., the largest discount house, failed with liabilities of £18 million. When the firm first got into difficulties, it appealed for help to the Bank of England. It was rejected, partly because of an old quarrel with the Bank, and partly because the Bank did not consider the bills in its portfolio to be of sufficiently high quality. When the house crashed, the Bank had to pay out £4 million in one day to try to prevent the panic from bringing down other City houses in its wake.

In the international long-term capital market, the two key institutions were the merchant banks and the Stock Exchange. The merchant banks had been set up mainly by foreign immigrants during and after the Napoleonic Wars. In the long-term capital market they issued the great majority of foreign loans. The earliest merchant bankers had already gained experience of floating large loans by raising funds for the British government, especially during the Napoleonic Wars when the size of the National Debt had bounded up. With the end of the wars, houses like Barings and Rothschilds were also raising funds for foreign governments. The English houses which should have been best placed to become successful merchant bankers failed almost to a man. The house of Boyd,

8

Benfield and Co., which was with Barings one of the biggest underwriters of government loans in the Napoleonic Wars, disappeared apparently without trace, while a high proportion of the immigrant bankers survived. Of the fifteen accepting houses, the City's top merchant banks, all but one (Robert Fleming) are directly descended from banks formed by immigrants – and the original Robert Fleming was a Scot from Dundee.

The traditional explanation for the success of these foreigners in merchant banking and the British lack of interest is that the foreigners had a ready made network of overseas contacts. Certainly this was true in the case of Hambros or Rothschilds, or indeed the later arrival Morgan Grenfell, all of whom had brother banks in other capitals. But what of Brown Shipley, founded by the son of an expatriate Belfast merchant and a Delaware Quaker, or Marcus Samuel, set up by the son of a Dutch Jew, or S.G. Warburg, started by a Jewish refugee from Hitler's Germany? Or indeed why did the British merchants fail to take advantage of their perfectly adequate foreign contacts? It cannot be the complete answer. Perhaps simply being outsiders in the City makes people run faster. If so, the next generation of City financiers could include an East African Asian.

The volume of overseas loans organized by these merchant banks was enormous. During the 100 years between the end of the Napoleonic Wars and the beginning of the First World War there was a growing stream of foreign issues, some on the London Stock Exchange, some issued directly by the merchant banks to other British banks and investors. In the early 1820s, a number of South American loans were floated, many of them disastrous, and in the late 1830s a succession of US state bonds, several of which also defaulted. Yet despite these early setbacks the trickle of foreign issues swelled to a flood. Between 1880 and 1914 well over £2,000 million was invested abroad; in the 1913 peak more than half of all British savings flowed overseas.

Borrowers continued periodically to default – with repercussions in Britain. After the Honduras loan of 1879, floated to build a railway to carry ships from the Atlantic to the Pacific Ocean, a parliamentary committee was set up to look at

9

foreign loans. In an important declaration it rejected the idea that the Stock Exchange Committee should be responsible for the quality of securities dealt on the market.

Just as the Overend, Gurney crisis helped to push the Bank of England towards taking ultimate responsibility for good order in the money market, so it was the need to ensure stability in the capital market that nudged the Bank towards accepting responsibility for good order in the City as a whole.

When the London market was threatened with the most serious collapse of the century, a collapse which in the words of the then Chancellor of the Exchequer would have made the failure of Overend, Gurney and Co. appear 'but a trifle', it was the Bank of England which had to organize the rescue. The Baring crisis of 1890 followed a boom in lending to Argentina. Barings, which had made the mistake of heavily committing its own money in South American stocks, was squeezed by rapidly tightening credit at home. With large blocks of temporarily unsaleable loans on its hands, it was unable to meet its immediate liabilities. A crash was avoided, but only by an unprecedented display of co-operation among the City's banks, which the Bank of England bullied into setting up a guarantee fund for Barings of over £17,500,000.

Did the City neglect British industry?

What possessed British investors to lend their savings to governments and industries 4,000 or more miles away, rather than invest it at home? The most convincing explanation is that the demand was overseas. The third quarter of the nineteenth century, when the main upsurge in foreign investment began, saw a vacuum in the stock market. UK government securities, which in 1860 still amounted to more than all the other securities quoted on the Exchange put together, shrank to only 5 per cent of the value of all quoted securities by the outbreak of the First World War. Moreover, the yield on government stocks never seems to have been very attractive compared with even the most impeccably secure foreign loans. But the real puzzle is why British industry did not compete more effectively for savings on the Exchange. The first barrier between industry

10

and the Stock Exchange was erected in 1720, with the fiasco of the South Sea Bubble, when the so-called Bubble Act was passed, outlawing joint-stock companies set up without parliamentary permission. This was rarely granted: until the Act was repealed in 1825, the only way for companies to obtain the safeguard of limited liability and the power to raise capital by public issue was by the lengthy and expensive process of Act of Parliament.

The Act probably helped to create a gulf between the young Stock Exchange and industry. By the time industry did need to raise money through public flotation the Stock Exchange was better geared to channel money abroad or into government debt. One industry that probably suffered was insurance: fire and, even more, life business both needed the framework of a company. But even without the Act, the early stages of the industrial revolution would have been financed mainly from family savings rather than on the Stock Exchange. Thanks in part to flourishing home and overseas trade, wealth was quite widely distributed and the scale of industry did not call for massive investment. The experience of the railways, which raised enormous funds in the 1840s, showed that when capital was needed at home, the City could mobilize it. It mobilized it with little help from those monarchs of the foreign loans market, the merchant banks. As Disraeli said of the railway boom:

> What is remarkable in this vast movement is, that the great leaders of the financial world took no part in it. The mighty loanmongers, on whose fiat the fate of kings and empires sometimes depended, seemed like men who, witnessing some eccentricity of nature, watch it with mixed feelings of curiosity and alarm.*

It was well into the nineteenth century before company law reached a stage which made floating a new joint-stock company both easy and advantageous. The public showed a clear preference for shares in enterprises with limited liability; yet it

*Benjamin Disraeli, *Endymion* (1880), Volume III, chapter 10, pp.97–98.

was not until two Acts had been passed in 1855 and 1862 that it became possible for companies to obtain limited liability simply by registering, rather than by going through Parliament.

Towards the end of the century an increasing number of firms, mostly in heavy industry or brewing, did come to the London Stock Exchange. They still faced powerful deterrents. Floating a company was extremely expensive. In 1909, the minimum cost was put at £2,000, and it could easily be ten times that amount. The big merchant banks were not, on the whole, interested in domestic industrial issues. With foreign issues generally so much larger than domestic ones, it did not pay them, and besides, all their experience and training had been in the foreign loan market.

Doubtless a substantial reason for British industry's failure to make greater use of the London Stock Exchange was that it did not want to. Either it did not need the capital or it preferred to remain private and finance expansion from retained profits. Even in the years shortly before the First World War only about a tenth of real investment in Britain was financed by new issues on the London Stock Exchange. Yet the fact remains that even if Britain's industry was not eager to raise capital on the Stock Exchange, the merchant banks and the Exchange itself gave industrialists little encouragement. If for the large firm floating an issue was expensive, for a small company raising public capital cheaply or quickly was virtually impossible. As long as the foreign loan market boomed, it paid the City to concentrate on this and leave industry to find its funds elsewhere.

In other countries, the obvious alternative would have been the commercial banks. In Britain the clearing banks might have become industrial banks, with shareholdings in industry, as did the German banks; or they might have offered long-term loans, like the American banks. In the event they did neither. They concentrated on attracting deposits and perfecting their system of short-term lending. By the end of the century they had become cautious and conservative, more interested in building up their size and their branch networks than in finding new industrial outlets for their deposits.

This hardening of the arteries is surprising in view of the

clearing banks' early aggression. It was not until 1826 that the Bank of England's monopoly of joint-stock banking was breached and not until 1833 that joint-stock banks (today, clearing banks) were allowed everywhere in England and Wales. Unlike the country banks the joint-stock banks were not allowed to issue their own banknotes. This had been the country banks' main source of profits. The joint-stock banks had to look elsewhere – and made their money by attracting the largest possible deposits and re-lending them at the best possible rate. To snatch deposits from the country banks and the London private banks they bid up rates on deposit accounts and even offered interest on some current accounts. Soon they realised that the best way to collect deposits from the largely unbanked middle classes was to create extensive branch networks across the country. As the century progressed and it became clear that the joint-stock banks had won their battle with the older banks, their interest in building up massive branch networks became predominant. One after another, joint-stock banks merged with each other or swallowed up country banks and private banks until by the 1920s the country's banking system was dominated by seven giant clearing banks, Barclays, Lloyds, Midland, Westminster, National Provincial, District and Martins.

The deposits for which the joint-stock banks competed so fiercely were re-lent not long-term but short – by discounting bills of exchange, or on overdraft. By the end of the century the banks had developed a highly efficient short-term lending system. Why were they reluctant to lend long-term to industry? They could, after all, have earned more on their deposits by doing so. It may be that the experience of frequent banking crises had given the banks a passion for liquidity. But the more important reason was probably that most firms wanted only trading capital. Those that wanted investment funds on a large scale could usually find them from their profits.

Thus with both the Stock Exchange and the clearing banks the story seems to have been the same. Neither, in the nineteenth century, appears to have set out to interest industry in their services as providers of long-term finance. Moreover industry, by and large, did not want their help, for it was

13

reaping the reward of leading the industrial revolution: its profits were generally substantial enough to pay for such investment as it wanted. Those enterprises which needed greater amounts of capital – the railways, brewers, steel firms – appear to have been able to raise what they wanted on the Stock Exchange. That British industry was not modernising its plants like its foreign rivals in the later nineteenth century was no fault of the City's. But the gulf that widened between industry and the Stock Exchange and clearing banks by the eve of the First World War has taken a long time to close again.

The twentieth century: decline and recovery

Thanks to decades of foreign lending Britain entered the First World War with overseas investments of some £4,000 million, giving her an annual income of over £180 million. It is now apparent how far the country had come to rely on this income; how it helped to conceal the extent to which British industry had fallen behind its competitors in Germany and the United States; and how the massive rundown of these investments to pay for munitions during the war could therefore leave the country more gravely impoverished than contemporaries could appreciate.

The First World War had a traumatic effect on the City. The German banks closed their branches; the London sugar market, largely run by Germans, was deserted overnight. Lloyd's suddenly found itself making a good profit as the main market for insurance against air-raid damage. The London money market was utterly disrupted. When war was declared some £350 million of bills of exchange, most bearing the name of an accepting house or clearing bank, were outstanding in London and only swift action by the government prevented a wave of bankruptcies. The London discount market by October 1914 was doing 5 per cent of its pre-war business, and rigid controls on issues of foreign securities dealt a hard blow to the Stock Exchange.

To some extent, however, the decline in overseas business was replaced by new UK issues, particularly of government debt. Thus the volume of Treasury bills outstanding shot up

14

from some £15 million at the beginning of the war to over £1,000 million by the end, while the general public became accustomed to holding securities, as they were encouraged to lend to the country by buying War Loan. The now notorious issue of 5 per cent War Loan in 1917 produced the largest block of securities ever created. Converted into 3½ per cent stock between the wars, it has still not been redeemed. Inevitably this rise in government debt increased the authorities' control of the monetary and banking system.

But the most profound impact of the First World War on the City came from its indirect effects on the British economy and specifically on the balance of payments. The massive income from investments abroad on which the country had depended to pay for its trade deficit disappeared. The trade deficit remained. The government struggled to restore sterling's nineteenth-century role and to rebuild Britain's investment income. But it failed to grasp how far sterling's international supremacy had been the result of Britain's special pre-war position as the world's largest trading nation and biggest exporter of capital. Instead it subscribed to the popular view that sterling's strength depended on international confidence, which in turn was reinforced by the pound's free convertibility into gold.

So attempts to rebuild the prestige of the City after the war were based on attempts to return to the pre-war gold standard. Ironically, the partial return to the gold standard in 1925 left the country with an overvalued exchange rate and plunged the British economy deeper into post-war recession. Efforts to revive foreign lending had to be financed with short-term funds, which in turn could only be attracted from abroad by keeping interest rates high. This then added to British industry's post-war difficulties and helped to convince industrialists that their interests and those of the City were diametrically opposed – a conviction which they have still not altogether relinquished.

It was the domestic economy, not the international, which provided the main source of City activity after the war. As soon as wartime restrictions on the Stock Exchange were lifted, a flood of companies came to the market for quotation. In the

15

1920s a great many of the firms which later formed the backbone of British industry were first quoted – Imperial Chemical Industries, Beechams, English Electric, Morris, Ford, Bowater. But the 1920s were essentially a period of consolidation for City institutions, rather than innovation. At the end of the war the clearing banks' amalgamation movement had its last spurt, inspired by the belief that, in the post-war reconstruction, large industrial companies would need correspondingly large banks to lend to them. The movement was finally checked by the Colwyn Committee's report in 1918. A parallel movement was reaching its culmination among the insurance companies. Since the beginning of the century, fire insurance companies had been gradually buying up accident and proprietary life companies, and the giant composites which dominate the market today were taking shape.

Such innovation as did take place in the City in the inter-war era was frequently inspired by the authorities. Thus the Bank of England initiated the creation of United Dominions Trust, touching off the growth of hire-purchase companies, and of Municipal and General Securities (today known simply as M & G), the first of a plethora of unit trusts. The established institutions tended to regard the new arrivals jealously: thus the clearing banks refused to help the finance houses by allowing them access to their clearing facilities.

The clearing banks did however co-operate in setting up the Industrial and Commercial Finance Corporation following the Macmillan Committee on Finance and Industry's report in 1931. The committee found a gap in financial services for medium-sized companies: companies that were too small to go public but too large to continue using family funds to finance expansion found it difficult to obtain additional long-term capital. It was to help fill this 'Macmillan gap' that ICFC was founded.

It was the worldwide depression in the 1930s which finally put paid to the City's efforts to recapture its international position of the previous century. Foreign lending virtually died out. The discount market, once the centre of international bill business, had already found itself driven to relying mainly on commercial and Treasury bills for business. When between

16

1929 and 1933, the number of commercial bills halved, several discount houses failed. Those that survived found interest rates ruinously low as a result of the government's 'cheap money' policy, intended to revive economic activity. To avoid extinction (and encouraged by the Bank), the discount houses made a series of defensive agreements with the clearing banks and among themselves. Thus the clearing banks agreed to buy their Treasury bills always through a discount house; and the discount houses avoided competing for Treasury bills, bidding for them jointly and then sharing them out by agreement, an arrangement which survived until 1971.

Britain recovered relatively quickly from the depression, and by the time the Second World War broke out, new British industries such as motor manufacture, electrical products and cinemas had once again restored City activity. But many of the defensive attitudes built up in the lean years of the late 1920s and early 1930s survived. Some have still to disappear.

The impact of the Second World War on the City was similar to that of the First, but far less devastating. This time it was the Italian and the Japanese banks that closed their branches. The government continued its cheap money policy – and persevered with it until 1951. Again, the volume of public debt rose swiftly. Exchange controls were maintained far longer than after the previous war. Sterling did not become fully convertible for overseas residents until 1958, and it was still not freely convertible for UK residents when Britain joined the Common Market.

For City banks the establishment of sterling convertibility in 1958 was arguably the most important event of this century, for it heralded the rise of the London eurodollar market. The steady flow of US dollars to Europe had replenished the reserves of the European central banks and was starting to find its way into private hands. Interest rates in the US were held down by a US banking control, Regulation Q. European banks, particularly those in the City, were able to bid higher rates for these funds. Thus British banks, baulked in the use of sterling for financing third country trade by the curbs imposed on sterling in the squeeze of 1957, switched to these dollars. US capital controls, in particular Interest Equalisation Tax, in effect closed New York to foreign borrowers. These borrowers, who included the growing numbers of US overseas subsidiaries, turned to London and other European centres. Merchant banks in Britain started arranging longer-term bond issues for them. At last London again had a currency in which to operate worldwide. Throughout the 1960s and 1970s it continued to develop this market, the most remarkable expansion being in the eurocurrency syndicated loan market, the international market in medium-term lending. It was only in the early 1980s, when people began to worry about the weight of commercial bank debt to the less developed countries, that this growth came to an end.

The phenomenal growth of the eurodollar has brought to the City a new era of international prestige. It has also had a considerable impact on the City's traditional institutions, giving a new lease of life to the merchant banks and providing the key attraction for the host of foreign banks in London. Merchant and foreign banks effectively destroyed the cosily demarcated world which the clearing banks and other established financial institutions had created for themselves. The clearing banks in particular had suffered from the ceilings on their lending which had repeatedly been imposed on them in the 1950s and 1960s. These had had the effect of discouraging competition among the clearers, while exposing them to competition from other institutions outside the controls.

Meanwhile domestic industry increased its demands on the City. The first effects were felt by the merchant banks – often provincial or West End issuing houses, rather than the old established names. Throughout the 1950s, they brought a stream of private companies to the market. Then, as industry went through the 1960s consumer boom, the merchant banks presided over a succession of takeovers and mergers. Before the middle 1950s, this had been handled by accountants, but the merchant banks spotted the opportunity to develop it and by the end of the decade had a virtual monopoly.

The 1970s saw a shift in the balance of power between the merchant banks and clearing banks. In the early 1970s, a whole generation of new merchant banks suddenly appeared – the so-called 'fringe banks'. Many of these new banks relied for their funds on short-term deposits bought on the money markets, which they lent long-term to property companies. In 1973–4, property values crashed. One fringe bank – London and County Securities – collapsed. Others found they could no longer raise funds from the market, and the City was threatened with a banking crash of the same gravity as the Overend, Gurney crisis or the Baring scare. The Bank of England intervened and supervised the winding down of many of the fringe banks, merged others into larger and more stable enterprises and encouraged (or bullied) the clearing banks into recycling funds from the money markets to provide others with cash. This recycling operation became known as the 'lifeboat', and was still carrying a passenger more than ten years later.

Most of the established merchant banks did not get into serious trouble, but the experience cast a long shadow over British banking. Even the best and most successful of the merchant banks found their growth curbed, while the clearing banks expanded rapidly into the areas from which they had been excluded by the restrictions of the 1950s and 1960s.

If the principal new feature in the City in the 1960s was the growth of international banking, the main new development in the 1970s was the growth of the financial investment institutions, designed to capture the funds of the personal saver and package them into investments of various sorts. Thanks to the rise of these institutional investors, investment became a professional activity, and the ownership of British securities switched from being mainly in the hands of individuals at the beginning of the decade to being mainly in the hands of institutions (on behalf of individuals, of course) by the end.

The growth of these savings media resulted in a dramatic concentration of financial power. By the start of the 1980s, Britain had a larger proportion of stocks and shares owned by financial institutions, as opposed to private individuals, than any other nation. It was alarm at this rapidly increasing concentration of financial power, often apparently unaccountable, that led the Callaghan government to set up the Wilson Committee in 1977, chaired by the former Prime Minister, Sir Harold (now Lord) Wilson. The Committee's

19

report was too divided to bring about any substantial changes, but the fact that investment is now overwhelmingly a professional activity has forced important developments in London's securities market.

The 1970s also saw another revolution, in financial information. While it was left to the national newspapers and a few specialist magazines to provide private individuals with their main source of information and comment, the professional dealers increasingly switched to computer systems, which gave them instantaneous information about prices and interest rates as well as instantaneous news. This made the City's financial markets sharper and faster. It also meant that London could gradually become the hub of a world-wide network of financial dealing centres. London had long been the main centre for foreign currency transactions. In the 1970s, it also became the main dealing centre for bank deposits, for international loans and for many international securities. But the changes in technology also made it easier for London's dealing skills to be challenged from abroad.

As the world of finance has become – very rapidly – more professional and more international, parts of the City have adapted quickly and easily. Other parts have found it extremely difficult. It is to one such part, the clearing banks, that we now turn.

TWO

Personal banking

The clearing banks and the building societies

When most people think of the clearing banks, they think first of the bank branch on the corner of the High Street. The clearing banks, indeed, still tend to present themselves as being first and foremost in the business of personal banking. 'Our roots are our branches,' said a famous National Westminster advertisement. Most of the people who staff the clearing banks, and many of those who run them, have spent much of their working lives in personal banking.

Through the 1960s and 1970s personal banking played a smaller and smaller role in the clearing banks' business. Individual customers do still account for a large proportion of the banks' deposits, though the proportion is falling, eroded by fierce competition from the building societies. But personal customers account for a small part of bank lending and have gradually become less important as a source of profits.

As the next chapter explains, the clearing banks today make most of their money by borrowing large sums of cash from companies or from the money markets, and by lending even larger sums to big borrowers – international companies, public utilities and even nation states. It is this 'wholesale' banking, particularly abroad, which has been by far the fastest growing part of the clearing banks' business, responsible for more and more of their profits.

The fact that the clearing banks have their roots so firmly in branch banking, though, helps to explain some of the difficulties that they have faced in transforming themselves into first-rank international banks. To be cruel, they are still largely run by former bank clerks whose experience and training has left them quite unsuited to the testing world of corporate banking. They have found it hard to get used both to the complexity of the service demanded by the big international companies and to the ferocity of the competition for their business.

The banks have also been inhibited by the clearing bank tradition of providing a public service, lavishly staffed and inadequately costed. This attitude has in turn been buttressed by the controls which successive governments applied to the clearing banks until the early 1970s, controls which encouraged the natural tendency of any small group of large institutions to avoid the unpleasantness of competition.

Most of the top men in the clearing banks today have spent two-thirds of their careers working under a regime of government controls which actively suppressed competition between the banks. Until 1971, the banks were encouraged to operate a cartel agreement which fixed the rates they paid for deposits and the minimum rates they charged for overdrafts. As both these rates were tied to Bank rate, they were effectively dictated by the Bank of England. The Bank also set limits on the total amount of money each bank could lend.

Not surprisingly, the banks attracted criticism from their customers, from official bodies like the Prices and Incomes Board and the Monopolies Commission, and from Labour politicians. There was the threat of nationalisation. The banks began to lose business rapidly to competitors, with the building societies taking an increasing share of their personal deposits and the US banks making inroads on their lending to companies.

In the early 1970s two major changes occurred in the institutional framework in which the banks operated. In 1970, the clearing banks were obliged to publish their true profits: until then, no bank knew for sure how much its rivals were making. Secondly, in 1971, the Bank of England changed the system of credit control, ending the banks' cartel and the ceilings on bank lending.

These changes did lead to more competition and to greater cost-consciousness among the banks. But even now, the clearing banks are self-evidently not providing their customers with all the services they want. In personal banking, the building societies now account for a larger share of deposits than the clearing banks, and collect them through a much smaller number of branches. And in corporate banking, the foreign banks are now firmly established.

It is with personal banking that this chapter is concerned. The most obvious measure of the clearing banks' failure is the simple fact that as many people in Britain now bank with a building society as with a clearing bank. Thirty years ago the banks had a virtual monopoly of the provision of personal banking services. But they lost that in the 1960s and 1970s to the building societies. Customer preference enabled the building societies, as a group,* to become a bigger banking sector than the clearing banks themselves. In private, senior bankers will admit that the battle is lost.

This needs some explanation, for customer surveys suggest that people are reasonably satisfied with the clearing banks' service. It is quite true that the clearing banks provide their personal customers with a convenient, secure and relatively sophisticated banking system. They have a gigantic network of branches. Current account customers can walk into any one of their bank's offices in England and Wales and, with a cheque card to guarantee it, cash a cheque for up to £50 on demand. It is virtually impossible for most customers to find themselves more than a dozen miles from a branch. This means that they can travel anywhere with just a cheque book – unlike Americans, who have to carry several credit cards, or Continentals, who frequently still need to carry banknotes. If the banks are shut, they can draw cash from automatic dispensers in every major town. They have 'free' financial advice from their manager. And they can still borrow on overdraft, an extraordinarily simple and flexible form of personal bank borrowing.

But if the public professes itself satisfied, that has not always shown up in the way it behaves. For a start, a smaller proportion of Britons have a bank account than in most industrial countries. Many of those who do have a bank

*Individually the building societies are smaller: the Halifax, the largest, is roughly a quarter of the size of Barclays in assets.

account now use it mainly as a way of transferring money rather than as a place to keep their savings. That role has increasingly been taken over by the building societies.

Unlike the clearing banks, which are broadly similar to their counterparts in other countries, the building societies are unique. They exist solely to channel personal savings into house purchase. They have no shareholders, do not make profits, and are very limited in the ways in which they can hold spare cash. In spite of their narrow role, they overtook the banks' share of personal savings in 1970. As of 1982, they took 46 per cent of the total pool, compared with 38 per cent for all the banks. (National Savings took 15 per cent.)*

When it comes to explaining why the banks have lost ground to the building societies, the banks and the societies, hardly surprisingly, differ. The banks point to the tax advantages which the building societies enjoy. The building societies, however, point to their costs and their hours. They have found their labour relations – so far – easier than those of the banks and have therefore been able to remain open for longer hours, including Saturday mornings (although the banks have experimented in a limited way with Saturday morning opening). And as the societies do not provide that expensive banking service, a money transfer mechanism, they have saved themselves much of the costs of running one. Instead they cash their cheques through the banks.

In short, the building societies are a much more primitive form of life than the banks. Because their function is simpler, their costs are inevitably lower. But the building societies can also point to the clearing banks' failure to control those costs which might be brought down. The 9 English clearing and Scottish banks have a total of 12,800 branches: the 227 building societies, a mere 6,500. They would argue, too, that the clearing banks still suffer from a stuffy image. Finally, they would point to the fact that the banks have been tardy in developing

*If you look at the proportion of the flow of new savings going to the banks and the societies during the 1970s, the figure is even more dramatic: in 1976 over 80 per cent of the growth of the savings pool went to the societies and only 2 per cent to the banks.

schemes to pay interest on their customers' current accounts, something that could greatly increase the attraction of the banks vis-à-vis the societies.

The clearing banks' defence looks stronger when one realises how little success their other competitors have had in breaking into the market for personal banking. The decade of the 1970s saw several attempts to do so: the promotion of National Girobank (set up by the Labour government in 1968 as National Giro), the expansion of the Trustee Savings Banks, and the rise and fall of a number of experiments in 'money shops'. All these aimed particularly at the unbanked lower end of the personal market. But none enjoyed the tax advantages of the building societies, and none has had anything like the building societies' success.

Perhaps the core of the clearing banks' failure in keeping their share of the personal banking market is that they have not adapted to the way in which inflation has altered their customers' saving habits. Inflation, and the high nominal interest rates maintained through the 1970s, helped to make the banks vastly profitable: indeed in 1979, Britain's largest bank (Barclays) first made bigger profits than her largest industrial company (ICI). The profits are made by borrowing for nothing (from current account customers) and lending dear. But customers are not stupid. Inflation has made them more aware of the need to earn interest on spare cash. The building societies offer not just a rate of interest on their deposits but a better rate of interest than most customers could earn from a bank deposit account. This has been partly the result of tax advantages which will be changed in 1985 (see p.32).

In the early 1980s the war hotted up. Banks went into home loans. Building societies started to offer a form of current account. Given the momentum of the building societies, the banks may well continue to lose their market share. Some bankers believe this may be a blessing in disguise, for they see the future of their banks as transforming themselves from personal banks to corporate ones. A few, particularly in Barclays, are wondering whether this is really the right direction and feel that the banks should indeed return to their roots on the grounds that personal business, run properly, may

25

prove a lot more profitable than its more glamorous, and competitive, sibling.

The 'big four' and their banking rivals

The names of the so-called 'big four' are household words: Barclays, National Westminster, Midland and Lloyds. Between them the banks handle four out of five personal bank accounts in the country and an even higher proportion of company accounts. Though they dominate the market for basic banking services, the big four do not have a complete monopoly even within the banking sector. There are a number of other banks which offer a comparable range of services: the Scottish banks, smaller deposit banks and to a lesser extent some of the merchant banks and foreign banks with UK branches.

All the big four live in very similar head offices: solid temples designed to convey an impression of unshakeable stability, with marble pillars supporting a grandiose dome. They still have different characters. By big-four standards, Barclays is the most aggressive. The Barclays group has long been the largest, though its lead has diminished. In Britain it was in 1984 behind National Westminster in UK sterling deposits, though worldwide it is larger by a fair margin. But the main difference between Barclays and the other banks is not size but character. It was formed out of a string of private family-owned banks and is still guided by the offspring of those families. The other clearing banks, by contrast, were forged from a series of mergers between joint-stock or commercial banks in the second half of the last century.

Barclays has an innovative zeal about it that the other banks have been forced to imitate. It pioneered bank credit cards in this country with Barclaycard and had a decentralised system of management control long before the other banks. Its main overseas banking arm is Barclays Bank International, with which it legally merged in 1984. Thus the Barclays' name appears above 5,000 branches, more than that of any other bank in the world, while Barclays was the first UK bank with a substantial branch network in the United States.

This international network of branches has been of

enormous benefit. While others have been able to compete with it quickly and effectively in some areas of international business, building up a chain of branches around the world is a slow and expensive business.

National Westminster has a less clear-cut personality. It was formed in 1968 from a merger between National Provincial and the Westminster Bank. It has been somewhat accident-prone. The most notorious episode in its short life was in 1974 when in the wake of the fringe banking crisis it was struck by rumours of serious financial trouble. It took the unprecedented step of issuing a statement that it was perfectly sound, and denying rumours that it had received financial support from the Bank of England. Since then its two most striking contributions to the City scene have been the building of its tallest office block, the 600-foot NatWest Tower, which houses the bank's international division, and the provision of the first clearing banker ever to become Governor of the Bank of England, Robin Leigh-Pemberton.

Midland, next in size of the big four, has tended to strike out in the opposite direction from Barclays and then been forced to turn back. It led the anti-Barclaycard lobby, and then when Barclaycard started (after five years) to make money, Midland joined a rival credit card scheme, Access, with the other banks. Midland too has begun to move away from a centralised management system towards the Barclays model and it plans to slim its over-large branch network. But it is in international business that Midland has most clearly headed off in the wrong direction. Unlike Barclays, Midland rejected the policy of setting up direct overseas branches and instead forged links with a powerful group of European banks. Together, these banks set up a number of joint ventures, including a subsidiary bank in New York. But that policy of cooperation does not seem to have worked.

In the early 1980s Midland changed course and set about building up a necessarily small chain of international branches and bought a controlling interest in Crocker Bank in San Francisco, an unsuccessful and costly move. It has also taken steps to improve its top management. Occasionally, too, Barclays has taken the wrong course and Midland the right one.

27

Midland pioneered personal loans, cheque cards, had a wholly owned hire purchase subsidiary and a stake in a merchant bank long before the others.

Lloyds, the smallest of the big four, originally concentrated on wealthy personal customers rather than industrial clients. It benefits from its relatively compact branch network centred in the rich south of England. Like Barclays, it has always had international aspirations. It owns Lloyds Bank International, an operation on the lines of Barclays Bank International. LBI and Lloyds plan to merge in 1986. Unlike other banks, Lloyds though has failed to make much impact in merchant banking.

The big four have interests in most of the other British deposit banks. But in general they regard these interests simply as trade investments. Lloyds owns 21 per cent of the Edinburgh-based Royal Bank of Scotland Group, by far the largest of the banks competing with the big four. This group owns the largest bank in Scotland, Royal Bank of Scotland, as well as Williams and Glyn's in England, formed out of Glyn Mills, Williams Deacon's and National Bank in 1970. In terms of deposits, the Royal Bank Group is little more than a third the size of Lloyds, and it has to run harder to grow as fast as the other banks: in Scotland it cannot grow by increasing market share as it already has 40 per cent of the business, while in England it does not really have enough branches.

The Royal Bank management, recognising these pressures, was prepared to lose its independence and in 1981 accepted a bid from the Standard Chartered group. This was topped by a counter bid from Hongkong and Shanghai Banking Corporation, much to the irritation of the Bank of England, which had supported Standard Chartered's bid. In the end both bids were blocked by the Monopolies Commission and the group remained independent. In 1983 it announced plans to merge Royal Bank and Williams and Glyn's under the Royal banner, and at the beginning of 1985, bought the merchant banking side of the Charterhouse Group.

Also north of the border is Clydesdale Bank, owned by Midland, and the venerable Bank of Scotland, founded in 1695, now best known for its North Sea involvement. Barclays has a 35 per cent interest in it, but would probably be prevented from taking full control after the Monopolies Commission decision on Royal Bank.

Elsewhere on the Celtic fringes, two of the clearing banks have Northern Irish subsidiaries; National Westminster owns Ulster Bank and Midland owns Northern Bank. Both are based in Belfast but have branches in Eire. There is really only one other regional bank, Yorkshire Bank, which is owned by four clearers.

Stronger competition comes from the Co-op Bank and, at the bottom end of the market, from 'money shops'. The Co-op Bank is owned by the Co-operative Wholesale Society and offers a conventional banking service, in some cases at a cheaper scale of charges than the others. 'Money shops' are owned by large financial groups, including the Royal Bank of Canada and the US Citibank. They offer a simple banking service aimed mainly at working-class customers, granting fairly high-cost loans for purchase of consumer durables.

Finally, a couple of curiosities: in the antique Coutts, formed in 1692, they will give their lunch guests a quill pen to sign their names in the visitors' book. The bank has a select air about it (it has only twelve branches, including one in Eton) which belies its ownership by the proletarian National Westminster. More precious still is C. Hoare and Co., a private bank which still had its statements written in longhand up to the early 1960s.

The really serious competition for the personal deposits which are the lifeblood of the clearing banks does not come from other regular commercial banks at all. Four other main kinds of institution – Trustee Savings Banks, National Savings Bank, National Girobank and the building societies – offer personal banking services, and all have one substantial advantage over the banks: their more convenient hours. The Trustee Savings Banks have 1,650 branches scattered across the country with 8·5 million active accounts, and the National Savings Bank, formerly the Post Office Savings Bank, operates from 22,000 post offices.

Until the late 1970s the TSBs were limited by their legal status, which amongst other things prevented them from offering overdrafts. The TSBs may well become more serious competition now they have become members of the clearing

29

house and offer a virtually identical personal banking service to the clearing banks. There are plans for them to acquire a Stock Exchange quotation. But their potential is limited by the size of their branch network and by a dearth of first-rate management.

The National Savings Bank, as it is at present organised, is even less of a threat, as it cannot offer a proper banking service. The challenge to the banks would come were the National Savings Bank to merge with National Girobank. The banks would then have a single public-sector competitor offering direct competition in most of the services they provide.

National Girobank offers both personal and business customers a money transfer service which it claims is more convenient and appreciably cheaper than that of the banks. It has made considerable headway in attracting payroll business from big companies and nationalised industries and has 1·4 million personal accounts. But complicated forms, badly briefed counter staff and poor advertising initially undermined Giro and made it less of a threat to the banks than they feared. It is now a modest success, making reasonable profits and gradually gaining market share. But it is not the banks' prime worry. That place is reserved for the building societies.

The advance of the building societies

Far and away the most successful of the clearing banks' competitors for personal deposits have been the building societies. In 1962, the building societies' share of the country's pool of deposits was 21 per cent, while the clearing banks had 43 per cent. By 1982 the proportions had dramatically changed. The building societies had 46 per cent of the pool; the clearing banks only 38 per cent.

The building societies are curious institutions. There are approximately 227 of them and they vary enormously in size. The Halifax, biggest of all with one-fifth of the entire movement's deposits, has 600 branches and 10,000 staff. The ten biggest societies (see table) control a total of 73 per cent of the movement's deposits. At the other end of the scale there are many with just one office and a handful of staff.

In spite of the way the building societies dominate personal

The Top Ten Building Societies: 1983

Society	Total Assets £ Million	Branches	No of Savers
Halifax	16,782,035	634	6,762,086
Abbey National	14,312,454	676	9,482,560
Nationwide	7,347,839	517	3,163,648
Leeds Permanent	5,075,350	464	2,079,192
Woolwich	4,853,300	380	2,359,000
National & Provincial	3,917,645	337	1,336,585
Anglia	3,642,000	379	1,797,072
Alliance	2,791,142	203	845,634
Bradford & Bingley	2,686,857	230	1,298,623
Leicester	2,476,899	243	1,042,362

Source: *Building Societies Association.*

finance in Britain, the City does not really see the building societies as part of itself, and the societies see themselves as standing a bit apart from the City. One reason perhaps is the character of the movement. The very word 'movement', which the societies always use when talking about themselves, is significant. It catches their rather non-conformist, crusading flavour.

Rather like the clearing banks a hundred years ago, the societies have their roots outside London. They developed in their present form in the mid-nineteenth century, taking in small savings and making loans for house purchase. From the 1950s onwards, with the enormous expansion of home ownership, the building societies enjoyed a period of phenomenal expansion. As they grow, the societies, like the clearing banks before them, will find themselves increasingly seen as part of the country's financial system, and subject to monetary control by the Bank of England.

There are perhaps three main reasons for the way the building societies have overtaken the clearing banks. First of all, they are performing an operation of extreme simplicity and can, as a result, work on very low margins. Almost all their depositors are private individuals. (There are also a large number of partnerships – solicitors and accountants, for instance – which place funds with them.) They make only one kind of loan, for house purchase, secured against the value of the house. Even the way in which they can invest spare cash is highly restricted by law. Most of it has to go into government securities; they are not allowed to hold equities. Unlike the clearing banks, they do not offer personal customers advice, overdrafts or other financial services. And they do not lend money to their corporate customers.

A second advantage they have over the clearing banks has been that very few of their staff belong to trade unions. This has allowed them to have more flexible opening hours. Many building societies are open on Saturdays – even on Saturday afternoons – a day when the clearing banks, by agreement with their staff, are generally forced to shut.*

Until the 1984 budget, the building societies enjoyed a third advantage: the way the tax system operated. The interest which the building societies pay on their deposits was taxed at the average rate of tax paid by all their depositors (the so-called 'composite rate'). Because many building society depositors are retired people who pay little or no tax, this allowed the building societies to offer the average taxpayer a better return on savings than the clearing banks could manage. In the 1984 budget banks and building societies were put on broadly the same basis, with the change becoming effective in 1985.

But tax was probably not the most important reason for the building societies' success. The essential fact is that the building societies, unlike the clearing banks, have been swept up in a growth market – house purchase – for the banks only started offering home loans in 1981. This heralded a new bout of intense competition for deposits. The interesting question will be what happens to the societies if home ownership starts to level off. Will the societies then slow down? Or will they try to find new outlets for their efficient savings collection machine? In 1984 a government White Paper set out plans for easing their legal straitjacket.

*Though some banks have reopened a few branches since 1982.

32

How the clearing banks are managed

Looking at clearing-bank management, two things immediately stand out. One is that the boards of directors of three out of the big four are largely comprised of men – rarely women – with no experience in banking (Barclays is the exception). The other is that the men who actually run the banks, the general managers, have little experience of anything else.

The gentlemen/players distinction survives. The boards of the big four are composed overwhelmingly of gentlemen who have either distinguished themselves in fields such as industry, politics, the Civil Service and the armed forces – but hardly ever in banking – or they have come from old banking families whose banks have long since been swallowed up. Taking Lloyds as an example, fourteen of the twenty-three main board members in 1984 had titles. Aside from the chairman, the six directors who did not have titles were the six who worked full-time in the group. Until quite recently, senior management could not expect a seat on the board.

The general managers, by contrast, are recruited from the ranks. They come from the same pool as the thousands of branch managers all over the country, though they have been singled out at an early stage and given a spell at head office. These men are quite able bankers: they have had to be to get to the top of a massive organisation. They have frequently been sent by their banks on management courses, and even occasionally on high-powered business courses in the US. But inevitably they are handicapped by their lack of more general experience. With a few rare exceptions, their whole career has been within the clearing banks, and within the same bank at that. Their training is slanted towards decisions on domestic banking matters, such as the creditworthiness of industrial and personal customers, rather than on management matters, such as the cost-effectiveness of a computerisation project, or on international banking.

There are three important qualifications to this. First, the chairmen of the big four are more or less full-time, and two of them are experienced bankers. Timothy Bevan of Barclays comes from an old banking family. The Bevan family bank was one of the private banks that combined to form Barclays. Those families – the Barclays, Bevans, Tukes, Trittons – still supply the bank with its chairmen and many of its executive directors. Sir Jeremy Morse of Lloyds is a career banker of a rather different kind. He began his working life as one of the bright young graduates at Glyn, Mills (recruited by his predecessor at Lloyds, Sir Eric Faulkner). He was pinched by the Bank of England and became executive director in charge of its international side. He has a reputation for extreme intelligence, a quality not widely admired by commercial bankers.

Midland is headed by Sir Donald Barron, a Scots accountant who was chairman of Rowntree Mackintosh, and NatWest by Lord Boardman, a former Tory MP who, as Tom Boardman, was chief secretary to the Treasury in the early 1970s.

The second qualification is that Barclays does not fit into the pattern of figure-head directors. It has organised a system of local head offices each with its own board. Through these boards, members of the 'special list' – composed of the cream of university graduates and scions of the old banking families that formed Barclays – can bypass the hierarchy and may ultimately become executive directors on the main board. The decentralised local boards enable Barclays, the only one of the big four to be formed from private banks, to ensure that it is run by executive directors rather than general managers. It has the added advantage of preserving respectable jobs for the private bankers' descendants.

The third qualification is the one that has become very important. The banks are increasingly being forced to employ specialists who do not fit into their caste system, and still less into the sort of salary structure that clearing banks think appropriate to people in their twenties and thirties. The instinct of the banks is either to train their own staff to do new jobs, or to hive off the new functions which call for these specialists into a separate subsidiary. This way the pay scales are not undermined. But this does not always work. The banks have had limited success in training their own people in marketing and public relations, while their original attempts to set up computer systems with their own staff were frequently unhappy.

At present the key man in the banks' domestic hierarchy remains the branch manager, the GP of the financial world. He (just occasionally she) is also one of the banks' two big staff headaches.

Look at his job. He has long had to run an office efficiently, to advise on personal financial problems, to judge credit risks and to sort out companies' balance sheets. Now he is expected to act as salesman for the bank too. Yet he has virtually no training – bar experience – for the job. Banks openly admit that they are finding it increasingly difficult to get branch-manager material, mainly because of the decline in the status of banking as a profession and of the spread of university education. Banks' rigid salary scales make it fairly difficult for them to attract graduates, and in private bankers complain bitterly about those they do get. As the banks try to increase the range of financial services they offer, so they increase the pressure on their branch managers.

The other staff problem of the banks is the marked increase in militancy since the second half of the 1960s. The banks, faced with their first ever strike by members of the National Union of Bank Employees in 1967, were forced to recognise the union alongside their home-grown 'unions', the staff associations.* NUBE has now changed its name to Banking, Insurance and Finance Union to try to broaden its membership. The staff associations have merged into a separate organisation called the Clearing Bank Union.

The clearing banks, then, have a grave management problem. This is not at all a criticism of the way the men who run the banks from day to day perform the tasks they have been set. The senior management have rarely been prepared, by experience or training, to guide a massive financial empire. As for the branch manager, his job is virtually impossible.

How personal banking works

The essentials of banking have not changed in three centuries. Banks borrow funds mainly from their thirty million or so

*Barclays, however, has recognised NUBE since before World War Two.

personal customers, lend them mainly to companies and run a money transfer system which allows their customers to make payments without using cash. In addition, banks increasingly offer a wide range of related services. For individuals they will do anything from keeping valuables safe to acting as executors; for companies, anything from managing payrolls to share registration.

But while the principles of banking have not changed, the practice has altered dramatically in the past fifteen years. Although the banks' personal customers may be unaware of the fact, they have become less important to the banks as a source of deposits and more expensive to look after.

Originally, the banks' branches were the key to their whole operation. Through them, they took in savings, and through them they made their loans. Today, the banks have an alternative source of funds in the wholesale money markets discussed in chapters 3 and 4. More and more of their loans, including almost all their expanding portfolio of foreign loans, are arranged through head office. The share of current account balances in the clearing banks' total sterling deposits has fallen from over 50 per cent in 1970 to under 30 per cent by 1982. (Barclays disclosed that in 1982 current accounts were only 23 per cent of its domestic deposits.)

While the banks' branches have become less useful to them, they have also become more expensive to maintain. Rising staff costs and property values have seen to that. So if the banks are going to go on making money out of personal banking in the future, they will probably have to change the way they do it.

Nearly three-quarters of the adults in Britain have some kind of bank account. To persuade someone to leave his or her hard-earned savings with it, a bank offers two inducements: convenience and interest. Its profit (or a great part of it) derives from the difference between the amount it pays for money and the amount at which it lends it out. There are basically two types of account: current and deposit. Most clearing-bank current accounts offer no interest, but only the convenience of being able to write a cheque and use the banks' other money transfer services.

In principle, personal and industrial customers pay for their

36

current accounts in almost exactly the same way, though the rates charged vary. For both, the banks calculate interest of between 3 and 8 per cent on their average balance and allow this against a charge of about £0·30 on each cheque. For industrial customers, the banks then translate this figure into a percentage of turnover on which they base future charges. Charges vary from nil to £0·25 per £100 of turnover, depending on the work involved, the balance maintained and on how much the bank wants the company's business.

There are no charges in deposit accounts but a personal cheque cannot be drawn on them. As money has to be paid in and withdrawn over a bank branch counter, they are less convenient. Interest is fixed at about 2 per cent under 'base rate' which in turn is fixed by the banks in relation to the cost of money market funds.

Banks – all banks – lend money in three different ways. They can grant loans, discount some kind of bill, or extend an overdraft. In Britain all three methods are used, though the overdraft is the most traditional. It does not matter whether the customer is a student wanting £100 until his grant comes through, a draper wanting £10,000 to finance a new line of summer dresses, or ICI wanting another £20 million to help pay its tax bill. All get (or in the case of the student, perhaps, do not get) an overdraft. The overdraft is a remarkably flexible instrument and has helped to make short-term borrowing in Britain cheaper and more convenient than anywhere else.

This is the way it works. A customer, either an individual or a company, is given an overdraft limit for a certain period, usually a year, and can draw up to that amount at any time. Interest is calculated daily, so that one only pays for the amount of credit actually used, at a rate fixed in relation to base rate. Rates for personal borrowing range from 3 to 5 per cent over base rate, with favoured customers (or customers borrowing for favoured projects) paying rather less. For commercial and industrial companies, the rate might be as low as 1 per cent over base rate. This bottom rate is called the 'blue chip' rate.

The overdraft is intended for short-term needs and is theoretically repayable on demand. In practice it is often used to finance long-term projects because it can be 'rolled over' from one year to another. A bank frequently requires what it calls 'security' against a loan. This is a claim against some asset of the borrower, often property, which it can sell should he default on the loan. In Ogden Nash's words:

> Most bankers dwell in marble halls,
> which they get to dwell in because they encourage
> deposits and discourage withdralls,
> and particularly because they all observe one rule
> which woe betides the banker who fails to heed it,
> which is you must never lend any money to anybody
> unless they don't need it.*

There is still a lot of truth in this. But in recent years there has been a shift in lending criteria. Instead of looking at the borrower's assets, the banks now ask about earning power. Often a bank will lend unsecured on the basis of an individual's expected future earnings, or a company's cash flow.

Attachment to the overdraft system (albeit a weakening attachment) distinguishes British domestic banking techniques from those of almost any other country. In the United States banks usually make loans for specific periods. In France, much short-term lending involves some kind of bill. Why are the English clearing banks so fond of the overdraft? It is not because it was their invention: a form of overdraft was introduced by the Royal Bank of Scotland in the 1720s. One of its greatest advantages is its simplicity. Initially there is no paperwork. There is no formal loan agreement (overdraft permissions are generally set out in a letter but may well be purely oral) nor any negotiable paper such as a bill of exchange. An overdraft, whether secured or unsecured, is fundamentally a statement of faith in the borrower's honesty and financial reliability. Compared with other systems of lending, the overdraft is remarkably convenient. American banks get into extraordinary contortions with their loans. Not only do loans become tied up with sheaves of legal documents but the actual

*©1935 by Ogden Nash. This poem originally appeared in the *New Yorker*.
38

agreement can be tortuous: until the early 1980s there was a system of compensating balances whereby the borrower had to lend back (at no interest) a certain proportion of the funds borrowed.

The overdraft allows the clearers to preserve the fiction that their loans can be recalled on demand. This, they pretend, protects their depositors – the primary duty of a bank. There are, however, two obvious flaws in this argument. Banks increasingly lend their depositors money medium-term; and in practice overdrafts are used for longer-term finance.

Since the early 1970s the fastest growing form of lending has been the term loan, where a bank lends a specific sum for a fixed period, typically two to five years. For industrial lending this is rapidly replacing the overdraft, but it is also making some inroads into personal business. In 1981 term lending to industry, then at £11·8 billion, overtook overdraft lending.

But for personal customers the simplest form of lending is through credit cards. These were an American invention, made necessary in the US by the absence of overdrafts and the limited acceptability of personal cheques. In this country they were pioneered by Barclays with Barclaycard and followed in 1972 by the other banks with Access. The interest rates on Barclaycard and Access are even higher than on a personal loan and far higher than on an overdraft.

Credit cards are also one of the three ways – apart from physically shifting cash around – by which the banks can move funds. The others are cheques, and credit or debit transfers.

The banks are the channel through which new notes and coins are distributed round the country and dirty notes removed. But the basic aim of any bank is to cut down the amount of cash that has to be carried around. The cheque, originally a written instruction to a goldsmith, is their traditional solution.

Legally, a cheque can be written on anything,* though it upsets the banks' computers if the magnetically coded cheque books provided by the banks are not used.

*Witness the court case about a cheque written on a cow. 'Was the cow crossed?' 'No, your Worship, it was an open cow.' A. P. Herbert, *Uncommon Law* (London, Methuen, 1970), pp.201–6.

39

Computers have enabled the banks to clear rapidly increasing numbers of cheques, which have to be returned to the bank on which they are drawn. Total cheque clearings through the London Clearing House rose by 98·4 per cent between 1972 and 1982 to 1,565 million a year, while the amount exchanged rose by 439 per cent to £5,771,350 million during the same period. In 1982 the banks cleared internally a further 547 million cheques, which were drawn and paid into different branches of the same bank. The London Clearing House operates the 'town clearing', a sort of wholesale high-speed clearing for very large cheques drawn on some City branches, and the 'general clearing' for banks all over the country. The cost? Despite computers, most banks reckon it at about £0·50 per cheque.

The personal cheque is widely acceptable in Britain, thanks to the cheque card which guarantees cheques of up to £50. But because cheque clearing is so expensive and cumbersome, the banks are backing two alternatives, the credit card* and the credit transfer.

The banks hope as soon as possible to use credit cards (and cash dispenser cards) through computer terminals in, say, retail shops, to allow instant and reliable money transfer. The technology exists. But for the foreseeable future, cheques will remain despite the banks' efforts to get rid of them. Even in America, where credit cards are firmly entrenched, cheque clearings are still rising almost as fast as ever.

Before credit cards replace cheques, the banks' other substitute, the credit transfer, is likely to be even better established. A credit transfer sounds more complicated than it is. Originally intended mainly for business customers, it merely means that the customer instructs the bank to add a sum to someone else's account and deduct it from his own. A debit transfer is simply the reverse – an account holder agrees to let a

---

*There are three kinds of credit card: bank cards, intended for all types of transaction, travel and entertainment (or T and E) cards, intended mainly for luxury items, hotel bills and so on, and gold cards. The best known T and E card is American Express. Gold cards are a sort of super credit card, granting extra privileges, including cheap overdrafts, and issued only to people earning more than about £20,000 a year.

40

body like the local electricity board debit him automatically when bills fall due. Standing orders are credit transfers made at regular intervals. The beauty of credit transfers is that they can be transacted entirely on computer. That is gradually happening. A company customer of National Westminster can instruct his bank to credit an employee with an account at Barclays. The NatWest computer simply feeds the instruction into the Barclays computer. No piece of paper has to be sent across the country.

Ultimately the banks want to get all types of transaction entirely onto computers: you would walk into a shop, buy something and have your account automatically debited over a phone line either to a credit card account, or direct to your current account. Pilot schemes are in operation, but meanwhile the banks have to stay afloat on a sea of paper.

Other clearing bank services

Besides banking, banks have long offered customers a number of other services. In the early 1970s, the banks developed these as 'loss leaders', a way of attracting customers and their deposits. But it gradually dawned on the banks that their loss leaders were losing more than they had intended. The banks began to cost out their services and to discover that they were highly unprofitable and not very successful in bringing in new business.

So in the second half of the 1970s, the banks did two things. They continued to offer facilities such as accountancy, legal advice and trusteeship but priced these economically so that now they appeal only to their richer customers. And they began to develop cheap packages of services, such as insurance deals and unit trust savings plans for the mass of their customers.

Company services, in general, are profitable. The banks can charge for them at an economic rate, which explains why they have been so eager to develop them. Many new services, too, use time on the banks' expensive computers which would otherwise be under-used. Thus the banks are offering to control inventories and to organise payrolls, taking over the whole business of making up wage packets. Ultimately, they would like to offer a complete computerised management information service.

Some of the more sophisticated company services offered by the big four are still organised through separate subsidiaries, though gradually the parent banks are tending to offer them direct. Some banks have also sought to provide what has previously been the province of the merchant banks – specialist financial advice. National Westminster has its own merchant bank, County, and Midland bought control of Samuel Montagu. Barclays has formed Barclays Merchant Bank, which competes directly with the accepting houses (see chapter 3). The banks have also branched out into near-banking activities such as hire purchase, factoring and leasing; and into non-banking ones, such as insurance broking. Lloyds has gone a stage further and owns a chain of estate agents. It is difficult to predict how important these specialist banking (and non-banking) services will become relative to the banks' original business. It is at the moment hard to see them being more than a sideline.

Branch banking: has it a future?

As many bankers recognise, one of the key questions facing them in the 1980s will be what to do about their branch networks. These are now extremely expensive to run, and they gather a diminishing proportion of the banks' deposits. This is essentially because company and institutional customers, who would once have put their spare money in deposit with a local branch, now increasingly place it either directly or through a bank on one of the money markets as described in the next two chapters.

The advantage of the branch network to the banks has in the past been that it is the way that the banks attract current accounts. Because the current account earns no interest, it is 'free' cash. The higher the level of interest rates, the more valuable this cheap money is to the banks. This so-called 'endowment element' has been the main reason for keeping the branch network going. Indeed the very high level of interest rates in the 1970s and early 1980s has allowed the banks to put off tackling the problem of their branches.

But the 'free' money has been costing the banks more. The

banks calculate that the true cost of acquiring current account cash is nearly 10 per cent. That does not matter so much at times when interest rates are in double figures.

High interest rates, however, make customers more aware of the alternatives to a current account. The share of current account balances in the banks' total sterling deposits has declined dramatically. The banks, moreover, have been slow to use their branches to offer banking to the mass of wage-earners. Though the banks have been pushing hard to encourage companies to pay wages through them, 42 per cent of British workers were still paid in cash in 1982. This has two consequences. Because the money comes into a family in cash, most of it stays in cash. And even where it is banked, weekly pay means a smaller average balance than a monthly salary cheque.

It is just conceivable that the clearing banks will eventually cut back their branch network to a bare skeleton. One large New York bank, Bankers Trust, decided to sell most of its personal bank branches. The big four have all been closing branches faster than they open them. But for the time being, all the clearing banks are concentrating mainly on finding ways of making their branch networks cheaper to run.

There are essentially two courses which the banks are pursuing. First, all are looking at ways of extending mechanisation. Lloyds has perhaps gone furthest along the road to robot banking, developing banking halls in which the customer is faced not by a row of tellers but a line of machines which dispense cash, take deposits or print out a statement. All the banks have been installing increasingly sophisticated cash dispensers, sometimes inside, but more often outside their banks. In 1983 they began to share each other's cash dispensers, as indeed the building societies plan to do.

The second line has been to reorganise the branch network, so that more skilled, well-qualified and expensive staff are concentrated at relatively few branches. For example, Midland has been grouping branches under one manager at a larger central branch. The smaller branches do little more than taking in cheques and dispensing cash. The office manager passes on any customer who wants specialist services, including lending,

43

to the manager of the central branch. Barclays is dividing its network into branches which specialise in corporate customers and others concentrating on personal banking.

With this branch reorganisation will also go a redefinition of the branch manager's job, possibly splitting the 'management' (i.e. the responsibility for the branch's profitability) and the 'banking' (i.e. decisions about lending) functions. Another way forward would be to have some managers concentrate entirely on company business, while others – the less good ones – just handle personal accounts. Somehow the banks have to deploy their scarce talent more efficiently: bank managers are expensive.

But there remains the nagging question: do the clearing banks really need their branches? Perhaps the most awkward fact to confront the clearing banks in the course of the 1970s was the incursion of foreign banks – particularly American banks – into the field of corporate lending. About a quarter of all the money borrowed in sterling by UK manufacturing companies is now lent by foreign banks. Yet the foreign banks have no branch networks: at most they have branches in a few large cities. They raise their money – as the next chapter describes – either direct from companies or through the money markets. If they can do it, then the clearing banks too can live without their 'endowment element'.

Most clearing bankers would probably agree that if they were starting from scratch, they would not today build up branch networks on their present scale. But the branches are there, often on extremely valuable sites. The building societies, unlike the banks, are actually opening new branches each year. It ought to be possible, with imagination, good management, technological advance and cooperative staff to make them pay.

It may be a race against time. If interest rates fall sharply in the course of the 1980s to below the cost of servicing current accounts, and the building societies continue to capture personal savings, the clearing banks may not find personal banking such an effortless source of profits as they have up to now.

44

THREE

Money market banking

Why 'money market' banking?

London's claim to be the leading world banking centre rests on a group of some 600 'money market' banks. They have all sorts of origins, ranging from the historic house of N.M. Rothschild to the Republic Bank Corporation of Dallas, or, indeed, the Moscow Narodny Bank. What they have in common is that they are all involved in money market banking, an activity which has grown since the early 1960s. This involves borrowing huge deposits from companies and financial institutions like pension funds – typically £1 million to £10 million at a time – and re-lending them in equally massive chunks, either to other companies, to countries, or on the money market. Through the money markets the banks lend any spare funds to other banks, and borrow other banks' funds when they find themselves short.

Because of their different origins, the money market banks vary widely in size. They fall into five main groups. At one end of the scale are the giants of world banking: the clearing banks themselves, and their foreign competitors, some of which (like the largest American banks) are even bigger. At the other are the merchant banks, of which even the biggest are smaller than a smallish commercial bank like Bank of Scotland. In between are the British overseas banks – a curious Imperial legacy – and a small group of consortium banks which have been set up by groups of other banks expressly to deal in the money markets.

There are two sides to money market business in London: sterling banking, where the borrowers are British local authorities and companies; and international eurocurrency banking, where the borrowers are usually foreign and overseas corporations (but sometimes British) and foreign countries. The international side is by far the larger. Both sides – and this is what has attracted so many different types of bank – were the most profitable and rapidly growing areas of banking during the 1970s.

The essential difference between all these banks and the traditional business of the clearing banks is the source of their deposits. While the clearing banks still collect their sterling funds* mainly through their branches in small amounts from millions of personal customers, the wholesale banks either take large deposits from companies and financial institutions or borrow them on the money markets described in the next chapter. They may have branch networks abroad, and even the odd branch in Britain, but these are secondary to their money market banking operations. The way they raise funds affects the way they lend. As their deposits are generally for fixed periods, the money market banks usually lend for fixed periods and not on overdraft like the clearers.

Until the late 1950s, the banks which were important were those with the largest networks of branches. Normally a branch network was the only way to attract a large volume of deposits. This remained true as long as the bulk of deposits came from personal customers, who cared more about the convenience of having a branch on their doorstep than the interest they received. But more and more, everywhere in the world, companies and financial institutions were becoming major lenders. It is their deposits that give a bank without a branch network a chance to rival a branch bank. For corporate depositors have little interest in the convenience of a branch and instead are concerned with earning the highest possible rate of interest.

In Britain, from the late 1950s on, a number of special factors allowed these wholesale banks to compete with the clearing banks for company deposits by offering better rates. One was the clearing banks' cartel on interest rates, in which the overseas and merchant banks were not included. Another was

*In foreign currency business the clearing banks are largely dependent on the money market for funds.

the demand for funds from local authorities, prepared to pay high rates for money for short periods. A third was the speedy development of new money markets, which allowed these non-branch banks to lend funds they could not immediately use, and to borrow when they were temporarily short. This meant that they could use their funds in the most efficient way and allowed them to pay the highest possible rates of interest. And finally there was the growth of the eurocurrency market, which provided them with another source of funds which they could lend to overseas customers who were not subject to the restrictions on sterling lending.

The growth of eurocurrency lending has gone hand in hand with one of banking's great inventions, the floating-rate syndicated loan. Floating rate means that the interest rate is fixed at a certain margin above the prevailing inter-bank rate, the rate on the money market that the bank itself would have to pay for its funds. It is usually changed every six months, as interest rates change. And syndicated means that the loan is split between anything up to a hundred banks, each providing a portion of the money, and each therefore taking a little of the risk that the loan might not be repaid. The bank (or handful of banks) that organises the loan is called the lead bank and will get a management fee as well as interest on whatever portion of the loan it takes itself.

The fact that the borrower, not the banks, takes the risk that interest rates might change enables the banks to lend for longer periods, up to ten years. But it also increases the danger that borrowers may be unable to repay if interest rates rise sharply. The fact that the loan is syndicated among many banks means that larger and larger loans can be made. The largest, by 1984, was the $4,000 million loan to the French government in late 1982. But the syndicated technique has encouraged banks to rely on the research of the lead banks rather than make their own assessments of creditworthiness.

The success of the syndicated loan market is evident from its growth. It only started around 1968, but in 1982 total funds lent were $84,200 million.* But success has brought headaches:

*Source: Morgan Guaranty World Financial Markets.

the worries that some Third World countries might default on their debts is the direct result of the way the syndicated loans market grew in the 1970s.

From the point of view of some banks, then, the growth of money market banking might seem a mixed blessing. At home, the clearing banks may have lost ground to foreign competitors in lending to corporate customers. But world-wide, London has seen the growth of money market banking, especially in eurocurrencies, turn it once more into an important international banking centre. In this revival, British banks, at least initially, played a small part. The lead came from foreign – mainly American – banks, which generate roughly half the invisible earnings from banking of which the City boasts.

To some extent, the American domination of international banking is inevitable. It is simply a reflection of the world-wide domination of US commerce and industry. An important part of the work of American banks in London is serving the overseas subsidiaries of their customers at home. But US domination has been helped by the fact that British wholesale banking was long split between the clearing banks and the merchant banks. To put it crudely, the clearing banks had the money and the merchant banks had the brains, but efforts to put the two together were not very successful.

The clearing banks moved into the industry's fastest growing area late in the day, when their competitors were already well entrenched. They did so initially on too small a scale, and with inadequate staff. They have suffered throughout from the fact that a man whose training fits him perfectly to run a branch in Sheffield is not necessarily equipped to decide whether to join in a $1 billion loan to Mexico, or how to help BP finance a North Sea oil field. The merchant banks, on the other hand, have suffered from the fact that they are too small to make loans off their own backs on a large enough scale to compete with foreign giants. As for the British overseas banks, they may have the necessary resources, but these tend to be tied up in the 'wrong' places – the Commonwealth and the developing world rather than the growth points of Europe and America.

Ironically, Barclays and NatWest, with a relatively small share of problem loans, may ride through the rough period in international banking in the middle 1980s more easily than Lloyds and Midland, whose exposure was greater. But if British banks avoid problems on quite the scale of their US and German counterparts, it will be, they would probably admit, largely because of good luck.

The merchant banks

The leading merchant banks have probably had more romantic nonsense talked about them than any other group of companies in the world. It should therefore be said straight away that merchant bankers are no longer the kingmakers of Europe; that even the largest houses are lightweights compared with the international deposit banks; and that they are hard pressed by increasing competition from their less glamorous competitors. Despite the fact that the banks, as a group, enjoyed outstanding profit and growth records during the 1960s, the 1970s were much more difficult. Indeed in 1983, in real terms, most of the banks were smaller than they had been ten years before.

There are two distinct sides to merchant banking. One is wholesale banking, in which the merchant banks compete with the other groups of banks described in this chapter. The other is providing industry and personal clients with financial services which do not involve the banks in lending their own money: the main ones are acceptance and issuing business, investment management and the newer moneyspinners, like advising on takeovers and mergers, the most publicised part of a group of services to companies dubbed 'corporate finance'.

Indeed takeovers and mergers were the largest single source of profits for some banks in the 1960s and 1970s. For years the banks have had, in Sir Edward Reid's famous phrase, to live on their wits rather than their deposits. Of course, many of the banks had long lent their own money on a small scale. But it was only with the development of the money markets that they could emerge as major bankers. This change has brought with it a dilemma: while being big is a positive handicap in providing some financial services, in banking it is vital to enable a reasonable spread of risks. In terms of their capital base, the merchant banks are tiny compared with the clearing

49

banks, the American banks and the British overseas banks. The difference is not only one of size. It is also one of attitudes and interests. The person adept at pushing through a contested takeover differs in training, skills and character from the person whose job is to take decisions on whether a company will be able to pay back a £30 million loan in three years' time. The first is interested primarily in making sure that the client wins; the second, in making sure that the depositors do not lose. Knowing how to raise money, long the merchant banks' special skill, is quite different from lending money wisely.

In the early 1970s, it looked as though the most important decision facing the merchant banks was whether to make a deliberate effort to grow, by borrowing from the money markets, in order to meet competition in lending to corporate customers on equal terms. In the event, the merchant banks never had the opportunity to take that decision. The reason was the fringe banking crisis – the collapse of a large number of small banks with aspirations to merchant banking. The crisis also curtailed the access of many of the older merchant banks to the money markets.

But the crisis, which we look at again in the chapter on the Bank of England, had another effect. It made it clear that the sheer diversity of the activities of the older merchant banks was part of their strength. The fringe banks which went to the wall – such as Slater Walker, London and County Securities – were all relatively new, and concentrated particularly in a small range of business, especially lending to property companies. For the remaining merchant banks, size is still a handicap: but they have come to concentrate more on the activities where it matters less.

Given the vast range of activities in which merchant banks are involved, and the fact that no two are quite alike, it is hardly surprising that there is no authoritative list of all merchant banks in the City. Perhaps some 100 institutions like to call themselves merchant bankers. Of these, the 15 most exclusive belong to the Accepting Houses Committee and are called accepting houses. A total of 55, of which 49 are based in London, belong to the less exclusive Issuing Houses Association and are called issuing houses. Some banks belong to both. To 'accept' a bill of exchange is in effect to guarantee it (see below), while 'issuing' means arranging an issue of shares or bonds on a stock exchange. But membership gives no particular rights, since non-accepting houses can accept bills, while roughly half the issues (by number, though not by value) on the London market (including the unlisted securities market) are organised by stockbrokers. Besides, accepting is only a small part of a merchant bank's business, while most issuing houses do many other things apart from new issues.

The descriptions below take the larger accepting houses roughly in order of size. The ranking is imprecise, partly because merchant banks still do not have to publish full profit and reserve figures; partly because, though two merchant banks may show similar balance-sheet totals, the spread of their activities and the way in which they are run may still be very different; and partly because taking group and bank assets gives a different ranking.

Until the end of 1983 the largest of the accepting houses, by a clear margin, was the Kleinwort Benson group. The Kleinworts were one of those immigrant families, like the Hambros and the Rothschilds, who came to Britain in the nineteenth century. In 1961 the Kleinwort bank merged with Robert Benson Lonsdale, a prominent home-grown merchant bank, the Bensons originally being Liverpool merchants. Its present form is largely the work of the late Sir Cyril Kleinwort, chairman until 1978. Kleinworts stands out from the other merchant banks because it is, in purely banking terms, much larger. In 1984 it organised the privatisation of British Telecom, the world's largest equity issue.

Next in size comes Schroders, which lives in a smoked-glass building in Cheapside. Schroders is a holding company which controls both J. Henry Schroder Wagg in London and J. Henry Schroder Banking Corporation in New York. The New York operation, now roughly the same size as the London side, was set up in the 1920s at the request of Benjamin Strong, then head of the New York Federal Reserve Bank. He was a great admirer of British merchant banks and wanted one in New York to teach Americans about acceptances and international money markets. Schroders' particular strength in the UK has long been in its client list, which includes many of the largest British industrial companies. It is liked in the City, but no longer admired. It suffered a serious drain of top talent after its chairman, Gordon (now Lord) Richardson, left to become Governor of the Bank of England in 1973. Only in 1984 did it appoint two bright, youngish Germans to run and revive it.

Samuel Montagu is one of the few accepting houses with links with a clearing bank. It is 60 per cent owned by Midland Bank, 40 per cent by the US insurance group Aetna. Samuel Montagu, however, has always been run as a quite separate operation from Midland, with the result that neither partner has benefited as much as it might from the relationship. Indeed, David Montagu, the last chairman from the bank's founding family, left because he could not work with Midland. He ended up joining arch-rival Jacob Rothschild. Samuel Montagu's particular speciality has long been foreign exchange and gold dealing. Only since the last war did it broaden into general merchant banking and its corporate finance department is still relatively small. In 1983 it started a new period of rapid expansion, increasing its Eurobond business and, the next year, buying into brokers W. Greenwell.

Morgan Grenfell has been one of the City's success stories in the 1970s. It used to be seen as sleepy and gentlemanly: 'We're not one of the largest banks, but we are one of the nicest to work for.' But it then emerged as one of the most successful banks at mergers and takeovers, while its non-Jewish background has helped to win Arab business. The Morgan name is a famous trans-Atlantic one, and for many years one-third of Morgan Grenfell's capital was owned by Morgan Guaranty, the New York bank. But the last portion of the shareholding was sold in 1982, though Morgan Grenfell still owns a part of Morgan et Cie in Paris. Most people in the City would bracket Morgan Grenfell with Warburg as the two best merchant banks.

Next come two banks which have, in different ways, found the 1970s difficult. At the beginning of the decade Hambros and Hill Samuel vied for the top of the accepting house league. Ten years later they were well down the ranking.

Hambros is a confident, energetic Victorian foundation, which became a public company in 1936 but is still controlled by the family under a system which Jocelyn Hambro, the group's chairman until 1983, dubbed 'enlightened nepotism'. His cousin, Charles, then took over as group chairman, while Jocelyn's son Rupert became chairman of the bank. Rupert's two brothers, Richard and James, are bank directors, while Charles's daughter Clare works in the corporate finance department. The best known Hambro, though, is Richard's daughter, Clementine, the tiny bridesmaid at the 1981 Royal Wedding. No doubt a place in the bank duly awaits her. . . .

Hambros needs its confidence, for it has recently had more than its fair share both of disasters and successes. Most dramatic of its disasters was the backing of shipping businesses, including that of the Norwegian shipping magnate, Hilmar Reksten. In 1982 it revealed total losses of some £70 million on shipping loans. Among its notable successes has been its support for Mark Weinberg's life assurance business,* which by 1983 had brought a total profit to the bank of well over £100 million. Hambros' success more than paid for its greatest disaster, but the bank lost both reputation and confidence.

Hill Samuel was largely built up by Lord Keith, who went on to become chairman of Rolls-Royce, the state-owned aircraft-engine manufacturer. Hill Samuel took on its present form in 1965 after a merger between the old City bank of M. Samuel and the aggressive West End issuing house, Philip Hill, which had previously swallowed up two other City banks, Higginson and Erlangers. Under Lord Keith it tried to gain size to compete with the clearing banks by seeking mergers with the property company MEPC in 1970 and Slater Walker Securities in 1973. Both attempts failed, and the bank had a pretty miserable decade, losing money in the Herstatt collapse and in its own insurance broking business. In 1980 a new thirty-nine-year-old chief executive, Christopher Castleman, took over under chairman Sir Robert Clark. Since then the profits have improved sharply and the group is more confident as a result.

Within the City, S. G. Warburg is widely admired. It has been very much the creation of the late Sir Siegmund Warburg, a German refugee who arrived in Britain in 1934 with less than

*See below, p.110.

53

£5,000 in his pocket. The bank has pioneered much of what has been new in merchant banking, from the aggressive takeover tactics which enabled it to win the celebrated Great Aluminium War of 1958–9,* to Eurobond issuing in the 1960s, and advising countries on their financial policies in the 1970s and '80s. In 1983 it further strengthened its position by buying an interest in London's largest firm of jobbers, Akroyd and Smithers.

Lazard Brothers is part of the Pearson empire, which also owns the *Financial Times*. This has not always ensured a good press in the City: the *FT* has found it difficult to criticise Lazard, but has also been deeply anxious to avoid being seen to support the bank. There are shareholding links (strengthened in 1984) with the New York investment bank, Lazard Freres, and the Paris Lazard. It has an important new issue business, a number of large industrial clients, and, since 1985, Sir John Nott, the former defence minister, as chairman.

The two great names of nineteenth-century merchant banking were Barings and Rothschild. Barings, once included in the duc de Richelieu's list of the great powers of Europe, has become something of a backwater. It is a shadow of its nineteenth-century self, seemingly happy to make a virtue of staying small. It is still controlled by the Baring family, who muster six earldoms or baronies among their number, including the Earl of Cromer, former Governor of the Bank of England. Sir John Baring is the present chairman.

At the end of the 1970s, the ruling family at N.M. Rothschild was riven by a row between cousins Jacob and Evelyn. Eventually Jacob left, and Evelyn took over the established bank. The rift inevitably damaged morale. But now N.M. Rothschild has rebuilt a highly talented group of staff, including some very bright women.

Jacob Rothschild left the family bank to run its investment trust subsidiary, RIT (Rothschild Investment Trust), which he

---

*Warburg engineered the takeover of British Aluminium by the American Reynolds and the UK Tube Investments, fighting off a rival bid from Alcan, represented by Hambros and Lazards. Ironically, when TI (as Tube Investments became) sold its interest in British Aluminium in 1982, it was because British Aluminium was losing so much money. Victory in a takeover may not spell long-term profit for the victor.

built up by buying interests in other financial institutions like the London stockbrokers Kitkat and Aitken, and the New York investment bank L.F. Rothschild, Unterberg, Tobin. (The New York Rothschild was no relation.) In November 1983, he merged RIT with Charterhouse Group, a medium-sized if rather nondescript merchant bank. For a brief period, this new enterprise was larger than any of the conventional accepting houses, and thus was the City's largest merchant bank. Then at the beginning of 1985 Mr Jacob sold the merchant banking side of the group to Royal Bank of Scotland, leaving himself with a tiny staff and some £400 million to deploy. The city, not surprisingly, is closely watching his next move.

Among the smallest accepting houses, there is Brown Shipley, which once employed Edward Heath, and Guinness Mahon, which was nearly sold in 1982 when its parent group Guinness Peat ran into financial difficulties shortly after its chairman, Lord Kissin, another central European refugee, retired. There is the tiny Rea Brothers, run by yet another European immigrant, Sir Walter Salomon. The newest member of the committee is Robert Fleming, which specialises in fund management and controls the biggest unit trust group, Save and Prosper. It is also seeking to expand its corporate finance business. It joined the committee in 1979. Until 1984 there was another member, Arbuthnot Latham, which dropped out when it was taken over by Dow Scandia, an American/Swedish bank. Foreign ownership means expulsion from the club.

For the merchant banks, the 1974–5 fringe bank crisis can now be seen as something of a watershed. Before it, new ones had sprouted almost every month. Many subsequently disappeared, including the largest, Slater Walker Securities.* Others, like Keyser Ullman, at one stage headed by Conservative politician Edward du Cann, never recovered their former status and were eventually taken over. Yet new financial groups, frequently starting in financial services with

*The unit trust business of Slater Walker survives under the name Britannia Arrow.

low entry costs like unit trusts, or commodity broking, are still springing up. A very few of these new groups will grow into the Rothschilds of tomorrow.* Others will go bust . . . or end up in the Old Bailey.

Because a whole generation of would-be merchant banks was wiped out in the fringe banking crash, the newcomers in the late 1970s and early 1980s have mainly been subsidiaries of foreign and particularly US banks. A new breed of international merchant bank has developed specifically to do business in the eurocurrency markets, such as American Express's Amex Bank.

The relatively small size of the UK merchant banks has meant that in wholesale banking they have gradually been elbowed aside by their bigger competitors. To understand why, one has to appreciate the need for size in this sort of business. The existence of the money markets made it possible for the merchant banks to compete with the branch banks by providing the merchant banks with an alternative, if expensive, source of deposits. But the money markets did not affect the size of the merchant banks' capital resources. Bankers generally hold that it is ultimately the size of their capital base that determines how much they can safely borrow and lend. Banks do not take deposits of more than a certain proportion of their capital and reserves.† So while the merchant banks were able to increase their banking business substantially, they could not hope to compete effectively with the clearing banks.

In the market of eurocurrency loans, where large loans are split among syndicates of banks the real profits are made in organising the syndicates instead of just participating in them. But because of their capital limitations, the merchant banks have only been able to take up small shares, and this

*Myth has it that Rothschilds' own prosperity had seamy origins. Nathan Rothschild is supposed to have received advance information of the British victory at Waterloo, gone to the Stock Exchange and sold stocks heavily. This precipitated rumours of a British defeat, prices slumped, and Rothschild stepped back into the market and made a killing.
†The proportion varies from country to country and depends on the type of business.

has reduced their ability to act as organisers of lead managers of the loans.

Luckily for the merchant banks, there are some areas of banking where they have hung on and which have been growing very rapidly. The best example is project finance: the provision of relatively small, hand-tailored loans for specific projects. For instance, it may be a loan for the development of a copper mine in a country which would not otherwise be creditworthy, and with repayments matched to expected copper earnings. By the late 1970s, this kind of complicated lending was growing much faster than the provision of huge 'jumbo loans', simple loans to countries, where the big banks had the unbeatable advantage of size.

In the early 1980s debtor countries like Mexico, Brazil, Argentina and Poland threatened to default on their loans. Because much of their lending was tied to individual projects, the merchant banks frequently found that it was better secured than that of their giant competitors. Biggest is not always best.

The other area of the eurocurrency markets where some of the merchant banks have been extremely successful has been in the specialised eurobond market, where they issue securities denominated in foreign currencies. This is simply a new variant of their old skill of finding other people's money, rather than lending their own.

If becoming big enough to compete in pure banking is fraught with difficulties, can the merchant banks expect their other services to go on growing? Accepting and issuing, two traditional merchant banking activities, can be extremely profitable. But the level of business fluctuates enormously – much more than banking profits.

Accepting is a way of providing a three-month loan by guaranteeing bills. The bill itself is like a post-dated cheque. Instead of paying for goods immediately, the buyer gives the seller a bill of exchange which says that he will pay (usually) in three months' time. If the seller wants the money immediately, he swaps the bill for cash, usually with a discount house, possibly with another bank. Since the discount house or bank has to wait three months for the money, it gives him a little less than the face value of the bill, the difference being the interest on what is in effect a three-month loan.

In order to make a bill more attractive to the money market, it may be taken to a bank to be guaranteed or accepted. Then if the issuer of the bill goes bankrupt, the bank will buy it back. In return for guaranteeing the bill, the bank charges a commission varying typically from 1/4 to 3/4 per cent depending on its judgement of the bill's soundness. A bill bearing a well-known bank's guarantee not only qualifies for the finest rate of discount (i.e. the lowest interest charges) in the money market, but if held by a bank, or a discount house, it can be pledged against a loan from the Bank of England (see chapter 4).

Acceptance business, which had virtually died out by the late 1950s, has tended to perk up each time that a government encourages it, for example by imposing controls on other forms of bank lending. It received a boost in the mid-1960s, until credit ceilings were extended to include acceptances, and another in the late 1970s. After 1980 there was an even more extraordinary boom in acceptances, because the monetary control system was changed to favour acceptances, and the volume consequently soared.*

Bankers admit that the system of acceptance is illogical. Why should GEC or Shell have to have a bill guaranteed by a bank it could buy up many times over for the bill to satisfy the Bank of England? The fact that acceptances are a favoured form of finance has led to ludicrous distortions. Some banks have been so eager to get into the business that they actually pay companies to be allowed to 'guarantee' their bills! Sooner or later these distortions will be unwound and while the business may have become temporarily profitable, anything based on such an artificial foundation can hardly be a secure source of income.

Issuing business, too, has fluctuated wildly in recent years, but because of changing economic conditions rather than artificial encouragement by the monetary authorities. New issues were £1,096 million in 1972, fell to £283 million in 1973, were back to £1,993 million in 1975, down to £967 million in

*See p.235 for a description of the present system of monetary control.

1979 and up to a record £5,033 million in 1983.* This is one of the two main areas in which merchant banks' corporate finance departments operate. (The other is mergers and takeovers.) A bank making an issue may be floating a private company on the Stock Exchange for the first time or raising additional capital for an established public company. In either case the banks face some competition from stockbrokers, who usually offer a cheaper service. The banks, however, have probably been increasing their share of this business. They claim to be able to offer companies better advice than the average new issue broker. It is only in small issues, for example on the unlisted securities market, where brokers dominate.

Many industrialists harbour deep suspicions about the way merchant banks price issues. If an issue is priced too low, it will be oversubscribed and the borrowing company will be raising less new money for its shareholders than it might have done. In the 1960s banks were open to the charge that they had allowed the issue to be oversubscribed so that they could pocket the interest on funds left for a few days by disappointed applicants. Now banks put the funds aside and any such profit goes to the company raising the money. But underpricing still brings back-door benefits in that juicy share offers can be doled out to favoured clients. Needless to say, all reputable banks deny that this happens. The truth is probably that the major merchant banks do try to price correctly, but in volatile markets it is difficult to do so and they may tend to underprice to play safe.

Businessmen also complain that the merchant banks overcharge for making issues. The banks deny this, claiming that issuing is not particularly profitable. But since banks rarely publish a scale of fees, customers feel that they are charged on the basis of what the market (i.e. they themselves) will bear. Typically, issue costs, including underwriting costs, range from 2 to 8 per cent of the money raised.

The banks claim that the problem with setting out a fixed scale of charges for any of their corporate finance work is that a large part of it is done free. A bank may groom a company for flotation for several years on the assumption that the fee it gets

*Source: Midland Bank and Samuel Montagu *News Issues Statistics*.

at the end will make it all worthwhile. And they argue that in practice large rights issues – where they are raising further funds for a company that is already quoted on the market – are the most profitable part of the business and are used to subsidise small new issues.

From the banks' point of view, the central problem with issuing is that the volume of business fluctuates so much. For this reason it is hard to see either issuing business (or acceptances) as reliable profit earners. The merchant banks' revival since the war has been founded on the other main aspect of their corporate finance work, takeovers and mergers. This is where the banks' biggest profits were made in the 1950s and 1960s. The fee of £250,000 that Hill Samuel received for merging GEC, AEI and English Electric was an example of the top rates at the beginning of the 1970s. By the early 1980s that would have risen to perhaps £1 million, and fees of £250,000 are quite usual for takeovers of £100 million or more. Hotly contested takeovers command the highest fees, but with a catch. The charge is for success, for few merchant banks would be able to persuade a customer to part with a substantial fee for a deal that failed to come off, still less a defence of a takeover where the defence fails and the victor has to foot the bill. Indeed a bank may get short shrift if it tries. In 1980, Lord Weinstock refused to pay the fee of some £250,000 which Schroders demanded for trying to fight off GEC's successful takeover of Averys.

In takeover business the merchant banks now have serious rivals in two of the 'big four' clearing banks. County Bank, owned by NatWest, handles a large amount of merger and takeover business, usually for relatively small companies (but sometimes large), while Barclays Merchant Bank has shown that it is fully able to compete with the established merchant banks in large-scale takeovers.

Stockbrokers also handle new issues but have been unwilling or unable to get into takeovers. This is mainly because they do not have the right people. But even if they had, a company could hardly feel happy talking about its takeover plans with a firm whose *raison d'être* is advising people on what shares to buy. This conflict of interest also exists in the merchant banks, for

60

banks act as investment advisers too. But reputable merchant banks make strenuous efforts to keep investment and corporate finance departments quite separate.

Profitable though takeovers and mergers have been, the post-war reorganisation of British industry that generated them may have drawn to a close. Merchant bankers acknowledge that companies are becoming more ready to withdraw their bids if the share price moves too high. And that means no reward for the bankers.

Of course, substantial takeovers will continue. The late 1970s saw a spate of British companies trying to buy US firms and most of these bids were handled by British merchant banks. Companies, even giant companies, that are badly run will still be prey to better, more aggressive managements. But skill at handling takeovers seems a relatively less important attribute for the merchant banks than it was during the post-war boom.

All the merchant banks offer a range of other services besides these main activities and most will have specialised in one or more of them. Thus all big merchant banks manage other people's investment portfolios, advising pension funds, unit and investment trusts (and a few rich private individuals) where to put their money. For most, this is a major, steady profit-earner. But for Robert Fleming it is its bread and butter. In 1984 it managed or advised over £11,000 million of funds.

Since the big oil price rises of the early 1970s, the merchant banks have developed a new and important version of this established skill. They advise the oil exporters on the investment of their funds, and help other developing countries, which have become heavy borrowers on the eurocurrency markets, to plan their finances.

The merchant banks noticed very quickly that there was a market for selling expert investment advice to OPEC. So Barings has advised the Saudi Arabian Monetary Authority. The Jewish merchant banks have had to specialise in non-Arab OPEC countries. Thus Schroders advises Venezuela. There is also a flourishing business in advising developing countries which borrow heavily on general economic policy as well as borrowing tactics. Warburgs, which probably has the biggest

61

business in this market and operates jointly with Lazard Freres in Paris and Lehman Brothers, Kuhn Loeb in New York, advises Turkey and Indonesia, the three banks being known as the troika. Elsewhere, Rothschild advises Singapore.

The banks have a number of sidelines. Leasing and factoring have both been growth areas, though here the clearing banks now own the largest firms. With leasing, a bank buys an aircraft, ship or piece of industrial equipment and rents it to the company that is going to use it.

While these are the main activities of merchant banks they are by no means the only ones. Among the bigger banks it is possible to find houses engaged directly or through subsidiaries in commodity dealing, property development, computer data processing, foreign exchange dealing, metal merchanting, insurance broking and underwriting, bullion market broking and dealing, life assurance and oil exploration. This range is remarkable, particularly considering the small size of a merchant bank's staff. Even Kleinworts, the biggest group, only employs 1,100 people.

In the course of the 1970s, the merchant banks as a group shrank both in size and in prominence. They no longer acted as a focus for much of the public criticism of the City which was directed at them in the late 1960s and early 1970s. Nor did they attract quite so much hostility from industrialists.

By the early 1980s, the merchant banks occupied a fairly small corner of the City. The larger merchant banks had done well enough. But some of the smaller and more second-rate banks had encountered real difficulties and either lost their independence (like Anthony Gibbs, bought by Hongkong and Shanghai Bank for a paltry £17 million) or disappeared (like Ionian Bank). In general, the merchant banks still attracted some of the brightest recruits in the City for some of the highest salaries. They still performed a number of specialised tasks extremely well. They still caught the headlines in takeovers. But beside the clearing banks and the US banks, they had become relatively unimportant. Size had won.

Since 1983 most of the larger merchant banks have been moving in a new direction, buying stockbrokers and jobbers and building up their security-dealing skills – as the securities market chapter explains. For some this will mean a renaissance. Others may well spend the 1990s regretting the alliances they so hastily entered. Size bought by merger is harder to manage than size generated by internal growth.

The foreign banks

Half of Britain's invisible earnings from banking are generated by the 450 foreign banks in London.* They employ over 35,000 people and their number has risen from less than a hundred in 1960. They range in size from Citibank of New York, with some 2,000 staff in London, to several representative offices with just one person, like that of Bank Schoop Reiff, of Switzerland, which installed Baron van Tuyll van Ferooskerken as its representative in 1981. There are more US banks with offices in London than there are with offices in New York. The Japanese are the next largest group, with branches of virtually all major banks. The Communist bloc is well represented: Moscow Narodny has 240 staff in London and Bank of China 160. The last major industrial country to open full branches after the First World War was Germany. German banks had been closed down in 1914 and for years only a few representative offices were subsequently reopened. In 1973 Deutsche Bank, Dresdner Bank and Westdeutsche Landesbank Girozentrale all opened branches in London, and the others followed, though Germany still has fewer bank offices in London than France or Italy.

These banks came to London for a number of reasons. Sometimes it was purely prestige. But most came to do one or more of three things: to finance international trade; to provide an information and liaison service; or, since the 1960s, to carry out international money market banking business. The third area is where most of their invisible earnings have been generated, and for most foreign banks in London it has become by far their most lucrative activity. Through the 1970s, foreign

---

*Some 450 banks were represented in some way or other in 1982. Of these 380 were directly represented either by a bank or a representative office, while the rest were partners in some 30 joint ventures. Source: the *Banker*.

63

banks began to move into a fourth area, that of UK domestic banking.

The importance of each type of business varies from bank to bank. Where there is just a representative office, it cannot conduct banking business and will simply give information to potential customers. Its main job will be to generate business for its parent bank. The London branches of the banks of developing commodity-producing countries, such as the Ghana Commercial Bank, are mainly concerned with financing commodity trade. For the banks from developed countries, international money market business is the most important. US banks will be doing a host of different things: borrowing eurodollars to package into international loans, dealing in foreign exchange or commodities, advising the London offices of their US corporate clients and so on. The Brazilians may be borrowing to finance their industrial development . . . while the Swiss banks may be investing the (possibly ill-gotten) gains of their anonymous clients.

Easily the largest single contingent of foreign banks is the American. There are some seventy-eight US banks, accounting for three-quarters of the deposits of foreign banks in London and generating foreign earnings of over £500 million a year.* A few have been in London since the 1920s, but the real onslaught did not begin until the 1968 squeeze in the American economy, when the US banks began to borrow eurodollars on a massive scale to supplement their funds at home. In the 1970s these banks had a tremendous impact, both on the development of the eurodollar market in London and on British banking practices.

It is largely because of the investment which the American banks have made in London that the eurodollar market has stayed here. They have brought to the market a number of American banking techniques. The most important is the term loan: in eurocurrency lending British banks invariably follow

*No firm figure is available. This rough estimate is based on the sort of profit foreign banks should be getting from the size of their deposits – excluding US bank repatriations – plus commission earnings on trade finance.

the US practice of making loans for a specific period rather than extending an overdraft.

For the larger American banks, the fastest growing activity in London by the early 1980s was international merchant banking. Most of the big banks have a merchant banking subsidiary of some sort. Citibank has Citicorp International Bank, Manufacturers Hanover Trust has Manufacturers Hanover Ltd, Bank of America has Bank of America International. These subsidiaries are rather more specialised than London merchant banks. The core of their business is in the euromarkets, organising eurocurrency syndicated loans and issuing and trading in eurobonds. Some of the banks undertake their eurocurrency lending through the parent bank. But under US law, eurobonds have to be traded through the books of foreign subsidiaries. British regulations have also encouraged the spread of foreign bank subsidiaries. Financing British exports in dollars under the export credit guarantee scheme has to be carried out by a UK registered bank and a number of foreign banks use their UK subsidiaries to do this.

This may seem a narrow base on which to build a business, and these international merchant banks are naturally anxious to try to get into other areas, such as arranging international mergers. Their central aim has been to generate fee income – to be paid for providing services, rather than earning money by granting loans. Fee business, unlike banking business, does not require capital to be set against it. But the extent to which commercial banks can build up fees is limited, and London is an expensive place to operate a bank.

The consortium bank is a relatively new species. It is usually owned by foreign banks, and developed especially to participate in eurocurrency lending. Its particular characteristic is that it is owned by a consortium of banks, rather than by a single one. In the late 1960s, when consortium banks were first developed, the partners were large commercial banks from several different countries. This proved something of a blind alley: the big banks soon found that they preferred to involve themselves directly in the euromarkets, rather than have to share the business with half-a-dozen competitors. What then tended to happen was that one of the partners would buy

65

out the others and convert the bank into a London-registered international merchant bank. Where the consortium bank still seems to have a future is as the London eurocurrency operation for a group of smaller banks from the same geographic area, for example, Scandinavia, where the owners do not want the expense and risk of a proper London branch, but still want to be represented in the City's international business.

British overseas banks

The British overseas banks are a relic of the Empire. A century ago, banks with such exotic names as the Ottoman and the Hongkong and Shanghai ran branch networks in the countries of the Empire and its allies, and financed trade between them and Britain. Then, as emerging nations either nationalised their branches (as in Egypt and Tanzania) or took a controlling interest in them (as in Zambia or Libya), the overseas banks were forced to look elsewhere. Today most have either disappeared or become transformed. Thus the Ottoman Bank has been split up; its branches in Turkey were conceded to the Turkish government, the rest to other banks. Hong Kong and Shanghai transferred its headquarters from Hong Kong to London during the war and back again to Hong Kong, where its business is centred. Both Australia and New Zealand Bank and the National Bank of New Zealand, which ran their networks in Australasia from London head offices until recently, have moved their headquarters back home. Only a handful have survived to carry on anything like their original overseas bank business, and these have remained partly because they have forged links with clearing banks, which have used them as ready-made overseas branch networks, and partly because they have moved into the eurodollar market.

The rump that could still fairly be described as British overseas banks in the 1970s was changing rapidly in the early 1980s. There were still four main groups: Barclays Bank International (formed in 1971 when Barclays Bank took complete control of Barclays DCO); Lloyds Bank International (also formed in 1971 when Lloyds Bank Europe was merged with Bank of London and South America [Bolsa], and now

66

owned by Lloyds); Grindlays Bank (bought in 1984 by Australia and New Zealand Bank); and Standard Chartered Group (formed in 1970 by the merger of Standard Bank and Chartered Bank). But Barclays, in 1984, was being merged into the main Barclays group, while Lloyds plans to merge with LBI.

Each of these groups has retained an extensive overseas branch network in the countries in which it originally specialised. Thus Barclays has branches in Africa – particularly in South Africa – and the Caribbean. LBI retains Bolsa's network in South America, as well as a handful of branches in fashionable European towns originally set up by Lloyds for its wealthy customers. Grindlays still specialises in India and Pakistan and has some branches in East and Central Africa. Standard Chartered combines Standard's branches throughout Africa with Chartered's Far Eastern network.

On the face of it, these far-flung branch networks look like an ideal springboard for international corporate banking. But these branches tend to be mainly in slow-growing, politically unstable developing countries. Occasionally the traditional territory of a bank has boomed and the bank has duly benefited. For instance, Hong Kong and Shanghai did so well out of the expansion of Hong Kong in the 1970s that it was able to buy control of Marine Midland, one of the biggest New York banks. Grindlays has done very well out of its branches in the Middle East. Overall, however, their branches provide a declining proportion of the banks' profits.

As profits from overseas branch networks have dwindled, they have been replaced by profits earned in London by borrowing on the eurodollar market to finance foreign trade and overseas investment projects. The invention of the eurodollar market has provided the overseas banks with an independent source of funds. The early development of the eurodollar market was to a large extent the work of Bolsa, and in particular of its former chairman, Sir George Bolton.

Eurodollars, however, are not an ideal substitute for retail deposits. Not only do they tend to cost more, but rates are much more volatile. So the overseas banks were forced to look for financial support from other sources. At the same time the

67

clearing banks, whose own efforts to build up networks of overseas branches had been unimpressive, began to look for ways of offering their customers international connections: hence the close links with clearing banks.

Of the four groups, Barclays Bank International now boasts the best-distributed branch network: it has a chain of retail branches in California and, taking advantage of the fact that only foreign banks can open branches in more than one US state, it has spread into New York and Massachusetts.

The only overseas bank independent of the clearers is Standard Chartered. It has a branch network which rivals that of Barclays International. It remains the least integrated of all the overseas banking groups, formed, as both banks admitted at the time, to fend off any possible bid from a clearing bank. Following its failure to buy the Royal Bank of Scotland group in 1981, its future is unclear: it will seek a stronger UK base, but how it will achieve this remains to be seen.

By 1986, a transformation which has taken two decades will be virtually complete. With two substantial exceptions – Hongkong and Shanghai (technically based in Hong Kong) and Standard Chartered – the overseas bank will have disappeared. The great names of Victorian banking will have passed into extinction.

The clearing banks and money market banking

If it is the foreign banks that have made London the key eurocurrency banking centre, the future of this business depends more on the British banks. Yet money market banking is an area into which the clearing banks in particular moved late in the day. That was not entirely their own fault. It was not until the revision of banking regulations in Competition and Credit Control in 1971 that the clearing banks were allowed by the Bank of England to bid for deposits in the money market under their own names. The banks were therefore forced to use subsidiaries to take part in a whole range of banking business, from hire purchase to the eurocurrency markets.

68

This history helps to explain the clearing banks' approach to money market banking both in Britain and internationally. They devoted a lot of effort in the 1970s to catching up, often by buying subsidiaries or expertise. In some cases, they have bought well. Lloyds Bank, thanks largely to its purchase of Bolsa, is the top British bank in eurocurrency loans – indeed, worldwide it was third in the first half of 1984. But other clearers are still years behind their competitors. Barclays, Britain's biggest bank, only started a eurobond issuing business in 1979, almost two decades after the market had begun. In still other instances, the speed at which they tried to catch up led to purchases of doubtful value – witness Midland Bank's expensive acquisition of a majority share in Crocker Bank.

The clearing banks use the money markets to fund two kinds of new business: term lending to UK companies, and international loans. Because they were able to offer term loans, US banks had begun to make inroads in the early 1970s into the clearing banks' traditional territory of lending to UK companies. The clearing banks were widely criticised for not following suit. But until they had developed a source of fixed-term deposits, it was difficult for them to expand their fixed-term lending. Since then there has been extremely rapid growth, so that in little more than ten years a form of lending which hardly existed had matched and then overtaken the clearers' traditional lending technique, the overdraft. With hindsight it seems extraordinary that the banks should have resisted moves to push them into what became such a boom business.

While the clearing banks' interest rate cartel has gone, remnants of the structure it encouraged still exist. Thus only in 1983 did Lloyds Bank get round to merging its two competing sterling money market departments – one a subsidiary, the other part of the main bank. A more visible legacy is the way in which the banks still carry out much of their small-scale term lending – to small businesses and to individuals – through the old 1950s-style hire purchase companies. Midland took over Forward Trust as far back as 1958, but the others only sorted out their holdings in these companies at the end of the 1970s.

69

Barclays now owns Mercantile Credit; National Westminster owns Lombard North Central; and Lloyds in 1984 bought the Royal Bank group's share of Lloyds and Scottish. Of the rest, the TSBs own United Dominion Trust, and Standard Chartered the Hodge Group. The only major independent finance house is now the First National Finance group.

The sheer size of the clearing banks made it relatively easy to move into eurocurrency banking once they had decided to do so. From a practical point of view this was an easy business to enter. All the bank had to do was to say 'yes' when it was offered a place in an international loan syndicate, and arrange for its chunk of the loan to be borrowed by the money market division. But as with all banking, there are risks. By the end of the 1970s, quite a few senior bankers were wondering whether they had been wise to increase their commitments so rapidly. As there are surprisingly few published figures on the amount that the individual British banks have lent to countries abroad, it is not possible for an outsider to judge how right they are to be worried, and no way of assessing what bankers call each bank's 'country risk'.

In increasing their international lending, the British banks have merely been following the example of their rivals. The business has been so big, and appeared so profitable, that no bank could afford to ignore it. But there are at least two possible criticisms of British banks. One is that they have by and large taken a passive role, tending to join in loans organised by other banks, rather than earning additional fees by taking the role of lead managers and going out and organising loans themselves. There is some evidence that this criticism is justified. Thus out of the top twenty lead managers in 1981, only three were British. The second is that the quality of their lending has been poor: that in their desire to boost their business they have lent too much money to doubtful borrowers at too small a margin. To gauge the justice of that, we simply have to wait and see if the billions they have lent have to be written off.

The clearing banks have other sides to their international business, of which the most important is trade finance. But here, most of the loans are either short-term, or are underwritten by governments. In lending to companies
70

abroad, the banks have been able to build on their long domestic experience of assessing the credit-worthiness of corporate customers. But no one – least of all the banks themselves – can know whether Argentina or Turkey or Nigeria will repay a loan which matures in 1993.

Indeed, the shadow of country indebtedness will linger through the 1980s, just as the shadow of the fringe bank crisis lingered through the previous decade. Bankers themselves find it hard to gauge the significance of country indebtedness. In 1982 Sir Jeremy Morse put the danger of the worst outcome, a catastrophic banking collapse, at 5 per cent, prompting a rival banker to growl: 'I'm surprised with his intelligence he couldn't tell us it was 4.78 per cent.' All agree that it will be a serious constraint on international bank lending for some years. But while it was country lending that expanded most rapidly during the 1970s, the majority of eurocurrency banking is lending to companies, not countries. This sort of business, which has weathered the recession far better, gets less publicity, but is a lot more profitable.

It seems sensible to assume that City banking will not see a boom in the 1980s comparable to that of the second half of the 1970s. It is quite possible, too, that the proportion of business organised from London may shrink *vis-à-vis* New York, which at the end of 1981 set up offshore banking legislation to permit US banks to book loans in New York without going over the hurdle of US tax and domestic monetary controls. Within a year these International Banking Facilities, as they are called, accounted for 8 per cent of the total euromarket deposits, as against London's share which has held steady at around the 35 per cent mark. In bank loans booked through the different centres, London's lead was narrower: 27 per cent against 14.5 per cent for New York.

It is a useful warning that London can be challenged. For the time being, to be sure, London may not have too much to fear. Not only do the American and other foreign banks already have an enormous investment in the City, which will tend to keep the business here, but New York has not proved as efficient a place to raise euromarket deposits as London, and most of the loans being booked through New York have to be funded by dollars

71

bought in established euromarket dealing centres, of which London is by far the largest. So perhaps the most important thing that will keep international banking in London is less the fact that the clearing banks have stirred themselves but rather the extraordinary quality of the foreign exchange and money markets in the City.

FOUR

The money and foreign exchange markets

What a money market does

Money markets thrive on adversity. Nothing seems to stimulate them more than government regulations, cartels and restrictive agreements designed to keep them under control. For money markets are mechanisms through which money is channelled from lenders to borrowers. Try to dam the flow . . . and it trickles round another way. Thus the tremendous growth both of sterling and of international money markets in the 1960s and 1970s was, to a large extent, encouraged by the attempts of the British and other governments to keep the lenders and borrowers apart.

Abstruse though they sound, money markets do quite a simple job. But before looking at what they do and how they do it, it is important to understand their structure. Until the mid-1950s there was really only one kind of money market in the City: the discount market, run by the discount houses and closely controlled by the Bank of England. During the late 1950s and 1960s, a whole new group of money markets sprang up, in which transactions are carried out through money brokers. These 'new' markets are commonly divided into two groups, depending on whether they deal in sterling or eurocurrencies. The sterling markets include the local authority, the sterling inter-bank and the certificate of deposit (or CD) markets. Some of them evolved to escape the regulations and cartels by which the discount market was trammelled. The eurocurrency markets, for which London is the main dealing centre, grew up to dodge attempts of national governments to keep lenders and borrowers apart.

The structure of the eurocurrency market is simpler than the sterling parallel markets: it divides only into one market in eurocurrency deposits and one in CDs. It is vastly larger. Its explosive growth in the course of the 1970s is the most important single development in international banking in the post-war period. It deals in every major currency (although by definition the euro-sterling market is not in London). And into the 1980s, in spite of challenges from other centres, London remained by far the most important dealing centre for the market.

This chapter also describes another type of market: the foreign exchange market. This is not strictly a money market, but it is operated by banks and brokers in much the same way: it was, in fact, the origin of the techniques used in the new money markets. Through the foreign exchange market, or forex market, the sterling money markets are linked to the eurocurrency market. Together these markets are the lynchpin of London's banking business.

Every important financial centre in the world has both a domestic money market of some sort and a foreign exchange market. Some may also have a market in eurocurrency deposits. London is unusual in two ways: in its discount houses, which are a peculiarly British buffer between the central bank and the commercial banks, and in the gigantic scale of its eurocurrency market.

There are 3,000 people in London who spend their day buying and selling money. About two-thirds of these work for 450 or so banks active in the money market, and the rest for the discount houses and money and foreign exchange brokers. To the outsider it may sound odd to talk about buying and selling money. But when bankers talk about 'money', they mean specifically money borrowed for a short period. So if they talk about 'picking up overnight money', they mean borrowing it (or buying the use of it) until tomorrow. The price is the interest. In a money market, people borrow and lend money for relatively short periods.

The actual sums involved look enormous. A typical unit for deals between big banks is £5 million in sterling and $20-25 million in US dollars. However, provided one does not want the money for long, it is surprisingly cheap: £1 million, borrowed overnight (the shortest possible period) at 8 per cent costs just

£219.18, the price of a couple of nights in the Savoy. To borrow overnight is by no means unusual: much of the funds on the London money market is borrowed for less than a week.

But what can you do with £1 million until tomorrow? The money markets use this very short-term money to do two jobs. First, they lend it to the banks to help them balance their books at the end of each day. If a bank finds it is a bit short, it goes to the market and borrows enough to tide it over. If it finds that it has spare cash, it makes a profit by lending it on the market.

Though very short-term money is useful to a bank, it is not much use to anyone else. So the second function of a money market is converting it into longer-term money that can be used by industry and the government.

This conjuring trick is done in different ways by the discount market and the money markets. In the discount market, it is the discount houses themselves that convert this short-term money into longer-term loans. The discount houses borrow the spare cash of the banks, mostly 'at call', which means that the banks can have it back whenever they want it. The houses then lend it to the government and to companies, usually for three months.

In the money markets, the trick is done by the banks. But they can only do it because they have the markets to fall back on. In money market banking, the banks borrow from financial institutions, such as pension funds, and industrial companies, usually for fixed periods of anything from a day to several years. They may borrow directly, or through the money market. They lend to company customers or to local authorities for rather longer periods. Thus a bank may lend for five years to one company and keep borrowing six-month money from the market to finance the loan. As long as it can borrow short-term from the market, it can go on lending for these longer periods.

But it can be a risky business. In Britain, in 1974 and 1975, a number of the banks which had relied on the parallel markets for their funds found that they could no longer do so. Some were small merchant banks – 'fringe banks' – which had lent unwisely on property and found themselves insolvent. But others were perfectly reputable. They found that because their solvency was suspect, they could no longer borrow short-term. They had to be rescued by the Bank of England. One of the major worries of central bankers at the start of the 1980s was that it might be much more difficult to stop a succession of banking collapses if it began in the eurocurrency market.

The discount market

Discount house men remain a dignified breed, renowned, slightly unfairly, for the short hours they put in and their enjoyment of the daily rite of putting on silk top hat to call on the major banks and the Bank of England. Despite this genteel atmosphere, the discount men are, like everyone else in the City's money markets, doing much the same job as a bookie. (The dealers in the money-broking firms actually look like bookies.)

In the 1960s, the sleepy atmosphere of the discount houses was reflected in the stagnation of their business. Throughout the decade, their total assets only crept upwards. The houses continued to do much as they had always done: to borrow the spare cash of the banks and to use it to back their purchases of Treasury bills from the Bank of England and commercial bills from companies. But the discount market was barely growing. Meanwhile a number of money markets which sprang up in the course of the 1960s enjoyed a dramatic expansion. These newer markets have indeed given the discount houses the opportunity to break out of their restricting traditional business. But to do so, they had to learn to operate in a radically different way.

Other attempts to diversify include borrowing money from commercial companies, rather than banks, and investing it mainly in Certificates of Deposit. Ironically, the main thing which kept the houses going through the 1970s was their traditional bill business. The reason is simply that whenever the government imposes controls on bank lending, companies tend to turn to bills as an alternative way to borrow. It is another case where controls can be a market's best friend.

The members of the London Discount Market Association carry out most discount market dealing. They vary in size from Union Discount and Gerrard and National, with balance sheet totals of some £2,000 million and £3,000 million respectively at

76

the end of 1984 and accounting for roughly two-thirds of the market, to Seccombe, Marshall and Campion, with a 1982 balance sheet of £175 million. All discount houses, however, have certain things in common. They are all small, intimate firms dealing in enormous sums of money. Even Union only employs about seventy people, but its balance sheet would make it as big as a large merchant bank.

Critics of the discount market say that there are really only two-and-a-half houses that matter: Union, Gerrard and National and Cater Allen. Union was long the largest, though it was passed by Gerrard in 1982. It lives in a beautifully restored set of 1890 offices in Cornhill and behaves rather like General Motors in the US: it has so much of the market that it is not anxious to increase its share. It is by tradition the most cautious of the houses, doing less well than the others in good years and less badly in poor. By tradition, too, the clearing banks have usually supplied it with non-executive chairmen. Its management is professional, competent, calm. The other large house, Gerrard and National, is completely different in character. It was formed in 1969 when a small but very successful house, Gerrard and Reid, took over the large but ailing National. It cultivates a slightly racy image, with everyone apparently on christian-name terms, young and enthusiastic executive directors and chairman, and discreet, comfortable offices in Lombard Street. Its success is built on well-judged gambling: it takes enormous risks, but knows when to cut its losses.

The 'half' of the two-and-a-half is Cater Allen, formed by a merger between two medium-sized houses, Cater Ryder and Allen, Harvey and Ross, in 1981. Both have been innovative as individual enterprises, and the Bank of England's aim in blessing their marriage was to encourage a proper third force in the market. It is admired by its competitors and may well succeed. A new rival may emerge following the successive takeovers by financial services group Mercantile House of the two discount houses, Alexanders – the oldest – and Jessel Toynbee.

The three biggest houses account for perhaps three-quarters of the business going through the market, inevitably raising questions as to whether the remainder should all merge or in some other way seek new capital resources. Of the rest there are two houses that in various ways ran into difficulties in the 1970s – Smith, St Aubyn and Clive. Gillett, another house with problems in the 1970s, merged with Jessel Toynbee in 1983. King and Shaxson, and the smallest, Seccombe, Marshall and Campion, which besides being 'special buyer' to the market also does some ordinary business, remained independent in mid 1984.

Apart from the discount houses proper, two other types of institution carry out money market business. There are an assortment of banks called the 'money trading banks' which deal in short-term securities; and there are six firms of stockbrokers which are confusingly called 'money brokers', which use money borrowed from the banks to trade in gilts. The task of these institutions is to oil the wheels of the gilt settlement system.

A discount house's day nowadays begins at about 8.15 when the CD dealers start. The traditional bill business gets under way at 8.30 with calls, usually by telephone, from the banks who have placed money with it 'at call' and now want it back. By mid-morning a large house might find that it needs £200 million if its borrowings are to cover its investments by the end of the day. During the morning, half a dozen of its men put on their top hats and stroll round to the money departments of the four main clearing banks and some of the other banks with which it does business, to find out whether they expect to call back even more of their funds – they have to do so by noon – or whether they expect to be able to lend substantial amounts back to the discount houses. Quite junior men in the house may go on these rounds, particularly to the smaller banks, and the conversation is as likely to be about cricket and the laziness of British workmen as about the bank's requirement. The tradition survives largely because everybody seems to enjoy it.

Throughout the morning some of the house's directors will be watching its investment position, perhaps wondering about the latest shift in US interest rates, and gauging the impact of this on the price of gilts and CDs, constantly comparing these with the price of money. Around midday a senior man from Seccombe

78

will ring up each house to sound out its position and to discover whether it is likely to be short of money later in the day. Thus Seccombe fulfils its role as 'special buyer', and its chairman, David Campion, is the Bank of England's link with the market.

Lunch will be a high-calorie affair, with a couple of guests, usually bankers or fund managers, and just occasionally a financial journalist. Afterwards the banks will be evening up their balances and the house should find money flowing in as the banks lend it their spare cash. If by mid-afternoon, however, it is clear that the house is not going to be able to borrow enough from the banks to make its books balance, Seccombe will tell it what the Bank of England wants the market to do. Usually the house will be allowed to sell Treasury bills to Seccombe; but if the Bank wants to squeeze credit, it may be forced to borrow either from the clearing banks (with which it has agreed overdraft limits), or even more expensively from the Bank of England itself.

This guarantee of help from the Bank is the discount houses' most important privilege. It puts them in a unique position, for they are the only institutions with the right to this assistance. It allows them to perform their conjuring trick of borrowing money at call – for a short period of uncertain length – and investing it for three months and longer.

Sometimes, of course, the discount houses' conjuring trick goes wrong. It only fails if they misjudge the trend of interest rates and hence the value of their investments. It failed for National in the late 1960s when the value of its portfolio of government bonds plummeted, and again in 1981 for Smith, St Aubyn for the same reason. But the major reason why the discount houses can borrow amounts which in terms of their capital bases looks dangerously large is that they know that one way or another the Bank of England will see that they do not go bankrupt.*

There is a special relationship between the Bank of England and the discount houses. The Bank protects the houses, and

---

*Anyone who thinks of the panic that followed the collapse of the discount house of Overend, Gurney and Co. in 1866 will understand the Bank's reasons (see chapter 1, p.8).

they in turn adjust their business to suit the Bank's control of the monetary system. Changes in monetary control, which seem to take place at roughly ten-year intervals, have an enormous impact on the relative importance of the various parts of the houses' business.

Thus in the 1960s their business was rather in the doldrums, as they feared that the Bank would dislike any attempt by them to get into the new, or as they were then called, 'parallel' money markets – the markets that had grown up parallel to the discount market.

Their business was distorted by two restrictive agreements between the houses and the clearing banks, legacies of the 1930s era of cheap money. The banks lent the houses a certain proportion of their funds at a very low rate of interest. In return the houses did not compete with the clearers for commercial funds by offering higher rates of interest than the banks charged under their cartel.

Then in 1971 these restrictive agreements were swept away in the new credit controls. With these the Bank conferred on the discount houses yet another special privilege. Money that the banks lent to the discount houses at call was to count as part of the banks' reserve assets. This was sure to be a strong incentive for the banks, clearers and non-clearers alike, to place spare funds with the discount houses rather than on the parallel markets.

When the system was revised yet again in 1981, the discount houses lost most of these special privileges, as the range of reserve assets was broadened. But the Bank still sought to protect them and required the 'eligible' banks to continue to place a proportion of their funds with discount houses.

The discount houses still borrow the bulk of their money from banks, half from the clearing banks, most of the rest from other banks and a small but growing amount from companies. They borrow almost all of it at call, and re-lend by investing in five main types of longer-term debt: commercial bills, Treasury bills, government stocks, local authority bills and bonds, and bank and building society certificates of deposit. These investments are usually offered by the houses to the banks as security for their loans. The mix of investments varies from house to house, but the more risky the investment the greater the restriction placed by the Bank of England on the amount of assets held in that form.

Commercial bills were the discount market's main asset during the nineteenth century. In the 1960s they again became important, as restrictions on clearing-bank lending forced companies to make greater use of commercial bill finance. The previous chapter explained how bills were guaranteed or 'accepted' by merchant banks. There are two kinds of commercial bill: those that have been guaranteed by a bank (bank bills or bank paper) and those that have not (trade bills). Bank bills can be either 'eligible', which means they have been accepted by a 'recognised' bank and that the Bank of England will lend cash to the discount houses against them;* or they may be non-eligible, which means they have been guaranteed by a bank not on the Bank of England's list. Until the changes of 1981 no foreign bank was on it.

Treasury bills are similar to commercial bills in that they are also three-month loans: but with Treasury bills the borrower is the government. As with eligible bank bills, the Bank will lend cash against them.

The discount houses buy their Treasury bills through a ritual called the tender. Every Friday the Bank of England offers a batch of Treasury bills to banks, discount houses, government departments and institutional investors. The amount varies, but a typical offer in the 1970s would be £300 million, although this shrank to £100 million in the early 1980s. The discount houses always bid for as many bills as have been offered, and this is the key part of the tender. It means that whatever happens, the government knows that it can always sell all its bills. This, historically, is why the Bank granted the discount houses their special privileges. An odd feature of the ritual is that the clearing banks rarely tender for bills for their own account. They usually buy them all from the discount houses.

Discount houses also lend to the government by buying

---

*In the textbooks these bills are described as 'eligible for rediscount at the Bank'. This means that they can actually be swapped for cash at the Bank. In practice the bank almost invariably lends against the security of the bills.

government bonds. It is here that they make their big profits or – as in 1979 and 1981 – big losses. Because they are longer-term securities, the prices of government bonds tend to fluctuate more than those of other discount market assets. Since the government decided to stop supporting the gilt-edged market, these fluctuations have become still wider and the houses' investments in bonds a more speculative component of their portfolios. A discount house that gets its bond portfolio right can make far more money on it than on all its other operations put together.

The last two types of security – local authority bonds and certificates of deposit – have become increasingly important to the discount houses. Local authority bonds (often called 'yearling bonds' because they were originally issued for a year) were the first, in 1964. They have not been particularly successful, because the local authority money market, described later, is more convenient both for borrower and lender, and because the amount of 'yearlings' which can be issued is closely controlled by the Bank.

CDs, by contrast, have been enormously successful, and are the discount market's fastest-growing asset. They work like this. A large company has £1 million spare on which it wants to get the highest possible rate of interest. It thinks that it will not need the money for a year, and since it can earn a higher rate the longer it lends it, it puts it on deposit with a bank for the whole year. But it is possible that it might need the money earlier. So when it puts the money on deposit it gets a certificate of that deposit in return. This says that £1 million has been left at such and such a bank at a certain rate of interest until a date one year hence. If the company needs its money earlier, it takes the certificate along not to the bank (which has by now lent the money to someone else and so does not want to repay it), but to the money market. The buyer, a discount house or bank, buys the CD at the going market price, which reflects current interest rates. Thus it provides what is called a secondary, or trading, market in CDs. If the buyer is a discount house, the money it uses to buy the CD is – as with all discount-house money – borrowed at call from the banks. The conjuring trick has worked again: the company can get its money whenever it wants . . . and the bank knows it has it for a year. In fact the CD has turned out to be so convenient that banks trade it between themselves. If banks want to lend to each other for short periods, they do so on the inter-bank market, but they tend to use CDs for longer periods.

CDs have given the discount houses their most important direct way into parallel market business. But the discount houses operate in the CD market in a different way from the money brokers. Whereas the money brokers simply match would-be sellers with would-be buyers, the discount houses buy and sell CDs as investments. More important, when CDs were first issued, the houses agreed to act as 'market makers' in them. This means that they will always quote a price at which they are prepared to buy or sell CDs. That the discount houses are prepared to perform this jobbing role in CDs has made this market much more liquid, and hence attractive both to borrower and lender.

Finally, the discount houses carry out a small but growing amount of foreign currency business. They do the same job in the dollar CD market as in the sterling market, and they discount bills of exchange denominated in foreign currencies.

Discount houses are virtually unknown outside the UK. No other major financial centre bothers with them. Attempts to introduce them into New York and South Africa have not been very successful. Do we still need them?

Their original function is to help the government to borrow short-term. They do this by guaranteeing, each week, to buy at each Friday's tender any Treasury bills which the government cannot sell. In other financial centres this function is carried out by the commercial banks. It could be in the UK too. As the Radcliffe Report on the working of the monetary system in 1959 concluded:

> It would not be beyond human ingenuity to replace the work of the discount houses; but they are there, they are doing the work effectively and they are doing it at a trifling cost in terms of labour and other real resources.

But even before the monetary changes of 1981 this job of the discount houses was becoming less important, both to them and to the Bank of England. Other institutions had begun to tender for Treasury bills, and Treasury bills in any case formed a much smaller proportion of the discount houses' portfolio. The Bank undoubtedly likes carrying out its money market intervention through small, specialised institutions which are – to some extent – in its pocket. But the Bank has a more general reason for wanting to see the discount houses flourish. They add greatly to something which London, as a financial centre, lacks in relation in particular to New York: market making capacity. The discount houses may be too small, but they have years of experience of what to do (and what not to do) in this most dangerous of financial functions. In their trading on the money markets, taking the risks they do, they help make those markets run more smoothly. While they can continue to trade successfully in the money markets, they not only earn themselves a living, but they help the rest of the City too.

The sterling money markets

For many years, the discount market was the only market in which banks could lend their spare cash short-term. These loans were always secured against some document – an acceptance, a Treasury bill, a short-dated gilt. In the course of the 1960s, a new group of money markets grew up whose essential characteristic is that money is borrowed and lent between institutions, companies and banks, unsecured, and without the direct guidance and control of the monetary authorities. The Bank of England does not formally act as lender of last resort to anybody in these money markets, as it does to the discount houses in the discount market. In some financial centres the bulk of this inter-institutional borrowing and lending is done directly between banks or companies. In London the bulk of it is done through the money brokers. While the discount houses make their profits on their own investments, the money brokers' job is simply to match up would-be borrowers and lenders, charging a small commission on each deal.

It is largely because the broking system is more widely used in London that the City has developed such a complex and sophisticated system of money markets. London brokers quote narrower margins than their counterparts elsewhere. And in turn the sheer size of the London markets has allowed the brokers to thrive. As the brokers have bought interests in other brokers abroad and set up subsidiary companies to deal in other centres, London has become the centre of an international network of broking offices.

Several of the main money brokers are descended from foreign exchange brokers. Others have a different line of ancestry: they were local authority brokers, formed in the mid-1950s to channel funds into local authorities. They are fiercely competitive, for money broking is the City's Wild West, where few holds are barred. Most discount-house men have been with their firms all their lives, but the money brokers' job market is a Mad Hatter's tea party, with dealers constantly on the move from one firm to another. They move for vast and spiralling salaries – and if they are still not satisfied, they go off and set up on their own. A good dealer, aged nearly thirty, would get about £40,000 a year. But while top dealers are paid as much as anyone else in the City, with the exception of a few merchant bankers and stockbrokers or jobbers, they probably need it. Their professional lives are short.

The broking companies themselves are a disparate lot. A few are large, highly professional organisations, able to place money in any market and deal in foreign currencies and sterling alike. These firms, employing 500 or more people and with a chain of offices and subsidiaries around the world, are by far the biggest operators of their kind anywhere.

The brokers are organised into two associations. Those which deal in either foreign exchange or currency deposits, or both, have to be members of the Foreign Exchange and Currency Deposit Brokers' Association. Those which deal only in sterling deposits are members of the Sterling Brokers' Association. Large brokers would be members of both, but FECDBA is very much the grander of the two clubs. To be a member, a broker has to be 'recognised' by the Bank of England, whereas anyone can join the Sterling Association.

The two largest brokers are public companies with shares quoted on the Stock Exchange. Both are gradually turning

85

themselves into financial conglomerates. The biggest is Mercantile House, which trades as M. W. Marshall in London and Lasser Marshall in New York. Mercantile House is run by John Barkshire, a small, energetic former discount house man who wants to move the company away from its money-broking origins and convert it into an international investment bank. To this end he picked up at a highly advantageous price in 1982 the New York investment bank, Oppenheimer & Co. He followed this by buying the two discount houses and an interest in stockbrokers Laing & Cruickshank.

Next in size, thanks to its ownership of the New York brokers Noonan & Co., is Exco, which in London owns Astley and Pearce, and Godsell. Just as the key step for Mercantile House was the coup of buying Oppenheimer, so Exco's success was underwritten by its clever purchase of a substantial share in Telerate, one of the two main computer-based market information systems used by dealers. It also owns stockbroking firms in Singapore and London.

The intriguing question with both Mercantile House and Exco is whether these firms will develop into the new international merchant banks of the next generation.

Other prominent brokers, though smaller, are Harlow Butler, owned by Mills and Allen, R. P. Martin (also a quoted company), Tullet and Tokyo, and Charles Fulton.

All the big firms of money and foreign exchange brokers are linked by direct telephone lines to main London banks. Dealers, both in banks and brokers, sit in rooms that look like a space mission control, surrounded by television screens giving rates and prices and by banks of buttons that operate the direct lines. Up to a hundred dealers could be on the phone in one room, ringing round the banks and brokers to find potential customers, and when they find one, phoning elsewhere for a 'match'. Deals on both the foreign exchange and money market are made on the phone. Written confirmation follows, but only after the deal has been completed.

There are three main sterling markets, distinguished by their borrowing instrument. On the local authority market, local authorities borrow largely from the institutions but also from banks, companies and a few private individuals on the security of a bond. On the sterling inter-bank market, banks borrow from each other against deposit receipts which cannot be bought or sold. On the sterling CD market, banks borrow from companies and other banks through CDs which can be traded. A fourth market in building society CDs is developing as building societies have joined banks as borrowers on the money market.

Of the sterling markets, two owe their existence directly to government controls on the UK banking system. Thus the local authority market was born in 1955, when the government tried to reduce local authorities' borrowing by limiting access to the Public Works Loan Board. In an effort to find a way round the squeeze, local authorities stepped up their borrowing direct from the private sector. By bidding for deposits in this way, they in effect invented a new type of money market.

By 1983, this oldest money market had been overtaken in size by the CD market. Of the total local authority loan debt of some £45,000 million, £5,000 million was borrowed on the market for periods of less than a year, representing what is conventionally thought of as the local authority short-term money market. The smallest lump of money that is usually lent on this market is £250,000 and blocks of £1 million and more are common. As of 1983, a further £9 billion of longer-term loans was borrowed in a variety of different ways: through loan stock (five years upwards), quoted bonds (up to five years) and money market mortgage bonds (one year upwards).

Shortly after the emergence of the local authority market, the inter-bank market grew up. Banks had found in the local authority market their first alternative to the discount market as an outlet for spare funds. The inter-bank market offered them a further way to even out spare cash among themselves. To do this through a discount house meant that they were paid only the discount houses' low rate of interest on call money. So to the amazement of the discount market they began to lend straight to each other through the broking network. Side by side with the growth of the local authority market has been a corresponding expansion in inter-bank dealing. The total

87

volume of funds deposited by banks directly with each other fluctuates and is swollen by some double counting. But the figure in early 1983 would have been £31,400 million if inter-bank CD dealings were excluded. The money is all very short-term, much of it overnight. The lumps tend to be much larger than on the local authority market, with £1 million the usual minimum.

On the sterling CD market the discount houses are all involved as traders, buying and selling second-hand CDs for their own accounts. Money brokers, by contrast, buy and sell these CDs on behalf of clients – sometimes dealing with discount houses and sometimes with banks and large companies. The total value of sterling CDs issued in early 1983 was £8,800 million.

All these markets intermesh. To take a simple sterling deal, a large company might lend £500,000 to County Bank, which issues it with a CD. County then looks at the local authority market, decides that rates there are too low, and instead lends the money for a week on the sterling inter-bank market to another bank that is short of cash. A week later, local authority rates have improved, and County lends the £500,000 to Greater Manchester Council. Meanwhile the large company has brought forward an investment project and needs its £500,000 to cover the down-payment on some machine tools. It sells the CD to Union Discount, which might either carry it to maturity or sell it to any of the banks in London – except County Bank. All these transactions, with the possible exception of the CD deals, will have taken place through a money broker, who sits at the end of the phone recommending clients to switch the funds from one market to another as rates move.

From time to time, another money market surfaces: the inter-company market. Companies frequently place money with banks or local authorities, on the money market, normally through brokers. But occasionally they have lent spare cash directly to each other. This market tends to appear at times of credit restraint – it was thriving in the late 1960s, and there was some evidence of it in the late 1970s. Although it offers companies the temptation of by-passing the commercial banks' mark-up on re-lending their cash, it has never really blossomed

88

into a formal market. One reason is that even small banks, backed as they are by the central banks, are deemed safer than industrial giants. Another is that the 1979 Banking Act would require companies to become licensed deposit-takers if they wanted to do so. And still another reason is that they could never be sure, unless they went through the formal money market, that they were getting the best rate at any one time.

The eurocurrency deposit market

The origins of the eurocurrency market are rather more complicated. The first eurocurrency, and still by far the most important, is the eurodollar. For any currency to become 'euro' it must quite simply be owned by a firm or individual resident outside the country where the currency was issued and lent to another non-resident. Take, for example, an oil-producing country which has been paid $250 million in royalties by Exxon. These funds were dollars when they were still on Exxon's New York bank account. But provided the oil-producing country lends them to someone else not resident in the US – even to an overseas branch of an American bank which lends them back to its New York office – they remain eurodollars. They only become ordinary dollars again if they are used to invest in American domestic securities or to buy some American product.

It was an American banking regulation which first helped to create the eurodollar market.* It came to Britain partly because London banks were among the earliest to find uses for these spare dollar balances. Not all were British. One early operator was the London-based Moscow Narodny Bank, which for political reasons wanted to employ its dollars outside the US and so helped supply dollars to the market. Since then markets have grown up in perhaps a dozen other financial centres and in other eurocurrencies. In Paris there is a small market in eurosterling (never europounds) and in Singapore a market in Asian dollars, eurodollars that happen to be

*See chapter 1, p.18, for its origins.

traded in Asia. But the City's dealing skills have helped to ensure that the lion's share of eurocurrency dealing goes through London.

The eurocurrency market is gigantic. By the end of 1982 the total pool of funds was over \$2,000 billion,* of which 81 per cent was dollars. This vast pool of money flows freely between the main financial centres. No one really knows how to control it. Just over one-third of this \$2,000 billion appears on the books of London banks. But unlike the sterling markets, the eurocurrency market is in no way a UK domestic market. The fact that London happens to be the main centre has, since foreign exchange controls were lifted, encouraged British companies to use it.

This \$2,000 billion, the main eurocurrency market, is mainly a short-term inter-bank market. Banks borrow from each other lumps of \$5 million up to about \$250 million for periods as short as overnight or as long as a year. (The longer the date, the smaller the unit of dealing.) The three-month and particularly the six-month interest rates (i.e. the interest rate on any one day for money to be repaid in either three or six months' time) is important, for the London eurodollar rate is used to set the rate on most eurocurrency loans. A loan will be quoted at, for example, 1 per cent above six-month London inter-bank offered rate, or LIBOR (pronounced 'lie-bore').

The eurocurrency market is almost entirely one between banks, hence the expression 'inter-bank'. If a company wants to place money on the market, it generally does so through a bank.

In practice, the large multinationals may well get as good a rate as a bank, and bankers argue that the treasurers of large multinationals are adept at getting the best rate for their spare cash. Equally, if a company or even a national government wants to borrow in eurocurrencies it cannot, unlike a bank, go straight to the market. Instead it has to borrow on one of the other two 'euro' markets, the eurobond market (see chapter 6)

---

*Morgan Guaranty figures. Morgan Guaranty and the Bank for International Settlements give the best account of market developments and the best estimates of its size.

or the eurocurrency syndicated loans market. The same institutions – big companies, public utilities and national governments – borrow on each. On the first, individuals are the main lenders; on the second, only banks. Both markets are run directly by commercial or investment banks: brokers are used only rarely.

New variations in ways of borrowing and lending money continually sprout in the euromarket. Since it is the fastest-expanding money and capital market in the world it has inevitably become a test-bed for new ideas. There have been experiments with loans and bonds denominated in groups of eurocurrencies, with issues of eurocommercial paper where companies borrow for three months by issuing a sort of IOU, or promise to pay, with mixtures of bond and loan issues, and so on. The line between bonds and loans is sometimes blurred, for banks sometimes lend to companies by buying their bonds rather than granting them loans.

All these eurocurrency markets have developed despite the fact that it often costs companies more to borrow on them than on domestic money and capital markets. The reason companies continue to do so is very often simply that the eurocurrency markets are the only places where they can find money on the scale they need. It may be quite impossible to raise funds on the domestic market at the time the company requires it. For unlike all domestic markets, the eurocurrency market has so far grown up entirely outside the control of any central bank. It is the supreme example of how domestic credit controls induce people to find ways round them. No doubt by the time the world's central banks have evolved an efficient way of controlling the banks' eurocurrency operations, the focus of the international capital market will have shifted elsewhere.

The foreign exchange market

The grandfather of all the money markets is the foreign exchange market. London's is still the largest in the world, but its dominance is being challenged by New York, which grew very rapidly as a foreign exchange trading centre in the late 1970s – largely thanks to British brokers. Now, more than ever,

London is only one link in a chain of centres dealing with foreign exchange as the time zones move around the world. Its dominance is being challenged in another way, for most trading in foreign currency futures is, as chapter 8 explains, done in Chicago.

On the London foreign exchange market there are some 600 British, foreign and consortium licensed banks that are allowed to deal in foreign exchange. In practice some 200 are active in the market. They trade one currency with another, frequently through the ten foreign exchange broking firms, members of the Foreign Exchange and Currency Deposit Brokers' Association or FECDBA.

The foreign exchange market has a history of restrictive practices, practices which were largely lifted at the beginning of 1980. But it was through FECDBA that these restrictions were enforced, backed by the Bank of England and the foreign exchange committee of the clearing banks. A broker has to be recognised by the Bank of England and join FECDBA to be allowed to operate in the foreign exchange market. Joining can be difficult. One Arab-owned broker, Sarabex, excluded from FECDBA, had to take the matter to the European Commission before it won, and only then despite strenuous opposition from the Bank of England.

Another restrictive practice prevented banks from dealing directly with each other in London in foreign exchange, even though they could, and did, deal direct with banks in foreign centres. This created the illogical situation where, for example, the London dealing room of Barclays would deal direct with Chase Manhattan's dealing room in New York, but not with Chase's London dealing room round the corner.

As New York developed its own foreign exchange market, this became a serious handicap. For most deals banks did want to go through brokers, as a broker tended to get a better rate. But sometimes they needed to make very large deals and needed to talk to someone who could give a direct answer rather than someone who would need to telephone round, during which time the rate might move.

When the restriction was lifted at the beginning of 1980, business boomed, roughly doubling overnight. The brokers lost some share of the market but overall their business grew too, and London regained some of the ground it had begun to lose.

The final restrictive practice prevented non-banks – large companies, for example – from dealing directly on the foreign exchange and eurocurrency markets, as they could on the sterling markets. In practice, whenever a company wanted to borrow in a foreign currency or put money on the eurocurrency market, it had to do so through a bank. A broker was not allowed to arrange deals between a bank and a non-bank. Opinions differed as to the extent which this restriction in practice penalised large companies, with many bankers arguing that company treasurers were sufficiently skilled to get as good a rate as any broker. At any rate, this restriction too was lifted in 1980 ... or so the companies thought. In fact, they found that though most banks would accept their deposits through a broker, they still could not place foreign exchange orders through one.

The most important recent development of the world's foreign exchanges is that they have become a true twenty-four-hour market, with trading starting in Tokyo and Singapore, moving to Bahrain, then to the European centres of which London is the most important, to New York and the west coast of the US and back to Tokyo. However, the volume of business in the Far Eastern centres and Bahrain is small compared with Europe or New York, and the west coast of the US has not developed as an important foreign exchange dealing centre.

Though the structure of the foreign exchange market has changed dramatically since the days when currency was traded on the floor of the Royal Exchange, the function of the market has not. The foreign exchange market's most obvious purpose is to exchange different countries' currencies as they trade with each other or make overseas investments. But it is also the mechanism through which the world money system is operated.

Between the Second World War and 1972, the exchange rates of the world's major currencies were fixed against each other. They were held within a narrow band on either side of their parity with the US dollar by central banks intervening as necessary on the foreign exchange markets. Since 1972,

93

currencies have been allowed to float: that is, central banks have not generally tried to hold their currencies in any particular relationship with each other. They have continued to intervene to try to reduce sharp movements in rates, and since March 1979 the EEC currencies, with the exception of sterling, have been linked together within a narrow band in the European Monetary System, the so-called 'snake'.

Under both fixed and floating exchange-rate systems, currencies move against each other, as the foreign exchange market balances supply and demand for each currency. Under both fixed and floating systems, central banks intervene in the markets from day to day. The difference is the rules, or obligations, under which the central banks operate.

Currencies are bought and sold 'spot' for 'immediate' delivery, which in practice means two days. They are also traded 'forward', which means that though the price between the currencies – the exchange rate – is agreed now, the buyer takes delivery in one, three, six or twelve months' time. Through the forward exchange market, traders can insure against exchange-rate changes. For example, a British company has bought some Swiss looms for which it will have to pay in three months. It fears that the pound may depreciate against the Swiss franc during this period. And so it buys 'forward' the Swiss francs it will need to make its payment. If most people believe that in the three-month interval the pound is going to depreciate against the Swiss franc, the importing company will have to pay a premium over the spot exchange rate for its forward francs, but it will at least know exactly how much it has to pay in sterling terms. If it waited until the payment fell due and bought the Swiss francs on the spot market, it would have had to gamble on the exchange rate. So long as exchange rates fluctuate, a forward market is essential for international trade.

In 1972 a new version of forward trading started in Chicago, the largest commodity trading centre in the world (see p.204). A market began in currency futures, buying and selling contracts in currencies several months ahead. Trading grew rapidly and it became possible to 'insure' against currency movements farther ahead than was possible on the forward

94

markets. It then devised forward contracts in interest rates. By 1983 currency futures markets had developed in most commodity dealing centres around the world, including London.

Almost anyone who buys or sells foreign exchange has to take some view of the way in which exchange rates are likely to move. In this sense almost everyone is speculating. But a line is conventionally drawn between those who, like the loom importer, are using the market as an insurance against exchange-rate changes, and those who are using it purely to make a profit and not to cover another transaction. In practice this distinction is highly arbitrary. For example, many large companies delay settling their accounts abroad if they expect their own country's currency to appreciate, and speed them up if they are afraid of the reverse. Because Britain is so heavily dependent on foreign trade, this phenomenon, known as leads and lags, can put very heavy pressure on the exchange rate.

Someone must speculate on currencies if forward exchange markets are to work at all. To go back to the loom importer: in order for him to buy his currency forward, someone (probably a bank) has to sell it, taking on the importer's exchange risk for the price of the forward premium. Still, the very term 'speculator' has an unsavoury and unpatriotic ring about it. Certainly if enough people speculate on a currency with a fixed exchange rate being devalued, it is not easy for the combined forces of the world's central banks to stop them proving themselves right. But anyone who thinks that this is the result of the malice of speculators rather than the inadequacies of the international monetary system should remember the fate of Laker Airways in 1982. It had borrowed heavily in dollars to finance its purchase of the Airbus. But virtually all its income was in sterling. When sterling fell against the dollar, it could not generate sufficient income to service its loan. If Laker had passed that currency risk over to speculators on the financial futures market it could, conceivably, have survived.

The 1970s witnessed some of the most turbulent moments the foreign exchange markets have ever seen. These crises have left a lasting scar on British economic policy: movements in domestic interest rates are usually triggered by pressure on the

95

exchange rate. In the 1970s, the Bank of England's experience was coloured by the memory of the devaluation of 1967. Up to then, the Bank was obliged to support the spot rate for the pound with limits set down by the International Monetary Fund. Before the 1967 devaluation, the Bank also chose to support the forward rate. At the time this was heralded as an important statement of the nation's faith in the parity of sterling. Had the pound not been devalued, it would have had the advantage of taking pressure off the spot rate without causing a drain on reserves. As it turned out, the Bank – that is, the country – lost £356 million on forward contracts in this futile defence of sterling. In effect, the Bank was speculating against devaluation. It got it wrong and suffered the largest single speculative loss ever recorded on the foreign exchange markets.

Understandably, the traumatic experience of the 1967 devaluation made the authorities far less willing to fight to save a shaky exchange rate. In June 1972 it took less than a week of severe pressure before the pound was allowed to float, and British resistance to joining the EMS undoubtedly has something to do with the country's experiences in the 1960s and 1970s.

But floating has been no panacea. Sterling's plunge in 1976, which caused the then Chancellor, Denis Healey, to turn back at Heathrow airport instead of attending the International Monetary Fund meeting in Manila, was only stopped by a loan from the IMF and a deflationary economic package. Indeed the fluctuations of currencies in the late 1970s and early 1980s – sterling went down to $1.56, up to $2.42 and back to $1.19 in the space of eight years – have led to suggestions that the authorities will try again to damp down currency movements by intervening on the exchanges in a more determined way.

During these currency crises, the foreign exchange market is chaotic. But at any busy period a dealing room looks like a madhouse. The best description is that of the ex-dealer of a clearing bank:*

*Jack R. Higgins in a symposium, 'A Day in the Life of a Banker' (The Institute of Bankers, 1963).

Calls from customers, calls from foreign banks overseas, calls from the brokers. Some merely seeking information, some seeking rates on which to base their day's work. There will be calls from Paris, Amsterdam, Copenhagen, Brussels, Hamburg and many other financial centres. Some with genuine propositions, some hoping for an advantageous quotation somewhere in the list . . .

The babel rises a few decibels as the linguists join the chorus. Rates are being quoted in French, Italian and probably German. Each operator will be dealing with the requirements of his own particular caller, whilst keeping his ear often cocked to any possible changes in rates by his colleagues as they effect their deals and look for a covering operation elsewhere. . . .

The textbooks discourse widely and wisely on spot rates and forward rates. They delve deeply into the mysteries of arbitrage. Unfortunately, especially when dealing with exchange for a forward delivery, it rarely works that way. When one wants to buy dollars for, say, three months' delivery, one finds the broker offers in lieu some two months or some six months, or he cannot offer the outright date, but can offer the swap.

What shall one do? Will one of the propositions fit the book? Many questions flit through the dealer's mind. Try another broker? But the first will already have scented blood and be out scouring the market for the chance to close up a deal. To put someone else in will accentuate the effect. Take him off? He might see the opportunity to deal and go elsewhere. Try Paris? They will read a change in the market and be nipping back on another line to clobber the market under one's nose. Try Germany? Might work against marks. Can the mark dealer help? Has he something on his books which will help the arbitrage price? Questions and answers are flitting through the dealer's brain and he alone must find the answer. Meanwhile he is probably dealing with a fractious importer who is demanding last night's closing price as shown in *The Times* for a cheque for $27.53 drawn on Milwaukee, Wis.

The details have changed over the intervening twenty years but the fundamentals have not. As exchange rates become increasingly flexible and movements of foreign currencies become larger, the foreign exchange broker's job becomes yet more hectic. Of one thing you can be sure. The more chaotic the world's foreign exchange markets, the more money will be made by the people buying and selling on them.

FIVE

The institutional investors

Why institutions?

The growth of institutional investors during the 1960s and 1970s has dramatically changed the face of the City. It has been the outward and visible sign of a revolution in the way savings are now channelled into financial securities. This is a revolution which is not confined to the United Kingdom. In every major industrial country there has been a tendency for individual shareholders to decline relative to institutional shareholders. But the decline has gone further in Britain than anywhere else, including the United States and Germany. As a result, all financial centres have seen the growth of a new centre of power, a new barony. But nowhere else has financial investment power become so concentrated in the hands of a very small number of institutions and individuals as in the City of London. Not surprisingly, this concentration of power has acquired political as well as economic significance.

It has attracted plenty of criticism. Institutional power and accountability were the chief concern of the Wilson Committee, the committee formed under the former prime minister in 1977 which reported in May 1980.* It found that the pension funds in particular operated without adequate supervision – one of the few aspects of the City's functioning on which the committee members could agree. And some members took the view that the institutions failed to invest enough in British industry. Since the lifting of exchange controls in November 1979, the institutions have been the butt of further attacks. They have been the principal channel through which funds

*Report of the Committee to Review the Functioning of Financial Institutions, Cmnd. 7937.

99

have been sent overseas, investing in the subsequent four years far more in foreign industrial and commercial companies than they did in British. This has given rise to further concern that institutional power is not used in the best interest of the country's economy.

When people talk of institutional investors – or just 'the institutions', for short – they generally have in mind four types of financial organisation. First, and largest in the volume of funds they control, are the pension funds, with some £89 billion at the end of 1983. In the early 1980s they overtook the life assurance companies which had some £87 billion. Much smaller are the investment trusts, at £11 billion, and unit trusts, with £8.5 billion. Together these four groups had by 1978 already reached the stage of owning nearly half of all British equities and Government stocks, as the Wilson Committee revealed. The latest figures of the Stock Exchange* show that the total institutional slice of company shareholdings was in 1981 even larger: no less than 58 per cent. Aside from the four types of institutions noted above, the Exchange's figures also covered funds invested by charities, banks, industrial companies, the public sector and foreigners, but these have not significantly increased the proportion of shares they hold.

This dominance of the British equity market by the institutions has come about with remarkable speed. In 1963 the financial institutions owned only 30 per cent of shares. There are a number of reasons for this growth. In part it is a result of the fact that people save more than they used to. The 1960s and 1970s saw a sharp rise in personal savings as a proportion of Gross Domestic Product, and a sharp decline both in company savings (their retained profits) and in the savings of the public sector (reflected in the rise in the public sector financial deficit). As a result, the financial system has had to recycle a vastly increased flow of personal savings into loans to industry and to the government.

These increased personal savings were much more widely distributed than before: instead of savings being generated by a small proportion of rich individuals, they were being generated

*The Stock Exchange Survey of Share Ownership 1983.

by anyone in the country with a life assurance policy or a funded pension. So the wider distribution of wealth went hand in hand with a shift of savings from people who – by habit – would tend to keep their financial assets in individual shareholdings, to people who would generate their savings through contractual obligation to a financial institution and who would have no particular interest in holding the shares of individual companies. The result has been the rise of the institutional investor – and the decline of the personal investor. Individuals in 1963 held 54 per cent of all UK listed company shares; by 1975 this had fallen to 38 per cent; and by 1981 this was down to 28 per cent.

Thus individual savers, instead of buying shares and gilts themselves, have increasingly come to place their savings with specialist companies which invest it for them. They may not have much choice in this. Take life assurance: anyone who buys a house on an endowment mortgage will be taking out a life assurance policy which includes a large element of savings. Many companies oblige their employees to join a company pension scheme. As a result, even people who are hardly aware that they have any life assurance probably do, and more than half of all UK employees belong to pension schemes and so have to contribute part of their salary into a fund which will be invested with the aim of providing them with a pension when they retire.

It is this growth of occupational pensions, particularly in the public sector, that has been the most important single force driving the growth of the big institutional investors. The actual number of people in pension schemes has not risen that much since the 1960s, but the quality of the benefits has been improving steadily. The result has been that contributions as a proportion of salary have tended to rise and that fund managers have been under enormous pressure to deliver the best investment performance. An accumulation of investments through capital gains has been the main way to generate the funds to pay increased benefits in a time of relatively high inflation.

The boom in contractual savings would not have occurred on its present scale had it not also been for the tax system. Saving through a pension scheme is encouraged in three ways. First, employees' contributions to a pension scheme are deducted from their gross pay before tax is calculated. Second, there is no tax on the investment income or the capital gains of a pension fund. And third, employees may draw out the equivalent of up to one-and-a-half times their final pay. The first two tend to increase the pool of funds locked into the pension funds; the third enables people to get at that pool more easily. Indeed the rules have gradually been changed so that people retiring early have found it possible to retire without losing any of their pensions, which has further increased the attractiveness of paying as high a proportion of salary as possible into the pension fund.

Life assurance had similarly benefited greatly from tax relief until the 1984 budget, in which this relief was removed. Until then, the whole premium had attracted tax relief, not just that part which insured the policy-holder's life. This had encouraged people to take out additional life assurance over and above what they might require, simply as a tax-efficient saving scheme.

Tax relief for pensions continues. It has undoubtedly been a very important factor in encouraging institutional growth, but no one knows whether, were it completely removed, individuals would start to buy more and more stocks and shares . . . or whether they would simply save less. Meanwhile the boom in institutional investment continues.

The pension funds

A company wanting to offer its employees a pension scheme has three main ways of organising it. One is to set up its own fund, run by trustees appointed by the company and its employees. The largest of these self-administered pension funds make their own investment decisions, with a staff to study the investment scene worldwide. This staff will, of course, take advice from the various investment specialists: British stockbrokers for UK equities and gilts; foreign securities houses for international investments; property specialists for investments in land and other property. But day-to-day decisions will be taken by the chief investment managers and their staff, going to the trustees for major strategic decisions.

A second option, chosen by smaller self-administered funds, is to hand over the day-to-day investment decision-making to a specialist adviser, usually a merchant bank or insurance company. The adviser (or advisers, as the fund may be split) will report regularly to the trustees on the investment performance of the funds, and take all the investment decisions. But they do not carry the ultimate legal responsibility, and the trustees can sack them if their performance is inadequate. Most medium-sized firms choose this second way of running a pension scheme, and advising these has been a large and growing source of business for the City.

The third option is for the company to encourage its employees to join an outside scheme, run usually by a large life assurance company, which will give the employees a package deal. The funds in this case will be added to the company's own larger funds. In the case of small pension funds, this has the advantage of spreading the investment risk over a wide range of different securities. The employer will probably pay a contribution to the pension fund, but the insurance company carries the legal responsibility for the pension and makes the contract with the employee.

The very largest funds, which almost invariably have a team of investment managers and an active investment policy, are those of the nationalised industries. Biggest of all is the massive fund of the old Post Office, although it will lose its place once it is split between the Post Office and the new organisation, British Telecom. In 1982, before it was split, it had a market value of £4.7 billion. Not much more than half that size are the two funds of the National Coal Board, one for white collar staff, the other for manual workers, which together had a value of £2.7 billion. The Electricity Council, British Rail, British Steel and British Gas all have a market value greater than the largest private sector funds, those of Barclays Bank, British Petroleum, Unilever and the National Westminster Bank. In 1982 eleven funds had a capital of more than £1 billion and a further twelve controlled more than £500 million.

The public sector pension funds have grown particularly fast

103

for two reasons. First their benefits are effectively (and in the case of local authorities, statutorily) indexed: as prices rise, so does the value of the pension the funds are required to pay out. Second, they are relatively new funds: the number of people contributing to them still generally exceeds the number of people receiving benefits. They are not, in the jargon of the trade, 'mature'. As a result, the net sums of new money they have to invest each day is vast; the Post Office alone has to find a home for well over £1 million every day.

The people who invest these enormous sums for the giant public and private sector funds are – to put it mildly – not well known. They are honoured guests at stockbroker lunches, for the business of a large pension fund has been immensely profitable for the brokers under the fixed commission system. And they attend City seminars on investment policy. But most of the time they remain incognito, watching the millions roll across their desks and flow into investments around the world.

On the rare occasions when they do appear in public, it is usually because they intend to make waves. Ralph Quartano, the donnish chief executive of the Post Office fund, will sometimes make a point in person at a shareholders' meeting. When he does so, he invariably chooses his words carefully to make sure that his views get maximum publicity; he was once a journalist himself. It was he who declared that, 'It is important that St Michael is on the side of the angels,' when he criticised Marks and Spencer directors for enjoying the benefits of low-rent mansions at the firm's expense without the approval of the shareholders. He also appeared in court during the dispute over the takeover bid by Robert Holmes à Court for Lord Grade's ACC, when he challenged the decision of the company to give a £560,000 golden handshake to the former managing director, Jack Gill.

The National Coal Board's funds, the next biggest, were managed by Hugh Jenkins, a Welsh surveyor, until early in 1985. During his time there he came to be regarded as the country's leading expert in the institutions on property investment, and has also played an energetic role in improving the accountability of pension funds. The Coal Board's pension fund has occasionally made investments which have not been to the liking of the National Union of Mineworkers, but independence from the NUM (or indeed the NCB) was one of Hugh Jenkins' most fundamental tenets. The NUM took the Mineworkers Pension Fund to court in 1983 to try to stop Jenkins investing so much in the United States. It lost.

The British Rail pension fund is run from modern offices just in front of Euston Station by John Morgan, a mild-mannered ex-banker. In fact, the British Rail investment policy has been one of the most controversial, with at one stage (largely before Mr Morgan took the helm) the fund making a string of well-publicised ventures into the art market. With the advice of Sotheby's, it bought a large collection of antiques, porcelain and paintings, including works by Cézanne, Renoir and Picasso. Outsiders, including a House of Commons committee, have pondered whether this is really the appropriate place to invest the savings of the railway workers.

Apart from these obscure giants, there are some 25,000 middle-sized and smaller funds, ranging down to tiddlers like that of the Lygon Arms in the Cotswold village of Broadway, whose members' contributions in 1982 were £9,600.

With such enormous variations in the size of the funds they invest, the quality of pension fund managers inevitably varies greatly. It is probably improving quite fast, for while pension fund management remains a vigorous growth area, it will tend to attract bright people. In the big funds, staff have been poached from other City institutions, and the performance of the investments of each fund manager is measured at least every three months. But elsewhere pension fund management suffers from the fact that until recently it was an unglamorous backwater. The funds themselves have made efforts to improve the quality of the profession, setting up the Institute of Pensions Management in the late 1970s to carry out examinations and establish a professional qualification. But in many companies the pension fund is run by the company secretary, with a bit of help from a couple of stockbrokers.

As a result, the performance of different pension funds must vary enormously too. But it is hard to measure pension management performance. Only local authorities have published figures which allow their average annual investment return to be compared (by anyone prepared to shell out £50 for the information). For other funds, the most one can say is that the pension provisions of the best schemes are much better than the worst: although this may have rather more to do with past contribution levels than with current management performance. There are no figures available to the general public on how well the various funds perform, so it is not possible to draw up a league table (as can be done for the life assurance funds).

There is virtually no public information about the size of most pension funds, their investment policies or their performance. Read through the *Yearbook of the National Association of Pension Funds* and you find that some funds give considerable detail, including their market value and the names of their investment advisers. Others, including the Stock Exchange, the *Financial Times* and the Labour Party, merely offer the name and address of their registered office.

Worse, there are often no adequate figures on performance available to the company's shareholders, sometimes even to the members of the pension scheme itself. Yet both have a key interest in fund performance. Pension fund contributions are for most people their largest single investment, often worth more even than the house they own. And if there is a deficiency in the fund, it will be the shareholders of the company who will suffer, as the company is usually required to make up the difference.

The reason for this extraordinary lack of information is partly that legislation has not caught up with the growth of the pension funds as an important part of our financial system, and partly that there is no natural competition between the funds to try to deliver improved performance. As far as legislation is concerned, most pension funds are set up as trusts and covered by trust law. This was developed mainly to cover family and charitable trusts, not to order the affairs of pension schemes with anything from ten to many thousands of members. It does impose a simple legal obligation upon trustees: to manage the assets of the fund solely in the interest of the beneficiaries. But it does not buttress this with any obligation on the part of trustees to give information that would enable the members to

106

determine whether they were in fact carrying out their duty adequately. Some schemes give their members considerable detail, publishing an annual report on performance and holding an annual meeting at which any member can ask questions. But they do this voluntarily, and are virtuous exceptions to the norm.

As long as trustees are perceived to be obeying their general duty to manage the funds in the interests of the members, there are very few constraints in law on their freedom to put the money where they like. If members are unhappy with the fund's investment performance, there is no obvious action they can take: they cannot take their pension to a better fund manager, despite the fact that it is their own money that is being badly invested.

One result of this lack of regulation is that there are alarmingly few constraints on the way in which pension funds can be invested. There are all sorts of ways in which conflicts of interest may arise. For example, when the J. Lyons food group was under severe financial pressure in 1975–6, it sold a number of its properties to its own pension fund. It sold with an independent valuation – but under trust law, it was under no obligation to have one. Or again, the Cavenham food group, controlled by Mr (later Sir) James Goldsmith, placed a sizeable proportion of its pension fund in a bank which was also controlled by Sir James. That bank also provided pension advice to the Cavenham group. Yet again, many of the Sainsbury pension fund's properties in the 1970s were in fact shops leased back to the Sainsbury group.

The lack of regulation also meant that during the 1970s the pension funds of some of Britain's most reputable concerns became involved in highly speculative investments. For example, the ICI fund lost a great deal of money in the fringe bank and property crash of the early 1970s, and as a result the company had to increase its contributions to the fund very sharply. The pension fund of the Electricity Council lent money on a large number of speculative projects and its managers were strongly criticised for doing so in a report by the accountants Cork Gully. One of the advisers to Unilever's pension fund continued to manage a large portfolio of

107

European property even after he had been described in a Department of Trade report on his other businesses as unsuitable 'to act as a director of a company'.*

Indeed the remarkable thing about pension funds is the extent to which they operate in a vacuum. There is no comprehensive framework, either laid down by statute or established as part of the City's self-regulatory mechanism, for supervising their affairs. There is no prudential control, no body responsible for monitoring their behaviour. The funds have a trade association, the National Association of Pension Funds, which has offices in Croydon and is supposed to represent their interests. But this body has no authority over its members, and though some 1,600 funds are members, there is no obligation to join.

There is the Occupational Pensions Board, a statutory body set up in 1973, which is supposed to ensure that pension funds comply with various regulations: like the preservation of pensions when people change jobs, or the requirement that funds provide a minimum level of benefit. But its powers are limited. In 1975 it undertook a study to see whether the industry needed strict controls on investment. It also recommended a code of good practice, regular publication of financial information, registration with a central authority and easier legal procedures for members who thought there had been poor administration and wished to challenge this. None of these recommendations was taken up.

Five years later, the Wilson Committee had another crack at the pension funds. It recommended that there should be a Pension Scheme Act, which would enforce similar provisions to those suggested in 1975. Again nothing happened. But Margaret Thatcher's government has promised a Green Paper, with new legislation to follow in 1984/5.

The life offices

Unlike the pension funds, the life assurance companies, or life offices as they are generally called, operate both under external

*For the best account of misbehaviour of pension funds, see *That's the Way the Money Goes*, by John Plender (André Deutsch, 1982).

supervision and in a highly competitive environment. They still have a very wide degree of freedom over where they should put their (or rather their customers') money, but their performance is closely monitored by insurance brokers and the specialist press. They also have to be registered with the Department of Trade and Industry, which grants them a licence without which they cannot practise. Most of the companies doing this business, though not all, are members of the trade association, the Life Offices Association.

The life assurance companies fall into two broad types: those which are part of a general insurance group, and those which only offer life assurance. The largest funds are all part of general insurance businesses, of which the two biggest are the Prudential and the Legal and General.

The Pru, from its red-brick gothic temple in Holborn, is the country's largest single investor, handling more than £1 billion a year and with total assets in 1983 (including non-life business) of £16 billion. Its life fund was £12.4 billion. It also runs a general insurance business, but it is the growth of its life assurance side that has enabled it to overtake the Royal and the Commercial Union to become the largest overall insurance group. The Pru is run in a curiously collegiate style: decision is by committee consensus. Of its ten board members, five are actuaries, including Brian Corby, its chief executive, and Ron Artus, its chief investment manager.

The Pru takes its size seriously, as it must. In any major company it is usually the largest single investor. It tends to pursue a more active role as a shareholder than most other institutions. It has a large team of analysts examining the performance of the main companies in which it holds investments, whereas most smaller funds can only afford a handful of managers who have to rely on the second-hand judgments of stockbrokers' research departments. But size also tends to lock the Pru into shareholdings, while its smaller competitors can sell their holdings without moving the price too much against themselves. Thus there is a double incentive to stay with a company that is doing badly and try to help or bully it into solving its problems. The Pru has more resources and less freedom than the other funds.

109

The Pru is consulted regularly by the Bank of England on matters of corporate investment policy. It took the lead in coordinating the institutional investment purchases at the end of 1974 which eventually succeeded in checking the catastrophic slump in share prices. After falling more or less continuously for two years, on 6 January 1975 the *Financial Times* index hit a low of 146. But during the last few weeks of the fall, institutions had started to build up their purchases following a lunch of the biggest investors at the Pru's offices. Thanks in part to this intervention, the rebound of the index was as sharp as its fall: it virtually doubled in the first two months of 1975.

There are only two other companies that have life funds even half as large as those of the Pru. One is Legal and General, whose speciality is pension fund management. It manages more pension funds than any other company: although it has a large personal pension business, its fastest growth area has been running schemes for commercial and industrial companies. The chairman is Professor (now Sir) Jim Ball, head of the London Business School until 1984, and the board is studded with distinguished City names. It is one of the rare places in the City where academic life mingles with finance; it manages the funds of a large part of the academic world and its senior staff have a vaguely donnish air as they go about investing the multiplying billions.

The other life company which is growing very fast is Hambro Life. It is completely different both in style and formula from Legal and General. Its speciality is direct-sale unit-linked life assurance. The company is very much the brainchild of Mark Weinberg, a charming and sophisticated South African who is married to actress Anouska Hempel. Mark Weinberg only founded the business in 1965, with funds from Hambros Bank, but he had previously built up and sold Abbey Life. He is therefore personally responsible for a very large proportion of Britain's direct-sale unit-linked life business. Competitors are snooty about Hambro Life, which in part may simply be jealousy but which also reflects a concern that too much energy goes into selling techniques and not enough into investment performance. But they find it hard to argue with Hambro Life's

110

growth, and acknowledge that it has pioneered a product that the market seems to want. That, at least, is what tobacco giant, BAT, thinks. At the end of 1984 it bought Hambro Life for £664 million.

With the exception of the Pru, the life assurance funds (and insurance company funds, for they too hold large balances) are even less happy to play the role of the interventionist investors than the large pension funds. This may simply be because they tend individually to be smaller. It may be because the fastest-growing funds, those with unit trust links, have a tradition of trading shares and so tend to sell an interest if they dislike the way a company is run, rather than try to change the management. It may be that much of the energy in life assurance companies goes into developing new types of policy, instead of devoting all their time to the investment side, while the pension funds can simply concentrate on investment.

The unit trusts and investment trusts

The other two groups of investor, the unit trusts and the investment trusts, are less visible even than the life funds in their investment role. But a few of them are taking on a different significance as they are becoming the nucleus round which new financial service companies are being built, companies which aim to offer a whole range of services beyond pure investment.

Investment trusts are much older than unit trusts. There were fifty-eight of them already in existence at the start of this century. In fact, they were the first institutions to offer investors a way of spreading their risks on the stock market. The last burst of activity was in the early 1970s. Then, some forty new companies were set up, mainly to invest in overseas shares in Europe, the United States and the Far East. The unit trusts, by contrast, were a 1930s' invention, which started to achieve widespread popularity in the 1950s and which look set to overtake investment trusts in size in the second half of the 1980s.

Both groups are very much smaller than pension funds or life companies. But aside from differing in scale, they also differ in the time horizon in which they work. A pension fund or a life company has to think up to forty-five years ahead, and has little incentive to chase short-term gains. It receives a steady monthly flow of new receipts from its policy-holders, and faces an equally steady outflow of payments. By contrast, a unit trust firm has to look at its performance on a daily or weekly basis and publish the results of that performance, the price of its units, in the newspapers. Depending on the performance, floods of new money will arrive and have to be invested in roughly the same mix of securities as the fund had before, or floods of money will go out and part of the portfolio will be sold. For an investment trust, the time horizon is a little longer, but an investment trust's shares are quoted daily and it has to report every six months on its performance, so it too will find its investment policy under close market scrutiny. If performance falls, the investment trust, like any commercial company, but unlike a unit trust, could face a takeover bid.

Thus unit trusts and investment trusts work in quite different ways. A unit trust is an open-ended fund: if you buy a unit in a unit trust, that money, after deduction of commission, is added directly into the trust's pool of shareholdings. An investment trust, on the other hand, is a closed-ended fund: if you buy a share in an investment trust, you are simply buying one of a constant number of shares in the company which owns the assets. The value of the shares obviously bears some relation to the underlying value of the assets, but for much of the 1970s and early 1980s investment trust shares stood at a fair discount to the value of the assets.

This is a reflection of the fact that investment trusts have not been very successful animals compared with unit trusts. There are a number of reasons for this. The principal theoretical advantage the investment trusts might have – their ability to issue loan stock and buy higher yielding equities with the funds – has been a disadvantage in a time when yields on fixed interest securities have in fact been higher than the return on ordinary shares. The disadvantage has diminished as the very high inflation in the second half of the 1970s has receded. Since then, the investment trusts as a group have in fact been producing a rather better return than the unit trusts. But they remain handicapped by the difficulty they have in

112

accommodating a steady flow of contractual savings. Unlike a unit trust, an investment trust cannot smoothly grow or shrink as money comes in or out.

While there are many specialist investment trust and unit trust groups, both types are usually run by other financial institutions. For example, the clearing banks all offer their own unit trusts across their branch counters; the merchant banks frequently run both types of trust and so do some stockbrokers. But there are independent unit trust groups which also run the odd investment trust, and independent investment trust groups which also have the occasional unit trust. A very few of these independent trusts seem likely to mature into more broadly based financial service groups.

The largest group of investment trusts, run by Touche Remnant, is a good example of this trend. It has £1.2 billion of funds under management, and is a limited company, owned by the trusts in the group. These trusts account for more than half of the funds it manages, but it also runs a number of unit trusts, and manages pension funds.

Next come half a dozen investment trust groups with between £500 million and £1 billion under management. The largest of these are the trusts run by the accepting house Robert Fleming, which also controls Save and Prosper, the largest unit trust group, and so are already part of a wider financial services company. This is followed by Electra House Group, a public company which is seeking to broaden itself and may well develop into one of these general financial service companies, and Ivory and Sime, the largest of a Scots mafia of investment trust companies, most of which are grouped round that most elegant example of Edinburgh architecture, Charlotte Square.

These Edinburgh trusts, which include Martin Currie, Baillie Gifford, Edinburgh Fund Managers, Stewart Fund Managers, together with Murray Johnstone (in Glasgow) and Paull and Williamsons (in Aberdeen), are largely responsible for the Caledonian nomenclature of most investment trusts. The names, like General Scottish, Edinburgh American Assets, Scottish Mortgage, Murray Clydesdale, and St Andrew, help to make the whole sector pretty impenetrable for the English

113

investor. The actual structure of ownership is designed to be impenetrable, too. There is a large element of cross-holdings between the various trusts, making it virtually impossible for an outsider to take over any of them.

This is not so in London. Jacob Rothschild used an investment trust, RIT and Northern, as his base from which he built up the investment bank Charterhouse J. Rothschild. Many of the smaller independent trusts have found themselves prey to takeover bids. As long as the asset value of an investment trust is much lower than its market price, it is naturally attractive to take it over: after all, the individual shareholdings can be sold off at a profit whenever the asset value is below the market price. A number of investment trusts have disappeared in this way. Others have followed the principle that if you can't beat 'em, join 'em, either by setting up unit trusts or, more radically, by turning themselves into unit trusts. This process, hideously dubbed 'unitisation', means giving the shareholders units that reflect the underlying value of the investments in exchange for their shares. This is expensive and complicated, but where a trust stands at a very large discount, it can show a good profit for the holders.

The unit trust groups are of much more recent origin than the investment trusts. Though the two largest management groups, Save and Prosper and M and G, both date from the 1930s, most of the actual funds they manage are post-war creations. The post-war boom gave a boost to the movement and by the late 1950s there were about 50 different trusts. In 1968 there were 176, in 1978 414, and by 1983 there were 630 unit trusts run by 110 management groups authorised by the Department of Trade. Most of these management groups, though by no means all, are members of the Unit Trust Association, which seeks to monitor practice, scrutinise advertisements and so on. If you include all the funds quoted in the *Financial Times*, the number is a lot higher. But the majority of these additional funds are not registered with the Department of Trade and Industry, and are intended for foreign investors or other institutional investors. These funds are not in general allowed to be advertised to the public, and in a number of cases have to be registered offshore: they are

114

technically based in the Channel Islands, Cayman Islands or some other location outside the UK tax law. Most of these additional funds, however, are run by the same management companies that run the authorised funds.

Unit trust management is a relatively easy service to get into, and new companies continually sprout. But the two largest are the two oldest. Save and Prosper, with well over £1 billion of funds managed and over 500,000 unitholders in 1983, is controlled by Robert Fleming, the merchant bank, with a large minority share owned by Bank of Scotland. It has tended to lose market share over the years, but has itself been innovative. For example, in 1983 it was the first British institution to launch, with Fleming, current accounts carrying a high money market rate of interest. It was rewarded by several hundred millions of pounds flooding in, far more than it had thought possible.

The other 1930s foundation, M and G, older but now second to Save and Prosper in size, had just under £1 billion in its unit trusts in 1983. It is a public quoted company, in which Kleinworts has a large interest. Like Save and Prosper, it has also branched out into pension and life fund management.

Quite a long way behind these two groups come Allied Hambro, the unit trust wing of the life assurance group, and Barclays Unicorn, owned by Barclays Bank. All the clearing banks have unit trust departments, which sell their units across the branch counters, while a number of other large unit trust groups are owned by the merchant banking groups. The other main independent unit trust groups are Henderson, a public company which originally managed a number of investment trusts but which has seen a very rapid growth on the unit trust side, and Britannia, the unit trust side of the old Slater Walker investment bank which collapsed in 1975. Britannia, the main part of Slater Walker to survive, is now an independent quoted company.

Many other bodies run unit trusts, from the TUC to Mencap, the charity for the mentally handicapped. At the very bottom of the scale are tiny trusts, with less than £100,000 under management and fewer than twenty unitholders.

Why have unit trusts been so successful as an investment vehicle? It must be partly the fact that for a small investor they are both a relatively cheap way of buying professional management advice and an easy way to spread risks among a large number of holdings. It must also be partly due to the flexibility of the open-ended fund that can be expanded or contracted in line with demand. But the key to their growth is that they are essentially marketing operations. They are the only way in which financial securities are advertised to the public.

If you look at any newspaper there will be hosts of advertisements for savings schemes from the banks and building societies. TV screens are packed with similar commercials. But there will be no advertisements from individual companies for people to buy their shares. Only when a company makes a new issue of shares does it advertise the issue, and then in the form of a legal document packed with fine print. Stockbrokers have only recently been allowed to advertise at all, and are not permitted to promote shareholdings other than through unit trusts in their advertising. Even investment trusts are forbidden by law to advertise. So the only way that most people hear of the products of the financial securities market is through unit trust advertising.

As a result, unit trusts are packaged to suit each and every investor's whim. There are trusts specialising in different types of situation, in geographical areas, in fixed interest securities as well as equities, in commodities and in property. Some unit trusts, called managed bonds, switch their funds between different types of security, property and cash to try to anticipate market movements.

The names of unit trusts, unlike investment trusts, are descriptive, designed to lure the saver seeking a particular sort of investment: names like M and G High Income, Allied Hambro Smaller Companies, Gartmore Japan, Target Gold or Chieftain Preference and Gilt.

This close identification with specific investment aims is also a help to the institutional purchasers. Even quite large institutional investors might want to invest in, say, Japan, but not have or want to acquire the expertise to build up a properly diversified portfolio. One of the less rich Oxford colleges moved all its investments into unit trusts on the grounds that the £2

116

million it wanted to put into securities was too small to attract proper skills and attention in a merchant bank. This might seem a rather poor comment on our merchant banks, but it is a feather in the cap of the unit trust movement. The sheer speed with which the unit trusts respond to a new investment opportunity is impressive. In the March 1982 budget, the government announced wider access to index-linked gilts. Within a month, a unit trust had been set up to offer a pension plan using investment in these to offer index-linked private pensions.

The expansion of the unit trusts will doubtless continue, particularly since it is the easiest area of financial services, aside from simply giving investment advice, for an outsider to enter. But its longer term growth is closely linked to the attraction of financial securities as a haven for savings, compared with bank or building society accounts. The sad fact is that when the stock market is doing well, the unit trusts boom, and when it is doing badly sales fall off. This means that many investors get into units at precisely the wrong time, when stocks are highest. They boomed in 1968–72, collapsed in the mid '70s, and then recovered at the end of the decade. But at the end of 1983, the actual number of unit holdings, at just under two million, was lower than it was in 1977.

So despite their innovation, the hard-sell tactics and the proliferation of different trusts, the unit trusts have not been particularly successful at attracting growing numbers of savers. They have not reached very far down the income and social-class scale. In the end it may well be that the main growth area for them will be as intermediaries for other institutions, rather than as channels for the cash of private individuals. Unless, that is, they themselves become part of larger financial service groups, the direction in which Allied Hambro and Save and Prosper, in particular, have already gone.

Power without accountability?

Inevitably, the concentration of investment in the hands of a relatively small number of institutions in a fairly short space of time has sent shock-waves through the financial system. The growth of these investment institutions has had an enormous impact on the way the City's other institutions operate – and, in particular, on the Stock Exchange. But it has also raised a whole series of questions about the extent to which the duties of the institutional investors should be tempered by a sense of wider responsibility to the country as a whole.

The institutions have come under attack from a number of directions. Some have argued that the concentration of share ownership increases the volatility of prices. Others have been concerned that the rise of the institutions has diminished the role of the small shareholder.

Like sheep, fund managers all tend to move in the same direction at the same time. Because the number of people involved is so small – less than a couple of hundred – and because they mostly know each other quite well, there is an inevitable similarity of outlook.

But the evidence, such as it is, seems to suggest that in fact different institutions have rather different investment policies. When the Wilson Committee surveyed how frequently the institutions sold their shares, it found that while the general trend over the years had been to trade more actively, the insurance companies and pension funds held onto their shares for longer, selling on average between 13 and 16 per cent of their ordinary shares each year between 1973 and 1977. By contrast, sales by investment trusts ranged between 17 and 28 per cent, and by unit trusts, which have to respond to investors' sales and purchases of units, between 38 and 57 per cent.

More tellingly, perhaps, there does not seem much increase in volatility as far as the general level of prices is concerned. It is difficult to argue that prices have been more volatile in the late 1970s and early 1980s than they were in, say, the late 1950s and early 1960s. Indeed, it is quite plausible that as most of the new institutional funds arrive in contractual form, their existence has actually smoothed out the flow of funds available for investment.

But that would only hold for the market as a whole. What about individual share prices? Here the growth of large funds may have increased the potential for a one-way market. Views become fashionable, be they views about the prospects for an individual company or for government financing in general. So a bullish briefing for the institutions from the finance director of a large company can drive its shares sharply upwards, at least for a while. Similarly, a circular by a firm of brokers with a reputation for understanding the intricacies of the Public Sector Borrowing Requirement can make or break the success of a new issue of government stock.

There may also be some element of deliberate institutional collusion over the decision on whether to subscribe for new issues. Here the institutions have a dual role. They help to underwrite new issues, guaranteeing that if the new shares are not sold, they themselves will take up what remains. For this they receive a commission. But they may also want to subscribe to the issues themselves.

So should it become apparent that an issue is likely to be undersubscribed, the institutions will not subscribe, because they will be likely to pick up all the shares they might have wanted from their role as underwriters. But of course an issue is only undersubscribed if the institutions do not subscribe it, for typically they would expect to pick up more than half the shares on offer. So how do they know what will happen? In practice they pick up the inclinations of the other institutions via the brokers, and though each institution would probably say that it makes up its own mind, they do give each other a fair idea of whether they will subscribe to an issue or not.

In doing this they would argue that they were simply seeking to do the best possible deal for their savers, as should individual shareholders do for themselves. But it is clearly worrying that the success of a new issue should be so determined by a relatively small number of people, whose judgment may well be proved wrong.

A more serious effect of the growth of the institutions has undoubtedly been to create two classes of investor. The big investor, wooed by the brokers, on first-name terms with company finance directors, working from an office packed with television screens giving instant information on prices and company results, is working in a quite different way from the individual with little more than native wit and the previous day's news in the *Financial Times*. In theory, the institutions should not be told anything about a company's prospects that an individual shareholder, seeking information from the company, could not learn. But everyone knows that is bunk.

Yet paradoxically, institutional ownership of Britain's companies may, in one sense at least, have increased the influence of shareholders. Most fund managers have to answer for their decisions every three months, and their performance is closely compared. One of the results of this pressure is that institutions are both more willing to intervene when a management is performing badly and less likely to support an existing management when a company is subject to a takeover bid.

Where concentration of power undoubtedly does have an effect is in a takeover bid. Here, in most cases at least, a handful of fund managers will effectively decide whether a bid should go through. To win a takeover bid needs only 50 per cent of the votes. Typically, the institutions will hold 60 per cent or more. A bidding company will usually only make its bid when it already has perhaps 10 per cent of the shares, so the proportion of votes that have to be swung is very small. Most personal investors will not vote, or if they do the votes they cast will split fairly evenly. So winning a modest majority of the institutions will usually win the company.

Does this bring about better decisions? It certainly leads to better-informed ones, for the dozen or two dozen people running the large institutions will probably have the opportunity to meet senior people in both managements personally, and be able to compare them with each other and with other companies in the sector. As professionals they are probably less likely to be impressed by a charismatic chief executive with a mediocre record than will 30,000 small shareholders whose main information comes from a glossy annual report, which will invariably state that the management is wonderful (if the company is doing well) or that the British economy is going to the dogs (if the company is doing badly). But no one can prove that the institutions make better decisions than the small shareholders, and there are plenty of examples where the small shareholders have done something that the

120

professionals universally thought was mad, and ended up making a fortune. Thus people who bought shares in the bankrupt Rolls-Royce in 1971 for less than a shilling, intending to paper their walls with them, found their investment worth anything up to twenty times the amount they paid when the receiver wound up the company. Much the same, though on a slightly less dramatic scale, happened to shares in British Leyland twelve years later. Just sometimes a private whim is a better guide than a host of computer print-outs.

Some of those who bewail most loudly the disappearance of the individual shareholder are also those who demand that institutions should use their rights as shareholders – something which the individual shareholder rarely uses at all. It is precisely because of the decline of the individual shareholder that we are witnessing a dramatic increase in shareholder power.

The most important issue of all in the debate over the role the institutions ought to play is how far they ought to use their considerable power to try to improve industrial performance. The pension fund and the life assurance companies are in precisely the sort of situation that some of the City's critics have wanted the clearing banks to achieve. Just as the banks in Germany or Japan own large chunks of industry – and so are forced to take an active interest in the way industry is run – so the funds are being driven to take an active interest in the companies they control.

It is an ironic situation. The nationalised industry and local authority pension funds (which have to provide for indexed pensions) are increasing control of British industry in a way which would cause uproar if such creeping nationalisation were formally proposed. Those employees of the public sector are, in turn, heavily dependent on the success of the private sector to provide them with a pension in their old age. A further irony is that the nationalised industry funds are the most vocal institutional investors: capitalism needs the voice of state-sector savers to keep it on the rails.

The ability of the institutions to monitor the performance of management varies. Only the biggest pension funds and life companies have the resources to do their own original research on the firms in which they own shares, or to make regular contact with more than, say, a couple of dozen each year. Most of the institutions prefer to step in – if they must – collectively through one of the three Investment Protection Committees run by the insurance companies, the pension funds and the unit trusts – or to use the more recently established Institutional Shareholders' Committee.

On the IPCs sit a group of senior investment managers. Most of the cases they handle each year come to them at the request of the companies involved, and deal with essentially technical problems such as the revision of lending contracts or capital reconstruction schemes. But there are also each year a few cases of principle, such as the issue of non-voting shares or the establishment of the rights of shareholders; and a few fire-fighting cases where a number of institutions have become worried about a management problem in an individual firm. In 1973, in response to pressure from the Bank of England, the institutions set up the Institutional Shareholders' Committee. Its intention was partly to coordinate the work of existing IPCs, and partly to stimulate 'action by industrial and commercial companies to improve efficiency'.

The ISC has probably done more to carry out its first aim than its second, more constructive goal. There remains a widespread feeling among the institutions – and, not surprisingly, among industrial companies – that the institutions do not have the manpower or the expertise to second-guess management. It is still fairly unusual for the institutions to install a director on the board of the companies in which they hold shares (although some of the insurance companies have directors on the boards of firms to which they have lent substantial sums). Without a presence in the boardroom, it is hard to see how the institutions can hope to become involved in a company's problems at an early enough stage to be able to do something about them.

A great deal of the contact which takes place between the institutions and industry does not become public knowledge. The institutions generally argue that a row which has a lot of publicity is harder to resolve. It is usually when one company bids for another, or when there is a boardroom row, that the institutions appear above the parapet. Frequently this is when there is a legal point at issue, such as an excessive golden handshake, or a charge that directors have cooked the books. In the case of a bid, they are simply responding to a proposition on which they, like any shareholders, are obliged to take a view. Only occasionally do the institutions intervene and initiate a major change of management, or indeed set up a takeover themselves.

The most radical example of the institutions taking the lead in sacking a management was the purchase of the controlling interest in the British F.W. Woolworth from its American parent in 1982. There, after many years of evident failure, the old management was eventually ousted and the British minority shareholders took charge. But though this was essentially at the wish of the institutions, it took a merchant bank, Charterhouse, to bring them all together and push the deal through.

The public feeling that it is appropriate and desirable for the institutions to take a more active role in monitoring the performance of companies has gone together with a belief that the public ought to have some say in how their funds are deployed. The concentration of investment makes it possible to talk about public control in a way which never made sense before: and the financial power wielded by the institutions makes it reasonable to ask what they do with their money.

Within the Labour Party in particular there has been pressure for the nationalisation of the clearing banks and larger insurance companies. It was to head off this pressure that James Callaghan, when he was Prime Minister, set up the Wilson Committee. A note of dissent to the Committee's main report, signed by Sir Harold Wilson and by four trade union representatives on the committee, called for the setting up of a new investment facility, jointly funded by the public sector and by the long-term investing institutions, to increase investment in British industry. The low level of investment, the note argued, was largely responsible for Britain's poor industrial performance.

Some of the widespread beliefs about the ways in which the institutions use their funds do not bear close investigation. For instance, there is the charge that institutional investors are less likely to take risks and to put money into small firms than individuals.

In fact, the Stock Exchange survey of share ownership for 1981 found that shareholdings by the institutions were evenly distributed among all but the smallest companies. It was only among firms with market values of under £20 million that the institutions were notably under-represented – but those tend to be the firms with the largest family shareholdings. Besides, there has been a tendency among the bigger institutions – especially the pension funds of the nationalised industries – deliberately to search out opportunities to invest money in small projects and companies. The Pru has a subsidiary called Prutech to invest in new high-technology enterprises. Other institutions have specialised in funding management buy-outs, others again in putting funds into the Stock Exchange's Unlisted Securities Market. These will probably have more success than the attempt by the Bank of England to foster institutional high-risk lending, by setting up Equity Capital for Industry in 1976. ECI, funded by the institutions, has made a series of disastrous investments including the carpet manufacturer Bond Worth and the truck manufacturer Foden. Both subsequently went bust.

Since the removal of exchange controls, the institutions have become the butt of a different line of attack: that they have been the main route through which British savings have been channelled abroad. It is perfectly true that in 1981 and 1982 the pension funds bought about as many foreign company shares as they did British; the insurance companies did much the same; and the investment trusts actually ran down their UK holdings while building up their foreign ones.

But it may still be wrong to cast the institutions as the villains or the victims of wider economic forces. If the returns on British industry are too low, the institutions will invest abroad; if British companies can deliver a good record, they will invest at home.

The fundamental question posed by the extraordinary growth of the institutions is whether it is really sensible for the tax system and for government policy deliberately to encourage

124

the trend. It may well be – as the rise of the institutional investor is an international phenomenon – that it would have taken place to some extent in any environment. But we have at the moment a system which gives every incentive to the saver to put money into a pension fund rather than buying securities directly. We have appallingly few controls on the way the largest of these investors, the pension funds, conduct their business. The next era of the financial markets, ripe for scandal or for reform, must be institutional investment and specifically Britain's 25,000 occupational pension funds.

SIX

The securities market

Public service or gentlemen's club?

Every stockbroker will assure you that the London Stock Exchange exists to serve the country.* To anyone who reads daily in the newspapers of takeover battles, daring coups by young financiers and gyrating share prices, this assurance might sound unconvincing. And to anyone who suspects that top jobbers in a good year are the best-paid men in the City simply because they possess a superior gambling instinct, it might sound positively outrageous. But in a sense, the stockbroking community is right. The Stock Exchange does exist for the mundane purpose of channelling personal savings into industrial and commercial investment and of providing a market-place for trading company shares. The criterion on which it should be judged is how well it performs these tasks.

The day-to-day business of a Stock Exchange is issuing and dealing in securities, which are of two kinds. In Britain, roughly one-half (by market valuation) are fixed-interest securities, some issued by companies (and called debentures, loans and preference shares) but most issued by the government (and referred to as 'gilt-edged'). These are, strictly speaking, stocks.† Shares (or equities or ordinary shares as they are known) are always issued by companies. Like fixed-interest

*Well, almost every stockbroker. Graham Greenwell, then senior partner of brokers W. Greenwell and a member of the Stock Exchange Council, wrote in a famous letter to *The Times* in June 1971 that the Exchange was a private gentlemen's club and not 'an institution which exists to perform a public service'. Greenwell's has changed since then: by the 1980s it had become one of the City's most aggressive brokers.
†Confusingly, in the United States stocks (whether issued by companies or the government) are called 'bonds' and equities, 'common stocks'.

stocks, equities are bought and sold at prices which fluctuate constantly; but while fixed-interest stocks pay their holders a known interest rate, equities pay a dividend which may be a different amount every half-year – or in a bad year nothing at all. Equity holders generally, though not invariably, have a vote in the company's affairs.

Taking the value of equity shares traded, a widely fluctuating figure, London always comes a poor third to the New York Stock Exchange and Tokyo. It is, however, almost as big as all the other European stock exchanges put together. It is twice the size of the next biggest, in Frankfurt, and it quotes roughly 8,000 separate securities, far more than on any other exchange. It is also one of the very few stock markets where the government raises money from the public; and where the public can buy and sell government securities after they have been issued.

This chapter deals with the whole spectrum of securities trading in London; not just with the activities of the Stock Exchange itself. There are two broad themes – two pressures which dominate the Exchange, and which are forcing sweeping changes in the way it works. First, there has been the rise of the institutional investor. The Stock Exchange still likes to think of itself as the bastion of the small shareholder. Yet the personal shareholder plays a far smaller role than in most other countries. Everywhere, funds invested in financial securities have come increasingly from the savings institutions rather than directly from individuals. But in Britain, this process has gone further than in other countries.

The rise of the institutional investor put pressure on the commission system, still (in 1985) the basis of charging for share deals; and it put pressure on the London Exchange's unique separation of the functions of stockbroker and jobber. But the institutional investors emerged as a problem for the Exchange in the 1970s. In the early 1980s, it became clear that the rigid structure of the Exchange would have to cope with a second change: the increasing internationalisation of securities trading.

The London Stock Exchange has, in effect, a near monopoly of trading in UK securities and UK gilts. But it accounts for perhaps only three-quarters of all securities traded in London. The remaining quarter – the proportion is a rough guess, for there are no figures – consists very largely of trading in eurobonds and foreign (mainly US) equities. In the course of the 1970s, London emerged as the main international centre for trading in dollar eurobonds and as the main non-US centre for trading in American shares. About 70 per cent of all eurobonds are denominated in dollars; and of others, the principal centres for bonds denominated in German marks is Luxembourg and Frankfurt, and for those in Swiss francs is Zurich.

But one of the remarkable aspects of the rise of the London eurobond market has been that it has largely by-passed the brokers and jobbers who make up the London Stock Exchange. The rigid distinction between broker and jobber has made it much more difficult for members of the London Stock Exchange to participate in the main growth areas of international securities trading – even when the growth is taking place on their own doorstep. In 1983 the Zurich-based Association of International Bond Dealers listed some 120 members as dealing in London in eurobonds. Only four were members of the London Stock Exchange. As the watertight divisions between national securities markets have broken down, the London Exchange has remained in splendid isolation.

But the days of isolation are drawing to a close. Through the first years of the 1980s, the main preoccupation of the more intelligent stockbrokers was the case taken out against the Stock Exchange rule book by the Office of Fair Trading in the Restrictive Practices Court. The case was due to be heard in 1984. Every new Secretary of State for Industry was lobbied to drop the case. Every one refused until, in the aftermath of the sweeping Conservative victory in the 1983 General Election, Cecil Parkinson announced the new government's intention to find a way to end the case. The government would introduce legislation to halt the case in exchange for concessions from the Stock Exchange, the main one being the abolition of fixed commissions.

It was partly because it attacked the system of fixed minimum commissions that the Stock Exchange was so

128

worried about the OFT case, for they have been vital in sustaining the unique division between broker and jobber. The interesting question which now faces the Exchange is whether the end of fixed commissions will make the Exchange better able to cope with the growth of institutions and the increasing internationalisation of securities trading. One thing is certain. The abolition of fixed commissions marks the first step in a revolution on the London Stock Exchange. In the mid 1980s, it will undoubtedly pass through a period of radical change. The final part of this chapter examines the form this change may take. But first, we describe the securities market as it exists on the eve of revolution.

The Exchange and its rivals

The Stock Exchange lives in a twenty-six storey tower, built in 1970, just beside the Bank of England. The tower itself houses the offices of the Stock Exchange council, and some of the brokers and jobbers. Alongside the tower is the 23,000 square feet of the trading floor of the Exchange. You can look down on it from a visitors' viewing gallery and see the jobbers sitting or standing round sixteen octagonal booths while the brokers scurry between them. Inside the booths sit the jobbers' clerks, who record deals and pass messages to the jobbers from their offices. In a busy period there might be a couple of thousand people on the floor, during a quiet one, a couple of hundred. Any one of these people can be contacted by his office by a 'bleeper' paging service. Some of the restaurants and pubs around the Exchange are also wired for the bleeper, so that the more convivial brokers can put in a full day's work in Throgmorton Street's Long Room and still remain instantly 'on tap' to their offices. Most of the larger brokers have gone one better, and equipped some staff with two-way radios.

The Exchange also has one of the largest private telephone exchanges in the country, big enough to serve a town of 50,000 people, and it has a price display system, called Topic, which relays the latest share prices and company news to television sets in the offices of brokers, jobbers and other institutions around the country.

The Stock Exchange's system of transferring shares and settling up after the transfer is completed has also been automated. This is possible because, like most American companies but unlike most European, British firms almost always have registered shares. This means that the names and addresses of all shareholders are kept on a central register on a computer memory bank. Being listed on this register is the shareholder's title to a share, and transferring a share from one owner to another simply means altering the register on receiving the necessary written instructions. The merits of this system over the European alternative of bearer shares have long been argued. With bearer shares, the certificate itself is title to the share and transferring ownership means transferring possession of the certificate. The system of registered shares has many advantages. There is virtually no security risk, it solves the problem of shareholders who lose their certificates and it allows firms to mail their reports to shareholders. It also makes it easier for a firm which wants to take over another to find out who the shareholders are. But it is expensive to operate.

After a share has changed hands, the deal is cleared through a computer-based system called Talisman. If a share is sold, it is held in a pool, technically in the name of the Exchange's own nominee company, called Sepon, which 'owns' it until someone else wants to buy it. It is then transferred out again into the new name. Foreign shares are gradually being added to the system, and the Exchange is looking at ways of putting gilt transactions onto a computer system too.

Running the Exchange is a council made up of forty-six practising brokers and jobbers, five so-called 'lay' or outside members, and the government broker, who gets an *ex officio* flat. The council meets about every fortnight under the chairman, who since 1976 has been Sir Nicholas Goodison. Chairmen are re-elected every year and there is no formal time-limit for the job. Sir Nicholas is senior partner of brokers Quilter, Goodison. He and his two deputies split their time between the Exchange and their own firms. Most of the real work of the Exchange, however, is carried out by the council's full-time staff, which in 1984 numbered 1,000, and by the various committees of the council. These usually meet at least once a week to consider such questions as whether a new company should be allowed a listing on the Exchange, whether new members should be admitted and whether brokers and jobbers are meeting the Exchange's solvency requirements. Technically, members only have to vote on changes in the Exchange's deed of settlement. Major policy issues (such as whether women should be admitted) and decisions to change the rules of the Exchange (such as whether to allow brokers to advertise) are sometimes voted on by all members of the Exchange. In practice, some important issues, such as the 1982 decision to alter commission scales, are resolved by the council, while some very minor ones, which involve changing the deed, such as technical changes to comply with EEC rules, have to be put to a full vote of members.

Whenever an issue has to be put to the vote, the smaller firms tend to dominate the outcome, for each member has a vote and small firms have more members relative to the amount of business they do than larger ones. This has resulted in a number of potentially dangerous decisions being taken on issues where the interests of the smaller firms run contrary to those of the larger. It is, for example, extremely difficult to persuade the small firms to accept an increase in the solvency margin of brokers, even when the council thinks it appropriate.

The fault lies partly with the people who serve on the council, for, with a few notable exceptions, firms have been reluctant to see their best brains spending time in lengthy committee meetings when they could be earning commission for their partners. But the democratic nature of the whole Exchange also makes it difficult to reach the right strategic decisions: the vote of the senior partner of one of the largest City firms is equal to the vote of a junior partner of a tiny firm in the provinces in anything that requires a vote by the whole membership.

In December 1984 the Exchange had a total of 4,540 members, of whom 3,849 worked for the 201 firms of brokers and 478 worked for the 17 firms of jobbers. (The rest were either corporate or inactive members.) In London there were 88 firms of brokers and 12 jobbers. To become a member of the Exchange, you have to have been with a broker or jobber firm for three years. Only a member can be a partner or a director of a Stock Exchange firm. But it is possible to go onto the floor of the Exchange on behalf of a firm without being a member: you need only be an 'admitted clerk'. There are two species of admitted clerks, unauthorised (or 'blue button', after the colour of their lapel badges) and authorised. Only authorised clerks can trade. Until 1971 you had to be British to be a member. Now foreigners are allowed to join. So are women. They became members rather by accident, as a result of the merger in March 1973 of the London and the country stock exchanges, on some of whose floors women could already deal.

Almost all the brokers are partnerships. They vary enormously in size. The largest have branches overseas, 40 or more partners and a staff of perhaps 600. The smallest have two or three partners and a couple of secretaries. Judging which are the biggest is a matter of informed guesswork, as there are no published figures. It depends, in any case, on the measure used. In terms of turnover, the largest are certainly those which specialise in gilt-edged securities, which are dealt in enormous blocks but at very low commission. Biggest of all technically is Mullens and Co., the government broker (see chapter 9, p.226). It is probably followed by Pember and Boyle, which is also very largely a gilt-edged broker, and general brokers like Phillips and Drew, Grieveson Grant and W. Greenwell.

On the more relevant measure of size of commission income, the largest firm is probably James Capel, formed by a string of mergers in the 1960s. It has fairly consistently ranked at the top of a table compiled by the US bank Continental Illinois, which polls City opinion on the quality of brokers' research effort. The more interesting distinction between brokers is not sheer size but the areas of specialisation. Thus Cazenove, specialist in new issues, is virtually a merchant bank. It takes a positive delight in its reputation for crustiness and has offices indistinguishable from a St James's club. Other brokers have chosen different routes. All big firms do every type of business, but each is known for different specialities. Thus Phillips and Drew specialises in managing funds – estimated to amount to

132

about £5 billion in the middle of 1984. It was also, in the 1950s, one of the first brokers to appreciate the importance of using research as a lure to attract institutional business. Grieveson Grant, by contrast, has an enormous list of private clients, whose business it has managed to organise profitably (thanks to computers); and Greenwell's has specialised in dealing for the huge institutions, particularly in gilts. Greenwell's senior partner, Gordon Pepper, has probably more influence on the gilt market than anyone else in the City, and is the nearest thing that Britain has to the US investment gurus like Salomon's Dr Henry Kaufman. In 1984, Grieveson Grant and W. Greenwell both sold stakes to British merchant banking groups – Grieveson Grant to Kleinworts and Greenwell's to Midland's subsidiary, Samuel Montagu.

Other brokers who have devoted a lot of energy to attracting institutional clients by developing their research are Hoare, Govett, who developed mathematical techniques of stock analysis,* and Wood Mackenzie. Hoare, Govett was the first London stockbroker to bring in an outside partner – Security Pacific, a Californian bank. Wood Mackenzie provides a fascinating example of how a small non-London firm (it started in Edinburgh) can become a top-flight City one. Until the early 1960s it was just another small 'provincial' broker. Since then, under the leadership of John Chiene, it has gradually built up so that it is now probably one of the top ten. Remarkably for a broker, it earns about one-third of its income from selling research and valuation services rather than commission. In 1984 it sold 29.9 per cent of its shares to Hill Samuel.

*Analysts belong to one of two sects, the chartists and the fundamentalists. Chartists draw graphs of share prices from which they deduce complex inter-relationships between events and expectations which, they believe, determine whether the market or a particular share will move up or down. Their graphs reveal patterns with wondrous names like 'head and shoulders' or 'double bottom'. As – retrospectively – each shape can be interpreted in several different ways, the chartists are usually right. Their rivals, the fundamentalists, believe that it is the fundamentals of a company, its earnings, profit records, etc. that ultimately determine its share prices. Though the market may 'get out of line' for a while, all you have to do is wait for investment opinion to catch up. If you are prepared to wait long enough, they too are usually right in the end.

Among the other large firms, Strauss Turnbull and Vickers da Costa built up large overseas interests (which Vickers sold to Citicorp in 1983). Rowe and Pitman, besides handling a large number of new issues, has made a speciality of put-through business (described below). Strauss Turnbull has a subsidiary which is a 'market maker' in eurobonds, while Vickers da Costa became the Exchange's main specialist in Japanese securities before it sold its Far East business to Citicorp, as part of a deal in which the giant US banking group also bought a 29.9 per cent interest in the London operation.

At the other end of the scale there are a host of tiny firms with just a couple of partners, mostly outside London, which can survive by providing an efficient dealing service and only carrying out minimal research.

Although both brokers and jobbers behave on the floor of the Exchange like overgrown schoolboys, setting fire to each other's newspapers and cutting off people's ties if they look too colourful, the brokers are regarded by the jobbers as rather sober. To become a broker you have, since 1971, to pass a qualifying exam. But it is the jobber who runs the biggest risks on the Exchange.

Jobbers are compulsive gamblers. They have to be: jobbers take massive risks, and can make equally massive profits. In a rising market they can hardly fail to make fortunes; in a falling one it is more difficult for them to make good profits; in a stable market it is hard to make anything at all. This is because, unlike brokers, jobbers hold shares as principals. Jobbers carry a 'book' of shares, basing the price of any one share on the state of the book in it and what they expect its price to do. If they expect a rise, they will build up a holding; if a fall, they will try to avoid making a loss either by holding as little of the share as possible or even by 'going short' – by selling more of it than they hold in the hope that they will be able to buy it back more cheaply later on. Holding large blocks of shares is not only risky, it ties up jobbers' capital. In recent years jobbers have tried as far as possible to reduce the size of the risk they carry over from one day to another.

Among the jobbers there are two large, three medium-sized, and the rest are minnows. Of the two big ones there is Wedd

134

Durlacher Mordaunt, the gentleman among jobbers. In 1983 it still had more dealers on the floor than its principal rival, Akroyd and Smithers, but in terms of turnover the two were roughly equal and with Akroyd gaining ground. Akroyd, traditionally second to Wedd, are the intellectuals among jobbers, insofar as any jobber is ever intellectual. The firm has been boosted by its strength in gilt dealing, and by the fact that as a quoted company it has been able to bring in capital from outside the partnership.

Between them, the big two jobbers are estimated to do over 90 per cent of all gilt trading by value, and perhaps 60 per cent of equity trading. A long way behind come Pinchin Denny, Smith Brothers and Bisgood Bishop. Pinchin Denny is the other main dealer in gilts; Smith specialises in company securities and particularly gold and mining shares; Bisgood Bishop, smaller still, has a general company business.

At the other end of the scale comes S. Jenkins and Son. It has four members and specialises in football club shares.

One of the remarkable – and ominous – facts about the London Stock Exchange is that no new outside firm has become a member since the Second World War. There have been mergers, and there have been splits – both of which have resulted in new names appearing in the membership list. But there has been no S.G. Warburg, no Hambro Life. The growth of competition has taken place outside. No foreign firm, under Stock Exchange rules, may become a member.

In world terms, London stockbrokers and jobbers are very small firms. They have remained small largely because Stock Exchange rules make it difficult for them to bring in outside capital. In their efforts to improve their financial strength, both brokers and jobbers have two courses open to them: to merge, or to look for corporate money. Twenty-five years ago the brokers might have tried a third course: recruiting rich young men and selling them partnerships. When brokers lived off personal clients, rich young men with wealthy contacts were also useful for the new business they could attract. But the professional skills that brokers need to pull in institutional business are no longer the prerogative of the rich.

So most Stock Exchange firms remain partnerships, a

135

curious anomaly when the *raison d'être* of the Exchange is to raise capital for public companies. There are, it is true, a small number of firms which are limited companies, but no brokers and only two jobbers have quotes on the London Stock Exchange.

Until 1970 Stock Exchange rules prevented both brokers and jobbers from being limited companies at all. This meant that the easiest way to find new capital was to merge, and throughout the 1960s a succession of mergers thinned the ranks of both. Since 1970 a few firms did indeed become corporations, but there remained further rules which reduced the advantage of so doing. One was that a single outside shareholder could not own more than 10 per cent of a firm's shares. In 1982 this was increased to 29.9 per cent. Another was that even where a firm was a limited company, its members would remain personally liable for its debts. Still another was that directors of Stock Exchange firms had to be members of the Exchange. Changes in these other two rules were promised when the Government intervened in the OFT case in 1983.

The effect has been that in broking, where the need for capital is relatively limited, the search for an outside partner at first moved quite slowly. But by the end of 1984 virtually all the large stockbroking firms had sold 29.9 per cent to outsiders, the only significant exception being Cazenove, which has a rather different business from the others.

Among jobbers the pressure was even greater. Wedd agreed to sell 29.9 per cent to Barclays (with an understanding that Barclays would increase its interest when rules permitted). Akroyd had sold the same stake to Warburg. The third largest firm, Smith Brothers, had sold to N.M. Rothschild, and the still smaller Bisgood Bishop to the NatWest group. Finally, Pinchin Denny sold to Morgan Grenfell.

The jobbers, as an independent breed, will clearly cease to exist. Their problem, quite simply, is that they are too small. Akroyd's market capitalisation in early 1984 was roughly £100 million, Smith's some £20 million.

By contrast, the market capitalisation of Merrill Lynch was over £2 billion. There are in London some 160 foreign brokers and investment bankers, including giants of Wall Street like

136

Merrill Lynch and Salomon Brothers. While these hardly trade at all in UK shares, they dominate London trading in US shares and eurobonds. Each morning, before the New York market opens, they operate their own market in North American securities, trading between themselves. None of them is a member of the London Stock Exchange.

The rules to which the brokers and jobbers of the London Stock Exchange subscribe have limited them to forms of organisation which make it very difficult to raise new capital and to become big. They also have been a very effective way of discouraging newcomers, either indigenous or foreign. On the stock exchanges of other countries, new companies – often of foreign origin – would seek to join as a matter of course. (Thus Akroyd is a member of the Hong Kong and the New York exchanges.) But in London, it is in practice not possible for a foreign trader to join the Exchange. So the competition has ignored it.

The Stock Exchange's trading mechanism

For the moment the London Stock Exchange remains the only one in the world where members are split into two groups, brokers and jobbers. Clients buying or selling shares place their orders with the brokers, who are not allowed to deal directly with each other except in circumstances explained later in this chapter. The broker carries out a client's order through a jobber, who is not allowed to deal directly with the general public. The jobber deals in and holds shares as a principal – on his own account; the broker only buys and sells shares on behalf of a client. The broker earns a living from the commission paid by a client on each transaction. The jobber earns his by setting a selling price for a share slightly above the buying rate. The difference is known as the 'jobber's turn'.*

The system of broking and jobbing (as of 1985) works – in theory – like this. A broker is given an order by a client to buy

---

*Jobbers point out that this turn is not necessarily clear profit. It would only be so if they could match each sale with each purchase. If they cannot, they may find themselves holding a share whose price is falling.

1,000 shares in ICI. He goes onto the floor of the house and asks two or three jobbers the price of ICI. Whatever his view of the market, the jobber will always quote a price in the shares in which he specialises. One jobber might reply '480 484', which means that he will buy shares at 480 pence and sell at 484 pence. Another might say '482½ 486½' and a third '480½ 484½'. At this stage the broker will go back to the first jobber, the one who has offered the shares at the cheapest price, and say he is a buyer for 1,000. Not until then does the jobber know whether the broker wants to buy or sell, or the size of the block of shares. If the block involved is very big, the broker may first ask the size of the market. The jobber might reply 'bid for ten, offered in twenty', meaning that he is prepared to buy up to 10,000 shares and sell up to 20,000.

Once the deal is agreed, both broker and jobber pencil it into their notebooks and go their ways. There is no other written record of their agreement: hence the Stock Exchange motto, 'My word is my bond'. At the end of the day all the notebook entries are put into a central computer which checks them against each other. When the two notebooks do not tally, as inevitably happens from time to time, broker and jobber have to work out a solution between themselves. Usually the jobber accepts the broker's word; but sometimes the two agree to split the difference.*

Yet what really happened on the Exchange was gradually diverging from the theoretical picture long before the OFT case was dropped. In practice, the broker might not find as many as three jobbers in any one share. He would certainly be hard put to it to find more. He might set up the deal in his office, making only formal use of a jobber's services. Thus the trading mechanism of the Exchange was coming under severe pressure. An increasing proportion of share dealing was already by-passing the floor of the Exchange; some by-passed the jobbers; and most international securities trading in London took place outside the Exchange altogether.

*As well as trading in shares themselves, the Exchange also trades in options to buy and sell shares at some future date. Most large companies can be traded on the options market, and these options can themselves be traded in before they mature.

138

In short, it is certainly not essential to have specialist jobbers. For shares to have a continuous market, someone has to perform the jobbing role, carrying shares for which buyers cannot yet be found and going short on the shares for which sellers have not yet appeared. It has, moreover, to be someone with enormous capital resources. But in many other financial centres, the roles of broker and jobber are carried out by the same institution.* Nor is it essential to have specialist brokers: in other centres, the commercial banks often dominate the buying and selling of securities. Nor, indeed, is it essential to have a central stock exchange building at all. In other centres – and indeed, in London's own eurobond market – securities are bought and sold over the telephone, like foreign exchange, rather than traded in a central dealing room. Even in London, when the Stock Exchange closes at 3.30 p.m., the jobbers cross Throgmorton Avenue and continue dealing over the telephone from their own offices for another couple of hours.

In practice, most other exchanges use one of two main trading methods. Small exchanges tend to use the 'call-over' system. This works rather like a London commodity futures market. An officer of the exchange calls out the name of a share and its current price, and members shout out their bids from the floor, if necessary agreeing on a new price to make a match. Inevitably this system sometimes leaves some shares unsold in the hands of brokers, who thus perform a jobbing function of sorts. The other main system, used in large exchanges like New York and Tokyo, is called the 'trading post' or 'specialist' system. Some brokers simply act as brokers; others act also as jobbers, trading with both brokers and the public and carrying books of shares. Each industry is traded at a 'trading post' or particular point on the floor of the exchange, from which the brokers 'specialising' in its share operate.

As of 1985, brokers still charged by a scale of commission, although the Stock Exchange had agreed to abandon this scale by the end of 1986 in exchange for the government promising to abandon the OFT case. On equity deals of up to £2 million

---

*Indeed until the 1960s provincial brokers in Britain often acted as jobbers in the shares of small local companies quoted on the regional stock exchanges.

139

there was a sliding scale, but above that there was a flat commission rate of 0.125 per cent. The commission on small deals failed to reflect the difference in the broker's costs, while the commission on a large deal was extremely high, bearing no relation to the relatively small amount of work involved. Just how uneconomic small deals were can be seen by comparing the commission on buying £500 of a share and £50,000 of it. Both deals could cost the broker much the same to transact. But the commission on the first transaction was £10; on the second, £309.50. To grasp how seriously the brokers overcharged their large institutional clients, compare the commission on buying shares worth £50,000 with that on £500,000 of the same share. On the first deal, it was that £309.50; on the second, £2,014.50. Yet, again, the difference in the work the broker had to do bore little relation to the reward.

Because they could not compete on price brokers came to provide a range of expensive research services to attract institutional clients, services from which private clients benefited but for which they did not pay. Thus brokers had to produce reams of paper about each industry's and each company's prospects. They had to visit major firms at regular intervals. If they wanted to be thought of as experts in a particular sector, they had to be in close touch with the directors of all the companies in it.

For large and successful brokers, the commission system has been extremely profitable, because it has consistently overcharged institutional clients. For other brokers, though, the commission system has not been a protection. For the second-rate firm, indeed, it may have increased the risks. For once a middleweight broker had built up a research team, it added considerably to its overheads without any guarantee that the institutional clients it attracted would stay with it. The client might switch allegiance overnight: or the star analyst might be poached by a richer rival, taking valuable business away.

The commission system has also inhibited the second-rate broker from pursuing the obvious alternatives: abandoning research and offering a cut-price specialist dealing system with no frills; or setting out to attract private clients.

It is still true that for the small broker, including most of the out-of-London firms, private clients are the principal source of income, and for any broker a client with more than £50,000 is worth having. But it was only in the early 1980s that the big London brokers began to show renewed interest in personal business. The reason for this change of heart was partly the increasing amount of discretionary business, where the customer turned over day-to-day investment decisions to the broker's discretion, saving telephone time in getting authorisation for deals; and it was partly that brokers realised that they could sell other services to customers and charge management fees. So several firms which had rather neglected their personal business decided to put more effort into it. This view, however, is by no means universal: in many firms of brokers, to be sent to the private clients' department is professionally like a spell in Siberia.

The effect of the commission system was to subsidise the expensive split between broker and jobber. But while the rise of the large institutions in the 1970s put pressure on the brokers to compete by offering better research, it brought a more direct pressure on the jobbers. For as the size of the blocks of shares which individual jobbers had to hold at any given time increased, so did their need for capital to finance them. In spite of mergers, in spite of an infusion of outside capital into some jobbers, the system has had to be patched up with a number of devices which ultimately undermine the arguments for keeping jobbing and broking separate.

One obvious device has been the merger. Whereas twenty-five years ago there would have been five or six jobbers making a market in a largish UK industrial company's shares, now there are perhaps three. In small, rarely traded shares there may be only one. There are now a number of important sections of the market, such as breweries and investment trusts, in which only two jobbing firms operate. Virtually all gilt trading is done by Wedd and Akroyd.

The decline in the number of jobbers has made it possible for them to adopt a number of restrictive practices, while the increase in the size of the blocks of shares they have had to handle has encouraged them to look for ways of reducing the

141

risks in what is, by its nature, a very risky activity. Thus, when faced with very large deals, jobbers occasionally go 'joint book'. Competing jobbers pool their positions, and deal as though they were one firm. Jobbers have also been criticised by the Monopolies Commission for agreements which fix the spread of their quotation, known as 'price-spread agreements'. But within the Exchange itself the most frequent criticism of the jobbers is that they will only quote a narrow spread on small deals. For any large transaction, spreads widen dramatically. In other words, the jobbing system does not really work in the text-book way. Large deals therefore have to be broken down into relatively small individual transactions, or the brokers themselves have to try to find the buyers if they have a large seller. The principal device they employ is known as the 'put-through'.

There are two kinds of put-through. Sometimes two clients simply want to exchange a block of shares, and ask the broker to organise it. Here the broker would only charge one commission. But though brokers say that no two put-throughs are the same, the usual pattern is this: an institutional investor, such as the Prudential, comes to a broker and asks to sell 500,000 Plessey shares. The broker will first establish a price, based on the market price. He may try to carry out the deal through a jobber, but this is a formality: no jobber would be likely to handle a block of this size. So he then rings round his other institutional clients to find out whether any of them can buy enough Plessey shares to make up the deal. If it is a large order, he may have a team of several dealers to do the phoning, and even split the transaction with another broker.

Once he has tracked down enough buyers, he tells a jobber and negotiates a turn. There is no agreed scale for this. The jobber has the right at this stage to take some of the shares onto his own book, and if the broker cannot match buyers and sellers exactly, the jobber may help him to complete the deal. The broker goes ahead with the transaction and the jobber then takes a commission from both buyers and sellers. Considering that the jobber has done virtually nothing, this is easy money for him. His justification is that if both client and broker default in a put-through, it is the jobber who carries the liability for the whole transaction and also that it is his market price that has provided the basis of the deal.

Not surprisingly, put-throughs are very ·popular with brokers and the proportion of deals done this way has grown steadily in the course of the 1960s and 1970s. Though the actual number of put-throughs is small, and the Wilson Committee put their value at about 10 per cent of all equity trading, for some brokers the proportion might be 25 per cent.

A few institutions have gone still further and quietly arrange share deals which completely by-pass the brokers and jobbers, using City solicitors to do the paperwork. It is impossible to know how large this business is. Stockbrokers say hopefully that it is tiny and not growing.

In 1972 the accepting houses attempted to by-pass the Exchange by setting up a rival computer-based system of share trading called Ariel. This worked by terminals connected to a central computer, the idea being that merchant banks and other financial institutions could trade shares simply by typing instructions into the computer terminal. In one sense the accepting houses' investment in Ariel paid off. A few months after Ariel was announced, the Stock Exchange cut commission rates on large deals. But Ariel never succeeded in attracting any volume of trading and was allowed quietly to disappear. Why did it fail? It may be that it was introduced before people in the City had become accustomed to using computer terminals and that it meant that an instituton had to reveal too much information about the shares it wanted to buy or sell. The Bank of England's opposition to Ariel stopped gilts being traded through it. Certainly, while everyone now relies on computer-based information systems – Reuters Monitor, Telerate, DataStream, Topic and so on – they prefer to do their trading over the phone.*

Ariel has been the most concerted public attempt to break the monopoly of the Stock Exchange in UK equity trading. It was beaten off: but the defeat has looked less important as time has gone by. For trading in UK equities is a dwindling part of all

---

*In New York, too, most securities trading is still done either on the phone or face-to-face on the New York and American stock exchanges. But in one regional US exchange, Cincinnati, all trading is now by computer.

the trading in securities done in London. The real erosion of the monopoly is taking place elsewhere. From the mid-1970s there has been an explosive growth in trading in foreign securities – mainly eurobonds, but also foreign equities – conducted largely outside the Exchange and largely by companies which are not UK stockbrokers. Although the Stock Exchange quotes 492 foreign companies and 887 foreign eurobonds, it probably conducts less than 10 per cent of all trading in eurobonds in London. The great bulk of the business is carried out in London between foreign investment banks and British merchant banks, none of which are members of the Exchange.

There is no easy way of gauging how many active traders in international securities there are in London. The Association of International Bond Dealers lists about 120 (including three jobbers) as making markets in a range of securities at any one time, but the number of active London traders is much smaller. Around the world there are some 800 members of the AIBD.

These big US, Canadian and Japanese investment banks and brokerage houses have trading rooms in London which buy and sell shares in the same way as London trades foreign exchange – over the phone. In doing so they may be acting on instructions for clients, or they may be trading for their own institution. The pattern of shares traded varies from house to house and even from morning to afternoon. Thus in the morning the US firms will trade in US shares before the New York exchanges open. The various nationalities will tend to specialise in their own shares, but some major British companies may also be traded, particularly those which are also quoted in New York.

Eurobonds, that is bonds denominated in eurocurrencies, are issued in London and Continental centres (see next section); but there is also in London a very large trading market in second-hand bonds, carried out by the issuing banks, partly as a service, partly to make money. It is a game that anyone can join, for it is wholly unregulated. But in practice the dollar side is run by the big US investment banks, and the smaller European currency markets by the Continentals. S.G. Warburg is the British bank with the biggest business in eurobonds.

144

How new funds are raised

Trading existing securities is only one side of the securities industry's work. Raising funds for industry and the government by selling new securities to the public is equally important: or logically should be. Yet the amount of time, energy and staff that members of the Exchange devote to raising new funds is a fraction of what they put into trading in existing securities. True, many brokers feel that new issues are the most interesting part of their work and some large firms, of which Cazenove is by far the largest, have specialised in them. A number of brokers have a separate department for handling new issues. But generally this department is tiny compared with, say, the research department, for by and large the new issues side of the brokers' business has not been promoted. They do not have young men scouring the country for companies which might be persuaded to raise funds on the stock market through them. And though the Exchange raises enormous amounts for the government by issuing gilt-edged (see chapter 9), its record in raising new industrial capital, at least in the 1960s and 1970s, has been less impressive.

This can be seen from a look at the eurobond market. In 1984 the Exchange raised a record £10 billion, roughly $12 billion, a figure which was itself 50 per cent up on the previous year. But the eurobond market raised some $75 billion in the same period, of which perhaps half was organised in London. Even if you add in the money the Exchange raised for the government in gilt sales – another £10 billion – the eurobond market is a much larger one than our own domestic capital market. Most of its loans are issued in London. Yet that is a business in which British institutions, with the exception of Warburg, play little part.

The mechanism for raising new funds in London is certainly more efficient than on a number of European exchanges, and the cost of new issues is not much higher. Issue costs are appreciably lower than on the eurobond market – though this has not stopped the eurobond market from growing far more rapidly.

If a company wants to raise money on the Stock Exchange, it

must apply for a quotation. If it does not immediately want to raise more funds (the most usual case being where a share quoted on a foreign exchange wants a UK quote too) then it is simply 'introduced'. All this means is that if full particulars of the company's affairs are not yet publicly available, it has to publish them. While a quotation on the Exchange implies that a company is providing adequate information about itself, it says little about the company's financial size or soundness: it is not a seal of approval. In practice, there is no problem for companies listed on major US stock exchanges, but some European firms have often found it embarrassing to have to unveil their full consolidated accounts in public.

More often, a company which wants a quote is going public for the first time. The issue is usually handled by a merchant bank in cooperation with a stockbroker, although in the case of smaller companies a new issue is frequently handled by a stockbroker alone. There are two main ways of carrying out a new issue. The more usual is called 'an offer for sale',* where the company offers its shares to the general public. Advertisements setting out details of the offer and of the company's financial position are published in the newspapers.

However, the offer for sale is expensive even for quite large amounts of capital. The cost of raising £3 million is as high as 8 per cent. The reason this is so high is the cost of advertising and underwriting the issue.

Underwriting means guaranteeing the sale of an issue. In an offer for sale, the issuing house, whether a merchant bank or a broker, gets underwriters – institutional investors like pension and insurance companies – to agree (for a fee) to buy any part of the issue that is not sold to the public. Thus even if the public does not buy all the issue, the company whose shares are being offered knows that it will get its money and the issuing house knows that it will not be left with the issue.

For smaller issues an alternative method called a placing can be used. Here the bulk of the shares are not offered to the public but 'placed' with institutional holders. A placing is cheaper

---

*A version of the offer for sale, which differs only in detail, is an 'offer by public subscription' or an 'offer by prospectus'.

than a public issue because it does not need to be underwritten or so widely advertised, but it does not get the shares into the hands of as many different holders.

There is a further, and even cheaper, way of raising money on the Stock Exchange. Instead of applying for a full listing, small companies can raise money through the unlisted securities market (USM). An unlisted quotation costs between half and two-thirds as much as a full listing to raise the equivalent amount of money. There is a further advantage, or disadvantage, depending on how you look at it. It is possible to raise funds for riskier enterprises on the USM than the Exchange would sanction under its full rules. So new companies and hazardous ventures, like the production of the Hesketh motorcycle which went bust, can raise funds on the unlisted market. Still, at the end of its first two years, out of the 149 companies brought to the USM, 136 were still there, 4 had been suspended, 2 taken over, and 7 had graduated to a full listing.

On balance, the USM has been a considerable success. It has brought the Stock Exchange into a type of business that was otherwise passing it by. The amount of funds raised is small – in those two years just £180 million out of a total of £5,914 million for all UK companies. But the successful USM companies will graduate to the main market as they grow larger and then be well placed to raise more capital if they need it. The very success of the USM, though, has added to the problems of policing the new issue market.

Both an offer for sale and a placing can be made on either the normal market or the unlisted market, though the placing has become the principal method on the unlisted market. The placing is a less democratic method of offering shares than an offer to the public, and carries a danger that if an issue is deliberately underpriced, shares can then be doled out to favoured clients at below market value. It is very difficult to prove that such practices take place, but most people in the City would accept that they do and duly tut-tut whenever there is a suspicious issue. Because each USM issue is controlled by a single broker, the danger of this form of fraud is greatest in the USM market, and both the Stock Exchange and the Bank of

147

England have been worried about it. But it is difficult to nail the culprits.

The public offer for sale avoids this particular abuse, but frequently generates another: stagging. Again, the issue has to be underpriced. When it seems clear that an issue has been priced below the likely market price, the stags move in. They are people who make a living by applying for shares at every suitable new issue and then selling them off at a profit as soon as the market opens.

There is a simple way to curb stagging. It is to offer shares by tender – to auction them, in other words. Would-be buyers write in the price they are prepared to pay for the shares and the amount they want to buy, and the shares are allotted at the lowest price at which there are enough buyers to sell them all. But the City does not like tenders.

There are two reasons for this. One is that issuers like to be able to groom the list of would-be holders of a share, to try to make sure that there is a fair balance of private and institutional clients. With a tender, issuers claim, there is the danger that a handful of institutions might put in the top bids for the entire issue, to make sure of being given a reasonable allocation, and end up owning the company. They are not convinced by the argument that the Prudential might not want the whole equity of J. Bloggs and Co. and might therefore be deterred from putting in an unreasonable bid for excessive amounts of a share.

The second reason for the unpopularity of tenders is that a tender may make sure that the share floats at the price the market is really prepared to put on it, but that means that a share is as likely to go down as up in its early days. No issuing house likes that idea – nor, admittedly, do the directors of the company coming to market, for they may well own the rest of the shares. So the stags remain.

Tender issues received a boost in the early 1980s from the Conservative government's privatisation programme. It was politically important to be seen to get a fair price for the taxpayer for any national assets being sold to private hands, particularly after one such issue, for Amersham International, was over-subscribed twenty-five times. The Government took

148

no such risks with its giant offer of shares in British Telecom in November 1984, and priced it cheaply enough to attract two million small investors.

Companies quoted on the Exchange can, if their shareholders agree, raise extra money in one of two ways. They can go to their shareholders with a 'rights issue'. This is so called because the company offers its shareholders the right to buy more shares, generally at a cheaper price than the ruling market price. Or they can issue a debenture.

The choice between equity or loan capital (debentures) is determined by a number of factors. Sometimes it depends on tax legislation. Thus the 1965 Finance Act made it cheaper to raise loan capital than equity, because equity dividends had to be paid out of taxed profits whereas loan interest was paid before tax. Between the early 1970s and 1982, high long-term interest rates caused companies to shy away from borrowing by issuing loan stock. Instead they raised money almost exclusively by issuing more equity through rights issues. But when interest rates fell in 1982, the market re-opened, with several companies, banks and some foreign countries* issuing loan stock.

The balance between equity and fixed interest capital is known as 'gearing'. A company is said to be 'highly geared' if it has a high ratio of fixed-interest capital to equity. Generally the more risky the business a company is involved in, the lower should be its gearing. A company which has a large amount of interest to be paid every year is more likely to be pushed into a loss in a bad year than one with a high proportion of equity capital on which it can reduce or if necessary pass its dividend.

The way in which eurobonds are issued is very much less formal. (There are no eurocurrency equities, though eurobonds can sometimes be converted into the shares of the issuing company, in which case they are called convertibles.) The documents are simpler, and the bonds usually in bearer form. There are two clearing houses, in Brussels and

---

*When a foreign borrower goes to a domestic market, the bond it issues is called a Bulldog (UK), Yankee (US) or Samurai (Japan) to distinguish it from a eurobond.

149

Luxembourg. It is also much harder for the small investor to buy an issue of eurobonds at the same price as the large institutions. The lead manager or managers get together a 'selling group' of banks and securities houses which place the bonds with their clients, keeping what they want for themselves. Instead of a public prospectus in the newspapers, all that appears is a 'tombstone' advertisement, so called because it appears as a matter of record after the issue has been completed. Not surprisingly, the London firms which are not active in the market are snooty about it, arguing that the private investor frequently gets a raw deal.

Takeovers and mergers

Like institutional investment, the takeover battle is largely a post-war phenomenon. As with the institutions, the Stock Exchange has not wholly succeeded in adapting itself to cope with it, though in the case of the takeover, the problem has not principally been one of the mechanism of the Exchange but of policing takeover practices. This task has confronted the Exchange with a whole batch of new and uncomfortable ethical questions.

Mergers and takeover battles are usually masterminded by the respective companies' merchant banks. Long before an offer is made, senior staff in the bidding company's bank will have spent days examining every available detail of the company being bid for. They will have worked out the price that their client can afford to pay, and discussed such finer points of diplomacy as whether the first approach should be made by the bank or the company, how to keep those directors of the victim company who are likely to object in the dark for as long as possible, and what should be said to whom and when. Throughout the bid, a reputable merchant bank has secrecy arrangements that make the Foreign Office look amateur. Bankers avoid naming their firm on the telephone, files never record company names and a minimum of staff are allowed to know of the bid.

If the firm being bid for is basically in favour of the deal, there will follow long negotiations between the two companies'
150

bankers on what the terms of the offer should be. At critical moments, tempers may be diplomatically lost, but the bankers are professionals and the next week they are perfectly likely to be enjoying an amicable lunch together.

It is when a firm is determined not to be bought that a takeover battle ensues. The bidding company often begins by making a 'silly bid' at a price level which is bound to be rejected. There are two reasons for this strategy. One is that it may be hard to find out enough about the bid-for company without forcing it to respond to a bid, which obliges it to send out a certain amount of information about its affairs to its shareholders. The other is that, as shareholders have grown more accustomed to takeover battles, they have come to expect not one bid but a succession of them. It may take several offers to persuade them to trade their shares.

For that is the object of the bid. The bidding company offers either cash, or more usually its shares or a combination of cash and shares, for those of the bid-for company. The company being bid for might, typically, have up to 60 per cent of its shares in the hands of institutions, and the remainder in the hands of private shareholders and of members of the board. The institutions play the game with sophistication, often delaying accepting the offer until the last possible moment and frequently having to be cajoled by the merchant bank to do so.

The takeover battle is an American and British phenomenon rather than a European one. There are a number of reasons. Industry in Europe is firmly in the hands of banks and family trusts rather than a broad spectrum of private shareholders. Disclosure requirements are not strict enough to make it plain when a company is undervalued. And shares are generally held on a bearer system rather than a register which, thanks to its useful list of names and addresses, makes it easy for the bidding firm to bombard shareholders with enticing offers. In Britain the takeover battle became common from the mid-1950s.

It became less common during the 1970s. The reason may have been partly a realisation that mergers do not promote industrial efficiency. In fact, the prime motive for a merger is usually to protect market share, or to buy out competition. But the depression in share prices in the second half of the 1970s was probably a much more significant influence. With share prices depressed, would-be bidders were unable to mount sufficiently attractive bids in terms of their own paper to win over the shareholders of potential victims. It is no coincidence that as share prices boomed in the early 1980s, so takeovers revived in both Britain and in the US.

One kind of takeover acquired a special notoriety in the late 1960s. It was again an American import: asset stripping. If the takeover is the only way the City is prepared to discipline sleepy companies, asset stripping is the most brutal form of this discipline. This was the activity in which firms such as Slater Walker and Drakes made their reputations. The stripper buys the company, sells off its under-utilised assets – usually property – to other companies who can use them more efficiently and closes down such remaining parts of the company as have no profitable future.

It may be true that asset stripping, by releasing assets which would otherwise be used less productively, contributes to a more efficient economy. Some of these strippers provide valuable managerial skills. But it is impossible not to question the enormous profits which accrue from what is sometimes no more than spotting a suitable firm, selling its land and laying off its workers.

This was certainly the view of the government, which took powers in the 1973 Fair Trading Act to block irresponsible takeover bids. As it turned out, asset stripping was brought to a temporary end by a fall in the price of assets: the property crash of 1975. The Stock Exchange has never sought to influence the decisions of the market; it sees its regulatory role simply to provide a fair market-place.

Originally, policing the Exchange was simply a matter of protecting customers from dishonest or incompetent members. In this, the Exchange has a sound reputation, aided by the enviable record of financial stability of broking firms, a record which contrasts sharply with that of New York. But ruling on the way takeovers and mergers are carried through is altogether a more delicate question. Policing the activities of dishonest managers and directors of companies requires an authority that the Stock Exchange alone cannot have.

For reputable merchant banks, there has always been an element of self-discipline in handling takeover deals, imposed simply by the danger of losing a reputation if the deal goes wrong. In the mid-1960s Robert Fleming, one of the smaller merchant banks not normally involved in takeover business, strayed into the field. The international merger it tried to put together was an unpleasant failure. For the next twenty years it did not handle a single major takeover.

With the battle for control of British Aluminium in 1959, it became obvious that something stronger than self-discipline was needed. The US stock exchanges have been governed since 1934 by a body with legal powers, the Securities and Exchange Commission. The whole idea of statutory controls was – and still is – repellent to a large section of City opinion. The alternative was the drawing up, by a working party set up by the Governor of the Bank of England in 1959, of the City Code on Takeovers and Mergers. Originally it seems to have been thought that the fact that the code had been drawn up on the Governor's word would be enough to make the City abide by it. By 1968 it was clear that some kind of supervisory body was needed to see that the code was enforced; but it was not until 1969 that the present Panel on Takeovers and Mergers was finally set up, equipped with sanctions.

Since then it has gradually – too gradually for many – increased its powers, while those powers have themselves been buttressed by changes in company legislation. In 1978 the Panel, along with the City representative institutions like the various banking bodies, the Exchange itself and the organisations representing the institutional investors, were brought together under an umbrella body, the Council for the Securities Industry, again at the behest of the Bank of England. The Panel remains effectively the executive arm of the CSI. It still does the policing of the takeover business, administering the code. The CSI represents the securities industry in matters like talks with the government over company legislation. Since 1983 the Panel and the CSI have shared a joint chief executive, called the director-general, a merchant banker seconded from a top bank.

In theory the wide membership of the CSI should enable it to

153

bully or encourage any City institution to heed its rulings. In practice the breadth of membership seems to have inhibited its ability to reach firm rulings in the first place. Within the City the CSI is not widely admired. Despite, or perhaps because of its more limited brief, though, the Panel is: it works very flexibly. Anyone who wants the Panel's guidance can simply ring the director-general or another member of the executive and get prompt advice. The panel executive's verdict is not, however, final. It has in the past been overruled by its governing board.

But the debate over whether this whole system of self-regulation is effective centres not so much on how the Panel and the CSI operate, but on the practical difficulties that face them, and at what points the voluntary system of self-regulation needs to be supplemented by legal controls.

The code itself deals exclusively with the ethics of takeovers and mergers. Its principal aims are to ensure the protection of the shareholder and the fair conduct of bids. The fundamental principle is that all shareholders be treated equally. This means, essentially, that those handling the bid are obliged to make the same knowledge available to all other parties.

One of the main achievements of the code has been to set out a clear set of ground rules for the conduct of takeovers. For example, a company which wants to increase its shareholding in another firm beyond 30 per cent must mount a bid for the whole company. Once a company has more than 50 per cent of the shares of another firm, and so has control over its management, it must offer to buy the outstanding shares on the same terms as it bought its original controlling interest. Further, all dealings must be disclosed to all: any person or company with an interest in the outcome of a takeover must declare dealings in the shares involved by noon the next day.

The code's strength is its flexibility and its responsiveness. It is constantly being altered and updated to take account of new market tactics. For example, in the early 1980s there was a sudden outbreak of 'dawn raids', where a broker was instructed to buy just under 30 per cent of a company's shares by offering well above the market price. Institutions, faced with a snap decision and the knowledge that share prices would

154

subsequently decline, usually sold. This put a company in a strong position for making a subsequent bid for control of the company, without committing it to an immediate bid. When it became apparent that this tactic seriously jeopardised the independence of medium-sized companies, and shut out the small investor (who was not able to take advantage of the snap offer of a higher price), the Panel altered the code. Among other changes, it reduced the proportion of shares which could be bought in a raid to 15 per cent, though not before several companies had effectively lost their independence.

Aside from dubious tactics, there are a number of clear abuses which the Panel has sought to regulate. For example, there is 'massaging the price' in a takeover bid. As bids are generally made wholly or partly in a company's shares, it is in the company's interest to raise the price of its own shares to keep up the paper value of its bid for the other company. A company is not allowed to buy its own shares. Its 'associates', however, may do so – and this could even include the manager of its own pension fund or the investment department of its own merchant bank – provided they declare the purchase. There is still no watertight definition of who is an associate.

A variant of this problem is over the 'concert party'. This is not a jolly evening at the South Bank. It is when a group of people 'concert' together to take over a company. The code forbids any one individual or company to buy more than 5 per cent of the shares of another without disclosing its interest. But a group of them can do so provided they are deemed not to be acting 'in concert'.

Most difficult to police by voluntary means has been the practice of insider dealing: using insider knowledge, usually of when a takeover is to take place, to profit from share dealing.

Until 1981, when the 1980 Companies Act came into force, insider dealing was not a criminal offence. It was left to the Stock Exchange and the Panel to seek out and punish offenders. This simply did not work, partly because it was so difficult to demonstrate that insider knowledge had been used, and partly because the Panel had no real sanctions. In 1973 the Panel and Stock Exchange recommended that insider dealing should be

155

made punishable by law, but the ousting of the Heath government and the relatively low priority given to companies legislation by the Wilson and Callaghan governments meant that it took seven more years before insider dealing became a criminal offence.

Insider dealing is still prohibited by the Council for the Securities Industry (with a wider definition than the legal one). But neither the CSI nor the Director of Public Prosecutions appear wildly successful. There is little evidence that insider trading has been reduced. And since November 1979, when all exchange controls were swept away, there has been nothing stopping insiders from doing their trading from the shelter of a foreign bank account, where they cannot be traced.

In early 1984 Professor Gower produced a report for the government on investor protection. In this he suggested that the entire securities trading and investment systems should be ordered through a series of self-regulating agencies whose work would be coordinated either by the Department of Trade and Industry or by a separate securities commission. The Panel, the CSI, the various insurance bodies, the Stock Exchange itself, would all become formal agencies ultimately responsible to government, and anyone wanting to carry out investment business would have to register. The government's response to Gower was published in a White Paper early in 1985, with legislation expected in 1985/6.

But even when the government's plans are put into action there will remain an enormous hole in the system. The whole structure can only be applied to dealings of UK residents carried out through British markets. A foreign company can conceal its identity when buying shares by dealing through its associates – as did the South African-dominated Anglo-American Corporation when it built up its 29 per cent interest in Consolidated Gold Fields in 1980. A foreign buyer of shares can further conceal its identity as it is not subject to UK companies legislation. If the foreign company buys shares in London, it has to persuade a London broker to act for it. But that requirement would not apply if he bought the shares abroad, and there is as large a market in New York for some British shares as there is in London.

At the moment only a small number of British shares are traded outside the Stock Exchange. But as this grows it will become increasingly obvious that there will be a need for securities trading to be policed on a world scale. We have hardly begun to think of how a securities trading Interpol might be established.

The growth of international securities trading

Through the 1970s, as we have seen, there was a rapid growth in a new market in international securities in London outside the Stock Exchange: the eurobond market. By the end of that decade, it had become the second largest capital market in the world, after New York. It is based in London. Its explosive growth came about at least partly because of its lack of formal structure and regulation. Because it is unregulated, borrowers find that they do not have to comply with complex stock market requirements; and lenders enjoy the advantage of anonymity. No one knows who they are, or can trace them for tax purposes. More than half the money flowing into the market probably comes through Swiss banks, and most of the rest through tax havens.

The eurobond market has been innovative and flexible. Loans can be tailored to suit each twist of the market: loans convertible into different currencies, from floating rates to fixed rates, from loans to equities and so on. But its success has come at least partly because it does not ask too many questions.

At the end of the 1970s, a new development in the collapse of barriers between securities markets took place. With the removal of foreign exchange controls in 1979, British investors became much more interested in buying foreign securities. At much the same time, the evolution of Margaret Thatcher's firmly monetarist economic policies made foreign investors more interested in buying shares in the UK. But like the growth of the eurobond market, this increasingly international market in domestic securities took place largely outside the London Stock Exchange.

In the first three years after foreign exchange controls were lifted, British investors bought £13,000 million of foreign

157

securities, most of them American, and almost all of them through New York brokers. Many of these brokers have offices in London. They include famous names like Merrill Lynch and Salomon Brothers, who were already in London in the 1970s to deal in eurobonds. A few London stockbrokers had offices in New York, or seats on American regional exchanges. But their offices were tiny, and an American investor wanting to buy British securities would not necessarily have bought through the New York office of a London broker, who would have to telephone London to place an order through the expensive mechanism of the London Exchange. Increasingly, the American investor would ring a New York broker, who would already be making a market (broking *and* jobbing) in the shares of the largest British companies. The New York broker, unlike the people in the British office, might very well be able to quote a price – and sell the shares.

It was the fact that the London Stock Exchange was being left behind in this rapid growth of international business that made the Bank of England, in 1983, desperate to break the log-jam created by the Office of Fair Trading's challenge to the Stock Exchange rule book. The Bank saw that it was to a large extent the provisions of the rule book which inhibited London firms from competing effectively for international business. For instance, a large jobbing firm like Akroyd and Smithers bought a New York broker through which it could deal directly with any institution in North America in any non-British security. Thus it could sell shares in Exxon to a British institution which had a New York office. But if it sold its shares in BP, the deal would have to be notionally passed through a London broker.

There again, a London merchant bank like Robert Fleming could have a licence to deal in Japanese securities through its subsidiary 8,000 miles away from its head office in Crosby Square, but could not then deal in British securities directly. Equally, no foreign securities house could become a member of the London Exchange, though all the big ones had substantial London offices.

There have been further oddities, particularly in eurobond trading. London jobbers were allowed to deal direct with British institutions, provided those institutions were also
158

members of the AIBD. So Akroyd could sell a eurobond direct to Fleming (which is a member) but not to the Pru (which is not). But while it could sell to Fleming a eurobond issued by a British company, say Hanson Trust, it could not sell to Fleming any of Hanson's ordinary shares.

The Bank of England realised that these eccentricities made it possible that trading in British shares would gradually move out of London, perhaps to New York, beyond the control of the British authorities. At the same time, London would lose out badly in the growth in trade in international securities. In 1982, the Stock Exchanges's foreign earnings were lower in real terms than they were ten years before.

On the face of it, the Bank's backing for the government's decision to call off the OFT case looked odd. After all, the three main charges levelled by the OFT against the Exchange were its system of minimum commissions; its distinction between brokers and jobbers; and its barriers to foreign entry into stockbroking. The only firm concession won by the government from the Exchange was an agreement to abandon the commission system by the end of a three-year transition period. The Bank and the Department of Trade were merely to 'monitor' the other two points.

But in practice, the walls began to crack very quickly. Some brokers indeed expect minimum commissions to be eased before the end of 1986. The consequences for stockbrokers and jobbers are immense. Most believe it will be impossible to finance the expensive division between the two without the subsidy that fixed commissions provide. It follows that the division must go.

The barriers to foreign entry likewise are crumbling. The principal protection of stockbroking firms is that no one owner may own more than 30 per cent of their capital. This is a restriction which no other British companies enjoy, and the Stock Exchange now favours abolishing this constraint on bringing in more outside capital at the same time as fixed commissions and single capacity are swept away. That date, some time towards the end of 1986, has been nicknamed 'the big bang'.

159

At the beginning of what is clearly going to be a period of enormous structural change, it is extremely hard to be sure what the London securities market will look like in the late 1980s. But London brokers might take some comfort from what happened in New York, where all commissions became negotiable in 1975. Many companies lost their individual identity in a rash of takeovers and mergers. But what appeared by the end of the 1970s was an immensely competitive securities market, which went on to enjoy, in the early 1980s, the biggest boom in its entire history.

SEVEN

The insurance world

The different faces of insurance

On the face of it, insurance is one of the most successful sections of the City. Despite growing competition from New York and the Continent, it remains the largest international insurance market in the world. The total net life and non-life premium income earned by Lloyd's in 1981 was £2,258 million; the income of the insurance companies* in that year was £17,988 million, and £22,821 million in 1983. Together this is some 7 per cent of world premium income and 10 per cent of the Gross National Product of the United Kingdom. It is also a big foreign currency earner. Indeed, insurance is roughly level pegging with banking as the City's biggest invisible earning, reaching £1.6 billion in 1983. It is also (thanks largely to life assurance) the second largest single source of investment funds in the country, after the pension funds. It finds a home for over £20 million of new money every day.

Insurance is divided into two categories, non-life and life. Between the two there are very considerable differences. Both aspects of insurance have two sources of revenue: premium income and investment income. The aim of a non-life fund is to make a small profit on its underwriting, that is, its premium income less its claims, and top that up with revenue from its investments. The investments are the premiums, which are collected before claims are paid, and thus give the company a

---

*Premium figures of Lloyd's and the companies are not strictly comparable. Lloyd's premium figures are published three years in arrears and are overwhelmingly from non-life. Those for the companies refer to the British Insurance Association members only, which do, however, account for over 90 per cent of the companies' business.

pool of funds which earn it interest. But as inflation increased, so the companies found it harder and harder to make a profit on underwriting. By the time a claim came up for settlement, perhaps several years after the premium had been fixed, costs had risen far more than anyone could have foreseen. So the 1970s saw companies plunging into loss on their underwriting.

Frequently, however, these losses were more than compensated by a rise in investment income. As inflation rose, so did interest rates, with the result that funds that had invested wisely and could contain underwriting losses were able to stay in profit. At first many companies plunged into loss. Gradually most of them came to terms with inflation, learning to adjust their underwriting policies to try to take it into account and turning down business that appeared unprofitable. But there has been a price: many UK companies have lost market share to their foreign competitors, both in Britain and overseas.

Life assurance is a very different activity from non-life. It is almost exclusively a form of investment. The risk of dying has long been so closely calculated that short of an outbreak of Black Death it is virtually impossible for the companies to make an underwriting loss. The nature of the business is different. Usually what you are saying to the company is, 'Insure me against dying before I am, say, sixty. And in case I don't die by then, save my money, invest it and give it back to me.' The main skill in life assurance is not judging the risk of someone dying, but investing their premiums to pay policy holders the best bonuses and selling policies which people are prepared to buy.

The total premium income from life assurance earned at home and abroad on the London market is nearly as large as that from all non-life business, and tends to grow faster. On the non-life side, fire and accident insurance, which includes both industrial and domestic business, accounts for about 60 per cent of the insurance companies' non-life premiums, while a further 33 per cent is motor insurance. Marine insurance is largely dominated by Lloyd's, but in aviation the companies claim to play the leading role.

There is one further distinction in insurance which should be explained here, and that is the one between direct insurance and reinsurance. Reinsurance is basically the taking-on of chunks of risks that have already been insured elsewhere – often abroad. It spreads the load more evenly and allows the cover for a large or particularly dangerous risk to be shared among a larger number of insurers. There are two main kinds of reinsurance: proportional reinsurance, where the reinsurer covers a certain proportion of the losses of the direct insurer, and non-proportional, in which the reinsurer covers all the losses of the direct insurer above a certain level.

London is still the world's largest international insurance market, although it has not been growing as fast as other centres. But overseas business still represents a very high proportion of transactions on the London market. In 1984 about half the fire, motor and accident premiums earned by insurance companies which are members of the British Insurance Association came from abroad, and about 15 per cent of the life premiums. About three-quarters of Lloyd's premium income is earned overseas.

Although London's share of world insurance business has been falling, it remains internationally important in three ways. First, it still leads the world in the markets of marine and aviation insurance. Second, London is still the only place in the world, apart from New York, which is truly an insurance centre. Zurich, for instance, is the headquarters of a number of extremely important insurance firms. But while most of them have branches in London, very few British insurance firms have branches in Zurich. As for New York, it is mainly a domestic insurance centre, taking the bulk of its business from the United States. And third, London is by far the largest reinsurance centre in the world. Lloyd's alone does more reinsurance that any other body.

At the heart of the insurance market are the underwriters, who assess the risks and pay claims. Underwriting is carried on by two very different bodies: Lloyd's, which accounts for about 10 per cent of the market's total premium income; and the 639 British and foreign insurance companies (many of them very small), which account for the rest.

The insurance companies sell insurance to the public both directly and through part-time agents and specialist broking firms. At Lloyd's the broker is the only link between the underwriter and the insured. Then there are a number of firms providing specialist services such as loss adjusters and specialists in loss prevention and risk control. The relationship between the brokers and the companies is a touchy one: companies resent the profitability of the big brokers, whom they feel make vast amounts of money without bearing any risk. The brokers, for their part, feel that the companies are bureaucratic and stodgy, sitting in their plush offices while the brokers scour the world to bring them business. In reality, of course, both need each other, a fact which doubtless explains much of the resentment.

Lloyd's of London: its organisation . . .

Lloyd's is the oldest, most eccentric and most controversial part of the insurance market. In the 1970s the grave weaknesses of its antique form helped to lead it to a series of scandals which eventually made necessary a complete recasting of its institutional structure, and led to the disgrace of several of its most prominent members. For Lloyd's, the period from 1975 onwards has been the most unpleasant of its 300-year history.

But Lloyd's' recent history has been a remarkable mixture of success and failure. On the 'plus' side it has managed to grow, attracting vast numbers of new members and only slowly losing its share of the world market for insurance. It has, broadly, increased its profitability through the 1970s, if investment income is added to underwriting performance. It has continued to pioneer new risks, such as cover against electronic crime and for commercial satellites. And, if imitation is the sincerest form of flattery, it has seen both New York and Miami start insurance markets rather on Lloyd's lines.

But there has been a minus side too, which has manifested itself in a series of 'New scandal rocks Lloyd's' headlines. For Lloyd's found that its outdated rules enabled a minority of members to behave at best incompetently, and at worst fraudulently. So it decided to beef up its rules. To do this it had to get an Act through Parliament. When it tried to do that, not only did Parliament force it to make a number of other changes
164

to its structure that most Lloyd's members would dearly have liked to have avoided, but a new set of even more dramatic scandals burst upon it, and the Bank of England stepped in to impose yet further changes.

To understand why Lloyd's should have got itself into such a mess, you have to look at its curious structure. Lloyd's has been essentially just a market-place with a relatively small degree of control over its constituent parts. It was born nearly 300 years ago in Edward Lloyd's City coffee house and it still has a whiff of Boodles about it. On the ground floor of a 1950s mock-Lutyens building in Lime Street is the huge Room, capable of holding 3,000 people at once. This is crammed with 'boxes': small tables cluttered with atlases and handbooks, and hideously uncomfortable hardbacked pews on which the underwriters sit. Upstairs is a maze of marble corridors and comfortable lounges, and the 'captain's room', a coffee-house relic, all bowls of flowers and genial waitresses. Above that are offices used by underwriters and the marine departments of some insurance companies. Beside this building, Lloyd's is building a brand new block round a courtyard which will house a new Room. It is designed by Richard Rogers, joint architect of the Paris Pompidou Centre, to which it bears a family resemblance. It will, by the time it opens around 1986, have cost some £160 million and may well turn out to be the most important new architecture in London since the war.

Lloyd's is a corporation and since 1982 has been run by a Council of twenty-seven members. Of these, sixteen are working members of Lloyd's and form its executive body, a further eight are external 'names' of Lloyd's (explained below), and the final three have no connection with Lloyd's but are there to represent the public interest. These are nominated by the Council but have to be approved by the Governor of the Bank of England. Until the 1982 Lloyd's Act, the governing body was the Lloyd's Committee, which was roughly equivalent to the sixteen working members of the new Council. At the head of the Council is the chairman, who usually serves for four years. Peter Miller has been chairman since 1983. Under him sit three deputy chairmen, two long-serving members of Lloyd's, the third – the chief executive – a new post

165

effectively imposed on Lloyd's by the Bank of England in 1982. The first appointment to the new job was Ian Hay Davison, previously managing partner of accountants Arthur Andersen.

Reporting to the chief executive and Council are the 1,900 staff of Lloyd's. They run a range of back-up services for members, such as the policy signing and claims settling offices, organise the investment funds of Lloyd's, handle external relations and, in theory at least, the policing of the market.

Apart from the employees of the corporation, there are four types of people connected with Lloyd's: the 'names', who put the money up, organised into syndicates; the underwriters, who assess the risks and sign the policies; the underwriting agents, who manage the syndicates; and the brokers, who place the business. Until the provisions of the 1982 Lloyd's Act are fully implemented these four groups remain enmeshed with each other: the tradition at Lloyd's is to own a bit of somebody else.

In 1984 there were over 26,600 names, grouped into 400 syndicates. The syndicates specialise in one or other market, and a name may subscribe to more than one. About 80 per cent of the names have nothing to do with the running of Lloyd's. These outside names include such well-known figures as Edward Heath and Susan Hampshire, and are elected after what must be the most exclusive means test in the country: British and other EEC names must be able to show £100,000 of wealth throughout their Lloyd's membership, though the charmingly entitled 'mini-names' have been allowed in with a mere £50,000. In return, names are eligible for a cut of the syndicate's profits and liable, in theory at least, down to their last silk shirt for its losses.

Lloyd's is, however, kind to names who for other reasons hit a spot of financial bother. When Sir Freddie Laker's airline collapsed in early 1982, he was allowed to put his Lloyd's membership into suspension, merely not writing any new underwriting business until his affairs were more settled. He did not have to resign.

The other 20 per cent or so of the names work at Lloyd's, as underwriters, as underwriting agents or as brokers. They too have unlimited liability; their wealth qualifications are less

166

demanding than those for outsiders but their underwriting commitments are correspondingly restricted.

It is on the second group, the underwriters, that the success or failure of the syndicate ultimately rests. They decide what risks to write at what price. These underwriters may also be names in their own right, or they may just work for a salary and commission from the underwriting agent.

The underwriting agents manage the third group, the syndicate. Apart from doing the paperwork and appointing the underwriting staff, the agent is the link between the name and the underwriter. With an outside name, it is the only link. There are two species of agency: members agencies, which recruit names, negotiate with them and probably handle their investments; and managing agencies, who organise the underwriting syndicates. But most commonly the two functions are combined.

Finally, the brokers: by and large, the only way in which a syndicate can get business is through one of the twenty-seven authorised Lloyd's brokers. The main exception is in the motor market, where many provincial brokers have direct access to motor underwriters at Lloyd's. But Lloyd's brokers can place business with the companies: generally more than half the risks they place are with the companies, not with Lloyd's. Feeding business to the underwriters is the brokers' main function, but they are also connected in two other ways. They may be names in their own right; and they may own the underwriting agencies.

The agencies were once owned by underwriters, but over the years many of them were sold off. As a result, by the early 1980s the overwhelming majority of the underwriting agencies were owned or partly owned by broking firms, and in particular by the handful of giant brokers, the broker barons. These brokers, through the agencies, controlled most of the syndicates and so indirectly employed most of the underwriters.

There was an obvious conflict of interest between an underwriter who wanted to write the best risks at the highest premium and a broker who had to seek the lowest premium possible for his client. Within Lloyd's opinions differed as to what extent this conflict mattered in practice, with some Lloyd's people complaining that brokers always tried to palm off their worst risks on the syndicates they controlled, while others grumbled that they kept the cream of their business for their syndicates.

If the brokers have been the moguls of Lloyd's, the underwriters are the stars. There is self-evidently an art to successful underwriting, a sixth sense that good underwriters have that enables them to distinguish between the good risk and the bad. Top underwriters typically earn more than £100,000 a year.

Watching the underwriting room you can see the way the underwriter is the core of the operation. He (for underwriters are almost exclusively male) spends most of his day sitting in his box in spartan discomfort, waiting for the broker to feed him. The broker weaves his way through the desks, collecting underwriters' initials on his 'slip'. This is a length of paper with the bare details of the risk typed at the top. Opposite his initials, each underwriter scribbles the proportion of the risk his syndicate will bear.

On any particularly large or difficult risk, the broker will go first to the 'leader'. This would be the syndicate which has built up a reputation as the expert in that particular type of insurance, and which would set the premium rate for the policy. In the non-marine market the system has not been working well, and has helped to aggravate relations between brokers and underwriters. The market is dominated by a few large syndicates, and brokers frequently have to queue for the signature of one of the underwriters before they can take their slips on to the next syndicate. Queuing is inconvenient for the brokers and not always to the underwriters' advantage. The leaders tend to be the biggest rather than the most competent syndicates, and the system makes the market less flexible. In the marine market underwriters are prepared to follow smaller syndicates provided they have a good track record.

... and its problems

The story of Lloyd's two turbulent decades is encapsulated in two reports, the first by a committee headed by Lord Cromer and completed in 1970, and the other in a committee headed by

168

Sir Henry Fisher, which reported in 1980. The Cromer report was commissioned in 1968. That year Lloyd's revealed that in 1965 it had lost nearly £38 million, a larger loss than Lloyd's had ever made in profits to that date. Lloyd's accounts are drawn up three years in arrears, as by then about 90 per cent of the claims of the base year will have been settled and a reasonably accurate reserve can be set aside for the balance. No one expected a golden year, but this loss set off a train of resignations amongst members.

Lloyd's became alarmed. The working party under Lord Cromer, then head of Barings and later British ambassador to the US, made forthright criticisms of the way Lloyd's was organised. Lloyd's refused to publish the report in full.

The shortened version of the Cromer report which emerged concentrated on the fact that Lloyd's capacity was not growing fast enough to keep pace with the world demand for insurance. The answer was to get new members. As it turned out, though, it was the return to profitability which had the most striking effect on the number of applicants, and Lloyd's continued to be profitable throughout the 1970s.

But neither Cromer's published criticisms nor the measures adopted by Lloyd's to meet them touched the most basic difficulty of the corporation: the relationship between underwriting agencies and their names.

The unpublished part of the report had made a stinging attack on the quality of information provided to names and on the way in which the agencies had been taking up to 25 per cent of the syndicates' profits in a good year, while making the names meet all the losses in a bad. Generally the agency not only received from each name a 'salary', a fixed fee, but it also got a cut of the profits of the syndicate. By contrast, the name paid virtually all the expenses of the syndicate and also bore all its losses. Lloyd's view is that the salary goes to cover the agent's expenses; the profits cut, to give him an interest in the syndicate's profitability. But to others it might look like 'heads I win, tails you lose'.

It was Lloyd's failure to take these criticisms seriously which landed it in trouble. In the second half of the 1970s there followed three public disasters which pointed to the unresolved

169

weaknesses in the Lloyd's system. First, the syndicates run by Timothy Sasse were found to owe a total of £21 million. One factor in generating these losses was that Mr Sasse had exceeded his premium limits. Another was that he had underwritten a lot of high-risk New York slum property. Second, a rather ordinary claim following a fire on a ship called the *Savonita* was contested and a row ensued which involved questions in the Commons. And third, Lloyd's as a whole lost some $400 million in insuring computer leasing.

Computer leasing was a straightforward commercial error. *Savonita* was a small row that became a public one. But Sasse ought not to have happened. It was to stop another Sasse failure that Lloyd's Committee called in Sir Henry Fisher.

The Fisher report is a 200-page document. Its diagnosis of Lloyd's problems was much the same as Cromer's, but its prescriptions were more radical. These can be summed up under three heads: it wanted the old Lloyd's Committee to be widened with the appointment of outside members and changed into the Lloyd's Council; it wanted the Council to have much tougher powers to impose discipline on Lloyd's members; and it wanted the shareholding links between Lloyd's brokers and underwriting agencies to be severed.

The idea behind the first was that if the Committee were widened into the Council (with the old Committee continuing as the executive body within the Council), it would have a greater natural authority in imposing controls on Lloyd's members. In particular the non-executive members would act as representatives of the public interest. The powers themselves were to be based on a different principle from Lloyd's previous sanctions. The powers of regulation, made explicit in a new Lloyd's Act, would replace the earlier system of contractual undertakings between members.

The chief powers recommended were over the admission and registration of members, agents and brokers, and the conduct of the senior people employed by agents and brokers. Fisher proposed a disciplinary committee with powers of fines, suspension and expulsion, with a right of appeal at an appeals tribunal. The Council should have the

170

power to veto the appointment of any underwriter, to carry out inquiries and to regulate the various safeguards like premium income limits.

All in all this might sound a pretty draconian set of powers. In fact the new regulatory powers aroused very little opposition within Lloyd's, which promptly began to draft the necessary legislation. What stirred up the opposition was the separation of shareholdings between brokers and agents. Unlike the rest of the Fisher recommendations, which had been unanimous, this was by a majority; in subsequent discussions it became clear that many broker members of Lloyd's would resist it, and when the Lloyd's Bill was first presented to Parliament, though it gave the new Council powers to force the brokers to sell off their agencies, it did not compel them to do so.

So Parliament was petitioned by some Lloyd's members (including people who had been bloodied by Sasse and *Savonita*). The Committee looking at the bill required Lloyd's to amend it so that the separation of brokers and agencies would no longer be at the Council's option: it would be required by law. By the middle of 1987, brokers must sell their interests in managing agencies, though they are allowed to retain their interests in members agents, as these merely recruit and deal with names and are not involved in actual underwriting.

With that amendment, and with the additional power of being indemnified against legal proceedings against the Council, Lloyd's finally got its new bill through Parliament in June 1982. It became law in January 1983.

But before the bill came into effect, Lloyd's was struck by a new wave of scandal which made what had gone before a mere aperitif. In the space of six months, Lloyd's saw the chairmen of two of its largest broking firms resign amidst allegations of fraud, its highest paid underwriter suspended, and a chief executive imposed by the Bank of England to try to clear things up.

The first scandal to break was the disappearance of $55 million from the accounts of brokers Alexander Howden. This was discovered because Alexander Howden was taken over by the giant New York brokers Alexander and Alexander, which uncovered the deficit and eventually decided that the best policy would be to reveal this to its shareholders. The full details will not be available until the Department of Trade reports on it, but in essence Howden directors set up small reinsurance companies in offshore tax havens through which business was directed, it was alleged, at higher than normal rates. The business was placed by underwriting agents owned by Howden. The chairman and four other directors of the company resigned. One of those directors was the star underwriter, Ian Posgate, 'Possie' to his friends, 'Goldfinger' to everybody else. He had been deeply critical of his fellow directors, and had argued against broker ownership of underwriting agencies before the Commons committee which scrutinised the Lloyd's bill, and had in fact resigned his directorship of Howden shortly before the takeover. It was, however, in his role as underwriter both for the Howden syndicates and those of his own company, Posgate and Denby, that he was suspended by the Lloyd's committee.

The second scandal concerned the broking firm Minet. Like the other big brokers, it owned a number of Lloyd's agencies. As with Howden, these agencies arranged reinsurance with offshore companies. It transpired that some $40 million had been diverted in this way, and that the chairman of the company, and some senior employees, had a personal interest in these. The resignation of the chairman of Minet, John Wallrock, particularly shocked Lloyd's, as he had been one of the principal defenders of the ownership of underwriting agencies by brokers. He wrote in his last annual chairman's statement before he resigned: 'I have never sensed any harmful conflict of interest' between underwriting and broking.

The combination of these two events was particularly damaging. The fact that it had been a New York broker that had uncovered the events at Howden meant that Lloyd's problems received maximum publicity in its principal market, the United States. The fact that John Wallrock had been regarded as one of the pillars of the Lloyd's establishment made people wonder who on earth could be next to be disgraced. And the fact that two of the half-dozen largest insurance brokers in the City should lose their chairmen and senior staff

172

undermined the notion that Lloyd's should be allowed to continue to regulate itself. The Lloyd's bill, then in its final stages in Parliament, was clearly needed to reinforce the powers of the Council, but would the Council be any more effective than the old Committee if something was not done to improve the bureaucracy under it? At this point the Bank of England stepped in and forced Lloyd's to appoint a chief executive from outside. It had no formal powers to intervene: merely persuasion. But it worked. The Governor himself then persuaded Ian Hay Davison to take the job.

It will take at least five years before it is really possible to assess whether the reformed structure of Lloyd's can cope with the strains put upon it. During this time there will be further disclosures as the new regime sets to work. Ultimately, Lloyd's will be stronger. But meanwhile it has lost not only reputation but also business and capacity. For Lloyd's to recover it must continue to attract new names. This in turn depends most obviously on its underwriting performance but also, at least as far as UK names are concerned, on the continuation of Lloyd's special tax treatment. For the individual name, one of the great attractions of Lloyd's membership is the ability to build up funds without paying full tax on them.

Lloyd's suffers from one further structural weakness. Because its capital and reserves are essentially the wealth of its names, it does not build up as large a cushion of investment income as do the companies. Such funds as it does generate are fragmented among 200 underwriting agencies and have to be invested shorter-term than do the funds of an insurance company which can pool its premium float. While investment profits have kept Lloyd's in the black in recent years, it is even more dependent than the companies on underwriting performance.

The ultimate question that will determine Lloyd's success is whether its antiquated and fragmented syndicate system actually produces better results than the more bureaucratic institutional system of the companies. It may be anachronistic to expect a few individuals, operating largely by hunch, to beat the massed ranks of the world's insurance companies. But clearly sometimes they can.

173

There are three outstanding reasons for supporting the syndicate system. One is the relative ease with which a new syndicate can be set up. Young men (rarely women) prepared to take risks – and able to persuade a handful of names to back their judgment – can come to the fore far more quickly and earn much more than they could in the more bureaucratic framework of a company.

The second is that the syndicate system is particularly suited to types of insurance where no two risks are the same, and where there is little experience or precedent to fall back on in rate-setting. This is not, unfortunately, the case with the most rapidly growing area of insurance, motor risks, nor with the most profitable, long-term life. It was once the case with marine insurance. It now applies to some industrial business, where rapid technological advance makes rate-setting a leap in the dark, and it applies to catastrophe risks, in which Lloyd's leads the world. This kind of business is not necessarily unprofitable. But it is by definition the most risky.

The third advantage may, in the long run, prove to be the most important. Its overheads are incredibly low: perhaps 2 to 4 per cent of net premium. No insurance company could touch that. For the balance of Lloyd's business is gradually shifting to reinsurance. Lloyd's finds itself shut out of direct business in many countries as governments strive to protect infant insurance industries. But these industries pass on their surplus risks to the world insurance market, including Lloyd's, through reinsurance contracts. Paradoxically, Lloyd's finds itself accepting more and more reinsurance, where someone else has done the basic assessment of risk, rather than the one-off business to which it feels itself most suited. That is why its low costs may ultimately prove a more important asset than the innovative zeal of the syndicate system.

Looking ahead, perhaps the gravest problem for Lloyd's will be to adapt to new standards of financial morality. Already in 1983, when the new structure had hardly been in place a few weeks, there were complaints that bureaucracy was getting in the way of business. Lloyd's, perhaps more than any other sector of the City, has been a close-knit group. Very few of its top people are prominent in other parts of the community, in

174

contrast to senior bankers, industrialists or even insurance company directors. Many Lloyd's members, seeing their friends and associates disgraced, deeply resent the fact that outsiders should be imposing new standards upon them, and often find it difficult to see anything wrong with the way their friends have behaved. Meanwhile they see business being missed.

Had Lloyd's heeded the Cromer report, in all probability the Committee would have caught and prevented the excesses of the 1970s. As it was, a morality was allowed to build up which, when exposed to outside scrutiny, was seen to be quite unacceptable to the rest of society. Now Lloyd's is paying the price for its hubris.

The insurance companies

There are 639 insurance companies operating in Britain, of which 392 are headquartered here. They vary enormously in size. At one end of the scale are a handful of giant composite groups, of which the ten largest underwrite between them some 80 per cent of all non-life company business. (The table on the next page lists them in order of size.) At the other end are such small and esoteric concerns as the Ecclesiastical, which insures churches and the lives of country parsons, to whom it offers, thanks to inspired management, one of the best bonus rates going. Finally, there are the life offices, some of which belong to one of the composites, some owned by other financial institutions, and some of which are independent.

All of the giant composite groups carry out both life and non-life business. All insure both individuals and companies. But there are differences both in their character and the shape of their business.

Measured by total premium income, the Prudential is currently second largest in the country. But it is fundamentally a life company, with a general business on the side, so it appears in the institutional investors chapter. The two largest general insurance companies are the Royal and the Commercial Union, both of roughly the same size, but with very different characters.

175

British Insurance Companies by Premium Income: 1983

		All business £m	General £m	Long-term £m
1	Commercial Union	2,178.1	1,808.0	370.1
2	Prudential	1,986.6	606.5	1,380.1
3	Royal	1,907.8	1,700.2	207.6
4	General Accident	1,358.1	1,233.0	125.1
5	Guardian Royal Exchange	1,232.1	967.0	265.1
6	Sun Alliance	997.9	798.9	208.0
7	Eagle Star	867.6	521.7	345.9
8	Legal & General	815.9	169.4	646.5
9	Norwich Union	722.0	251.3	470.7
10	Phoenix	640.5	484.1	156.4

Source: *Policy Holder.*

The Royal is something of a Rolls-Royce of insurance companies. It has the reputation of being cautious about the business it takes, but very prompt in settling claims. Its staff are sensitive to any criticism of the insurance industry and anxious that the Royal itself should always be whiter than white. Its UK business is run from Liverpool, where it had its headquarters until 1960. It now has a relatively small group headquarters in nineteenth-century offices in Cornhill. It does 80 per cent of its business outside the UK – and more than half in the United States.

By contrast Commercial Union has a certain brashness about it. It lives in a tower block with smoked-glass windows, and has a board room whose walls are covered with bottle-green suede. It has been aggressive in selling insurance, and aggressive in trying to pinch business off rivals. But sometimes its efforts to chase business have come unstuck. It expanded at the wrong time in the US in the late 1970s, ran into heavy underwriting losses and ended up getting rid of its chief executive.

Next largest in terms of general business is one of the two

176

companies in the top ten to have headquarters outside London, General Accident, which is based in Perth. General Accident grew initially because it was better and cheaper at motor insurance than its competitors. At one stage motor insurance accounted for 60 per cent of its premium income. It also benefits from not having to pay London costs for both a City headquarters and a City staff.

Guardian Royal Exchange was formed in 1968 when the pushing Guardian swallowed up its rather Trollopian partner. The company is mostly run by Guardian people, but it has inherited from Royal Exchange virtually free offices in the most central site in the City: the Royal Exchange itself. You go to the right of the central steps, and its offices run round the outside of the old central courtyard which, since 1982, has been let to the new financial futures market. Its calm, slightly shabby corridors contrast with the hubbub of financial futures trading that goes on in their midst.

Sun Alliance is built on three ancient companies, the Alliance (once the most aristocratic of insurers), the Sun and the London. It regards itself as strong on household insurance, and has extensive connections with building societies. It probably sells more insurance through them than any other large company.

Eagle Star, until 1984 a quoted company, was built up by one family, the Mountains. This meant that it was left out of the wave of big insurance mergers in the 1960s, but it found itself vulnerable to a 'dawn raid' in 1981, when the German insurance group, Allianz, swept onto the market one morning and bought 14.9 per cent of its shares. It subsequently increased its interest to 28 per cent and then in 1983, tried to buy control. Eventually it mounted a full bid. The Mountain family resisted this and supported a rival bid from tobacco giants BAT. BAT won control of Eagle Star in what was Britain's biggest takeover battle, paying just under £1 billion for it.

Eagle Star is followed by Legal and General, essentially a life company and described in the institutions chapter. Next in overall size is Norwich Union, with headquarters in Norwich. It also has a large amount of life business, but has an unusual structure in that its life society owns the shares of the rest of the group. The life company is mutually owned, so anyone who takes out a life policy with Norwich ends up owning a tiny part not just of the life company, but of a large general insurance business too.

Finally there is the Phoenix, which is just under 30 per cent owned by the US Continental Insurance of New York, with which it pools its American business. It is a reputable, if slightly retiring company that may well eventually be taken over by its US partner.

Apart from these ten firms (which were the same top ten in 1972, though in a different order), there are a sizeable number of other general companies, many of them very small. Several foreign insurers have branches in London: the Zurich handles easily the largest amount of general insurance, and Sun Life of Canada is the biggest life office. Then there is a group of specialists such as the British and foreign reinsurance companies of which the largest UK company by far is Mercantile and General.

Finally, there are the life offices. There are 304 insurers writing life business in Britain. Life assurance differs from all other forms of assurance in a number of important ways. First, it is not so much a way of insuring against risk – even the risk of dying – as a form of investment. Second, it is profitable. Because the life offices offer an outlet for savings rather than cover against risks, they suffered none of the massive underwriting losses of the general insurance companies. Third, partly because of strict legal restrictions in other countries on selling life assurance and investing life funds, they do a far smaller proportion of business abroad than non-life insurers. Finally, the life offices provide the main exception to the rule that insurance companies are ordinary publicly quoted companies.

A number of life offices are mutual. This means that all the capital comes from the policy-holders, among whom the profits are shared. This gives a mutual company a built-in edge over a quoted or 'proprietary' life company. In theory the proprietary companies are potentially at a perpetual disadvantage, as their profits must also be split with their shareholders.

But mutual organisation has its drawbacks too. It is

extremely hard for a mutual company to expand. It always takes a long time to get a new life fund off the ground and in that time expansion has to be financed from the parent company's capital – which in the case of a mutual belongs to the existing policy-holders. The management of mutual companies often seems sleepier than that of proprietary ones, perhaps because there is no chance of a mutual fund being taken over. For thanks to their peculiar structure it is impossible for a mutual fund to be owned by another company: thus the substantial life funds run by many of the big composites are almost all proprietary. The exception is Norwich Union Life, a mutual fund which owns shares in the rest of the Norwich Union group.

Of the largest life offices, most are part of composite groups – such as the Prudential, Legal and General (with its massive pension business), Norwich Union, Guardian Royal Exchange, Commercial Union, the Royal and Eagle Star. But there are also some independent life offices. Most are mutual, such as Standard Life and Scottish Widows', but a few, such as Sun Life, are proprietary.

Although the life assurers have not had to suffer the traumas which shook the general underwriters, their industry has been undergoing a revolutionary change. The change has come from outside the traditional life companies and as much as anywhere else from Mark Weinberg,* first at Abbey Life, the company he started in 1962, and subsequently at Hambro Life, where he moved in 1970. At the end of 1984 Hambro Life was taken over, like Eagle Star, by BAT.

The particular product that Hambro Life (and Abbey Life) developed was the unit-linked life assurance contract. Unit-linked funds have been followed by property bonds, where the maturing value of the policy is linked to the value of a property portfolio. Property bonds in turn have been followed by managed funds, where the value is linked to an investment fund managed by the life office.

Unit-linked and similar forms of life assurance were major growth areas in the later 1970s, despite the fact that unit trusts did not perform particularly well. On the whole, the

*See chapter 5, p.110.

old-established life offices have limped along behind this movement. By and large they have been content to concentrate mainly on their traditional with-profits policies, though most now offer a unit trust-linked policy too. But only a few of the older offices have made a feature of these new types of policy and most of this expanding market has been pre-empted by the newcomers.

In any endowment policy, the proportion of premium going towards providing life cover is extremely small. Typically 90 per cent of net premiums go towards investment, and a mere 10 per cent into life cover. With life assurance increasingly just one more savings outlet and serving a diminishing social function, it became impossible to justify tax relief on the whole of an endowment policy on any grounds other than as a means to encourage contractual savings. Recognising this, the Chancellor of the Exchequer, Nigel Lawson, ended tax relief on new policies in his 1984 budget.

The other major growth area for the life companies has been occupational pensions. Insurance companies, led by Legal and General, run these for smaller companies and for the self-employed. (Pension funds are discussed at length in chapter 5 on institutional investment.)

The broker barons

The insurance industry's marketing is haphazardly organised. There are three main ways of selling insurance, none entirely satisfactory: through brokers, through part-time agents and directly by the companies themselves. The pattern of marketing varies with the kind of insurance. Lloyd's relies only on brokers, while the companies use all three methods. Brokers sell 94 per cent of all domestic marine and aviation business (thanks largely to their connection with Lloyd's), 80–85 per cent of all UK insured pension business and 76 per cent of all non-marine business, other than motor, which is largely industrial and commercial insurance. Their hold on the market for personal insurance is weaker: they sell only about half of personal motor cover,

20–25 per cent of all ordinary life business and perhaps the same of household insurance.* In these areas agents and direct selling are much more important.

Since the 1978 Insurance Brokers Registration Act, people who want to call themselves an insurance broker have to be members of one of the groups of brokers that have been brought together under the British Insurance Brokers Association. In 1983 BIBA had some 3,500 members. But there is no law against people calling themselves insurance consultants, who may or may not offer much the same services as an insurance broker. The Federation of Insurance Consultants alone had 531 members, and there are many more. Apart from the large international broking firms with operations in London, the cream of the brokers are the 265 members of Lloyd's Insurance Brokers' Committee, now part of BIBA. Most of the big brokers draw nearly half their income from overseas, the bulk of it from the US. Willis Faber, for example, probably the third or fourth largest broker in the world, finds about 75 per cent of its business abroad. And most of the larger brokers are geared mainly to wholesale business – industrial, commercial and marine insurance – though one, Leslie and Godwin, does a considerable amount of pension business.

For the biggest risks, insurance broking has been booming. As risks have got larger and more complex, and more and more companies compete internationally for business, so the scope has increased for a broker who ferrets out the best deal for a client, and if necessary bullies the underwriter into prompt payment. One sign of this dominance is the way the brokers were able to take control of many of the Lloyd's agencies. Another has been the fact that they are immensely profitable: in 1983 Sedgwick had income of £207 million, costs of £140 million, and a pretax profit of £80 million. And a third sign is that the Americans want to buy them.

Already three of the big brokers have been bought up. In 1980 C.T. Bowring was taken over by the New York firm of Marsh and McLennan, the largest broker in the world. Sedgwick Forbes, Britain's biggest broker, nearly joined forces

*Source: British Insurance Brokers Association.

with Alexander and Alexander, another big US broker, until the deal was aborted, and Alexander and Alexander embarked on its ill-fated purchase of Alexander Howden. Earlier, the smaller Leslie and Godwin had been bought by the US insurance company, Frank B. Hall.

Yet if insurance broking has been a considerable success story, it may not be so much longer. It is the commission system which has made broking so profitable, and the commission system is now under attack from both insurance companies and some customers.

The commission relates the payment of the broker to the size of the deal. It is not easy to defend. It means first that the client in effect pays for the broker's services whether he wants them or not. For unless the client is sophisticated enough to lean on the company or the broker, he pays a premium that includes the commission price. Next, the broker gets paid the same whether it simply arranges a straightforward policy or offers its client valuable advice; and it gets more on a large policy than a small, even if they involve the same amount of work. Finally, the commission system means that the broker has a built-in financial interest in getting the client to buy the policy with the highest possible premium, whether it suits or not.

All brokers strenuously deny that this last point enters their calculations. But they tacitly acknowledge the first two. Thus large companies may get remissions on their premiums from the brokers, while ingenious personal clients can – though less and less – act as their own insurance agents and thus pocket their own commission.

Though commissions are usually on a fixed scale, they tend to be higher at Lloyd's (where in theory, though not in practice, they are all individually negotiated) because a broker for a Lloyd's policy has more work to do than he would for a company.

Many of the difficulties facing the broking profession are the result of the commission system. It has meant first of all that few of the largest brokers find it worth their while to try to make personal insurance pay, although many smaller brokers have succeeded and it is certainly a market with enormous potential. On life insurance policies the commission is particularly profitable. Many smaller brokers are prepared to sell motor and household insurance in the hope of attracting more life business. Thanks to the commission system, there is, incidentally, great pressure on firms to try to sell endowment policies as there is enormous profit for the broker in these, rather than term life policies, which are very much cheaper in terms of sum assured.

Most large companies tend to handle personal business from an office outside London, or to pass it on to a smaller firm to handle on their behalf. There are exceptions: some big brokers do subsidise a small amount of personal insurance from their industrial customers in the democratic belief that the small motorist of today may be the ICI chairman of tomorrow. But Norman Frizzell and Partners is the only really large firm with a personal business of any size, made up mainly of motor insurance.

In marked contrast to personal insurance, the fastest growing area of broking, reinsurance, involves vast premiums and relatively little work. Commissions are tiny but the sums involved are so large that reinsurance brokers are looked on as an elite. A reinsurance broker, say his lowlier colleagues, is the sort of man who excuses himself from a committee meeting saying he has a dinner appointment in Paris.

Thus the bread, butter and jam of the big brokers is industrial, commercial and marine insurance. Here the unsuitability of the commission system is most evident. The brokers are increasingly finding themselves called on not to sell insurance but to act as consultants; and they are wondering whether they should not be paid on this basis. Once a big company can spend £200,000 a year or so on its insurance bill, it can justify the appointment of a full-time insurance manager. As the insurance bill gets bigger, the company may set up its own insurance department. At this stage the broker can only earn his commission as a specialist adviser. In some cases brokers have actually set up special consultancy arrangements with large companies which already have their own insurance departments.

The big insurance companies have long been dissatisfied

with the commission system. As far back as 1969, Kenneth Bevins, then chief general manager of the Royal, said:

> Acting on the one hand as 'professional' adviser to your 'client' and on the other as an agent for the insurers . . . is a feat of acrobatics which is obviously perfectly possible, but it does seem to be uncomfortable and to create a number of difficulties. At some time in the future I imagine it will be necessary for you to decide whether you wish to be a profession or whether you wish to be in business, because the two seem to me to be incompatible.*

Yet the system has survived. It survived the one organised effort to break it. A committee of the British Insurance Association suggested in 1969 that clients buying more than £1,000 worth of insurance should be able to choose to buy policies net of premium direct from the companies, and pay a fee to brokers if they wished to buy their advice. Sooner or later the system will break down, but fifteen years after that report insurance commissions – and the brokers that get them – still flourish.

Other ways of selling insurance

One can understand the reluctance of the brokers to bother with personal insurance when they see their main competitors, the part-time agents, earning almost as much commission for doing little more than arranging introductions. A network of perhaps 500,000 agents† – garages, bank managers, estate agents, accountants, solicitors, building societies, even staff and ex-staff – act for a number of insurance companies, earning 'perks' every so often by selling their clients and friends insurance. The agents almost always just introduce the client to the company; they do not pretend to give the sort of advice that

*Talk to Corporation of Insurance Brokers Conference, 26 April 1969.
†Not all of these are active. One of the largest firms has 80,000 agents, but reckons that only half of these actually generate new business.

a broker should in theory be able to provide, and the chances are that they can only give clients details of the policies of one or two companies.

Part-time agents are dying out. Some companies have already begun to drop those who do not generate enough business and the drive to cut costs may squeeze others out. The clearing banks, too, have set up their own insurance servicing organisation to replace the private agency of the branch manager. But agents still provide about 16 per cent of motor business, while building society agencies still provide 27 per cent of household business.

Direct selling, by contrast, has bounded ahead. As the size of composite companies has grown and competition in insurance marketing has intensified, the insurance companies themselves have been selling more and more insurance direct. Direct selling has rarely been used for company business: the companies are too frightened of the brokers to risk that. Direct selling of personal insurance, on the other hand, has been developing rapidly through branch offices, through newspaper and direct mail advertisements, and through tie-ups with other institutions.

The large companies, particularly Commercial Union and the Royal, have tried revamping their branches and conducting some imaginative if not entirely successful experiments in selling insurance over the counter in big stores. One company, the Co-operative, has been particularly successful at mastering the economics of selling direct by keeping down its costs. But for most companies the more profitable approach has been to link with banks, clubs and associations. The particular value of these to the insurance company is the mailing list: thus everyone who is a member of the AA automatically must be in the market for motor insurance and probably other insurance besides. One of the hazards of answering mail order advertisements is of ending up on an insurance company's prospect list.

There are two very different worlds of door-to-door selling. There is the old-fashioned institution of industrial life, or 'home service', which grew out of the nineteenth-century burial funds. (The 'industrial' refers to the industrious classes, a Victorian euphemism for the working class.) And there is the slick hard sell – geared to the telephone and aimed at the middle class – mainly of unit-linked life policies.

Industrial life assurance is essentially expensive life assurance: as a general rule, its premiums are higher and its bonus rates lower than other forms of life policy. Its only justifications are that it is better than none, and what many people want.

The reason is that industrial life is not only sold door-to-door; the premiums are collected from each house every week or month. To do this the 19 members of the Industrial Life Offices Association (the biggest by far is the Prudential) employ an army of 35,000 full-time staff in the field. They call on two out of every three families in Britain, gathering premiums averaging only £60 a year in 1982. The average sum assured under an industrial policy is only £1,050, while the average policy in ordinary branch business is nearer £10,000. Yet these offices write nearly half of the country's life business in terms of premium income written individually – that is, not as part of group schemes – and roughly half of that is collected from the homes of policy-holders. The offices claim that industrial life is still expanding at a healthy rate. The Pru in particular has done well in modernising and adapting its systems to cut the cost of home service. But as a form of policy, industrial life has tended to die out in the US and Australia, and eventually may do the same here.

The industrial life offices also sell personal general insurance at the door, but their methods could never be described as high-pressure. Despite the arrival of the newer door-to-door salesmen, whom they regard with alarm and contempt, they remain entrenched in their belief that selling life assurance aggressively ultimately leads to high lapse rates.

Unit trust-linked and property-linked life policies, usually sold directly, have been the most important development in life assurance in the 1960s and '70s. The products themselves are not particularly impressive. More staid companies growl that if you compare the return on most of the unit-linked life policies and their own with-profits ones, they generally come out well ahead. If only the public would realise . . . Reluctantly many of

186

the old-style life offices have started to sell unit-linked policies, but usually with much less success than the more aggressive companies such as Abbey Life, Hambro Life, Save and Prosper and Sun Life of Canada. These policies have not been sold exclusively door-to-door or over the telephone, but those have been the fastest growing outlets. Roughly 65 per cent of Save and Prosper's new regular business comes from its direct sales force.

Some companies, especially the foreign-based ones, employ foot-in-the-door tactics and heavy 'front-end' loading. This means that a large part of the early premiums go to salesmen's commission and company management charges. There have been efforts to try to police this, in particular by insurance companies that were members of the Life Offices Association agreeing to limit commissions to brokers. The more aggressive firms solved this problem neatly – by resigning from the LOA – and the agreement was abandoned.

How can underwriting be made to pay?

The fact that underwriting seems usually to end up losing money raises two obvious questions: why, and does it matter?

There are several reasons why most underwriters lose money, but the reasons vary from year to year and from underwriter to underwriter. Both the companies and Lloyd's have found that as soon as they get one sort of loss under control another seems to pop up. In the 1960s and '70s much of their energy was devoted to trying to cope with the problems of inflation and technical change: inflation, because it was for most of that period tending to rise; and technical change largely because it inflated the size of individual risks.

So underwriters have devoted a lot of energy to linking their premiums to inflation, and to trying to anticipate the effect of, for example, rising repair costs on claims. And they have tended to rely more and more on reinsurance to spread the load of insuring jumbo jets and the like. Coping with pure technical change, and in particular with completely new risks, is more of an art than a science, and it is something

187

at which Lloyd's (or rather the most profitable syndicates in Lloyd's) excel. When a risk is misjudged, as it was with computer leasing (see page 170), the losses can be enormous.

But does it actually matter if underwriting is unprofitable provided it generates the cash flow to fuel investment profits? Insurance people feel uncomfortable about this. All their instincts are that there is something fundamentally unsound about relying on investment profits to offset underwriting losses. And indeed, should interest rates and hence investment income fall sharply, the impact on the insurance business would be as serious as some great natural disaster. Put another way, if investment income falls, a lot of people are going to find themselves paying more for their insurance.

The other issue in international underwriting is the extent to which it is becoming a reinsurance business. One of the reasons why British companies are so heavily involved in the US is that it is the one big market where foreign companies can operate directly. There is obviously a strategic danger in dependence on one market. For Lloyd's and for the large brokers, the US accounts for half their income. Yet efforts to diversify have run into barriers. Despite EEC membership, British insurers are still effectively barred from conducting most types of insurance within other member countries. The highly profitable endowment life assurance is largely a national monopoly, despite the fact that British companies seem to be able to offer much more competitive terms than their Continental rivals. It certainly seems illogical that freedom of trade in goods has not been complemented by freedom of trade in services – that German cars are allowed to be freely sold in Britain but British insurance is not allowed to be freely sold in Germany.

Nor has the Third World offered an alternative outlet. Insurers have found their direct overseas business gradually whittled down. Each developing country wants its national insurance company, along with its national airline, partly because such a company offers an easy source of savings which the government can tap. So British subsidiaries overseas have found themselves subject to direction of investment, or have been ousted by the new national insurance company. Much of this business will find its way back to the international market and hence London via reinsurance contracts, but the company will have lost its direct business.

So insurers tend to find themselves concentrating on North America. Indeed, as the US alone accounts for roughly half the world's insurance market, any British company doing international insurance inevitably finds itself involved there to some extent. For four of the major composites, Commercial Union, the Royal, General Accident and Phoenix, the US market is more important than the UK.

Yet the UK underwriters cannot seem to get the US market consistently right. The problem is not just that sometimes they become loaded with bad risks, like Tim Sasse's syndicate's houses in the Bronx which suddenly experienced spontaneous combustion. Most of the British insurers seem to go through periods when everything in the US goes wrong. There are the troubles with the courts granting liability settlements far greater than any insurer predicted. There are the problems with insurance regulation, with premiums in many states still fixed by law. But these problems are common to all insurers, domestic as well as foreign. Part of the difficulty may be that British insurers have been particularly anxious not to lose market share, and so have been reluctant to withdraw from potentially unprofitable business in case they never get back again. If you tax the companies with this, they say they are learning to be more robust in turning away business and to be more sensitive to the US insurance cycle. But they also argue that even with unprofitable underwriting in the US, by and large, investment profits have been very good. It grieves underwriters to admit it, but high dollar interest rates can pay for a good deal of underwriting mistakes.

But the problem of unprofitable underwriting is by no means confined to the US market. In all international insurance, premium rates have been shaved. If you ask insurers why this has happened, they tend to talk in terms of the swing in the cycle, of the desire of new companies, backed perhaps by OPEC money, to increase their market share, of the fact that insurance tends to follow trade and that the shift of Britain's trade relationships away from the US and the Commonwealth and towards the Continent has weakened their hold on international business.

In fact, there are really two reasons why underwriting has tended to become unprofitable. First, as long as there are some companies which deliberately lose money on underwriting, cutting rates to increase their market share, and living off investment income, then other companies have little option but to lose business or lose money. Secondly, given the size and power of the insurance broking industry, and the homogeneity of the product, companies have little to compete on except price. There are areas in insurance, particularly in life policies, where developing a new product and selling it hard can yield excellent profits. But in international business there is less of an opportunity to operate in this way.

So insurers run the risk that if investment profits come down, they may find themselves with their underwriting losses exposed. To judge by past history, it is perfectly possible that a large insurer in the second half of the 1980s might suddenly be unable to meet claims. In Britain in the 1960s and early 1970s a string of insurance companies collapsed, including the Vehicle and General, whose demise left 800,000 British motorists without cover overnight. That was followed by the 1973 Insurance Companies Act which greatly increased the power of the Department of Trade and Industry to control the industry. The Department acquired powers to impose and vary solvency standards, to keep unsuitable people from senior positions in insurance companies and to examine the detailed returns companies are required to provide. Its powers to investigate a company were also strengthened.

Given this level of supervision, it seems unlikely that a major failure by a British company would occur without the government having some warning. But there is little corresponding control over international insurance companies business. This could affect British companies. The nightmare of a British insurer would be to take on a large risk, reinsure most of it with a foreign company, and then find that foreign company was unable to meet its part of the subsequent claim. The original insurer would then have to foot the bill for the lot.

190

Optimists in the industry argue that nothing much has changed: that there have always been swings in the insurance cycle, and the squeeze on underwriting profits is just one more instance of this. When investment profits decline, insurance premiums will be adjusted upwards. Before that happens, perhaps some foreign insurance companies will go under. But that will be no bad thing: it will teach the market that it ought to insure only with top quality firms.

This may be right. But it would be easier to be really confident about the future of the British insurance industry if one could also be confident about the quality of the management of the companies and of the administration of Lloyd's. Both have suffered because of the success of the brokers. Being a broker in insurance is – relative to turnover – a lot more profitable than underwriting the risk. While the British insurance market remains mainly in the hands of domestic insurers, Britain's share of the international market has been shrinking steadily since the last war: it has fallen from more than 10 per cent when the BIA gave evidence to the Wilson Committee in 1978 to about 7 per cent in 1982.

Of course it would be unrealistic to expect British insurance to keep the dominance it had in, say, the early 1950s. The worry is rather that the relative solidity of the big British companies will not be perceived as a market virtue when set against foreign competitive rates – until, that is, a couple of big international insurers fail to pay up.

For that is what the British industry needs. Just as at home the big companies reaped enormous benefit from the failure of the rate-cutting competitors of the late 1960s and early 1970s, so they would be able to charge more profitable rates abroad if there were a big failure in international business.

In a way that is fitting. Insurance needs external disasters, or no one would need to insure against them. So it is just that the industry should also need disasters in its own back yard to enable the companies that remain to make a living. British industry has an ambivalent attitude to insurance in general. A risk which is properly insured is one which does not need to be taken so seriously.

Insurers will always face the attitude reflected in W.S. Gilbert's description of *The Wreck of the Ballyshannon:**

Down went the owners, greedy men, whom hope of gain allured.
O, dry the starting tear, for they were heavily insured.

*The Bab Ballads, 'Etiquette'.

EIGHT

The commodity markets and the Baltic Exchange

What a futures market is

If you ring up your broker in Atlanta, Georgia, he may very well put you into pork bellies or frozen orange juice rather than General Motors or ITT. But you would look a long time in the City before you came across a private investor who had just bought into greasy wool tops or cleared a small profit on the copper market.

The commodity markets do not generally welcome private speculators. This may be one reason why they tend to reach the notice of outsiders only when they are overtaken by some esoteric disaster, such as an epidemic of black pod in Ghana cocoa crop; or when, as periodically occurs, someone tries to 'corner' the market and send prices gyrating skywards; or when someone reveals yet another massive loss from commodity speculation. Just occasionally, two of these events are linked, as for example when the Hunt brothers of Texas tried to corner the silver market at the beginning of 1980, failed, and lost an estimated $1 billion in the process.

When people talk about London as an international commodity centre, they may mean one of two different things. They may mean 'merchanting': arranging the buying and selling, insurance, shipment and financing of raw materials, usually between third countries thousands of miles away. Or they may be referring to the organised commodity markets, the ones where dealing is organised round a specific meeting place. A few of these are 'physical' markets, on which raw materials are bought and sold; more are 'futures' markets (in London usually called 'terminal' markets), on which people insure against price changes.

It is with these organised markets that this chapter is mainly concerned. They are in two main groups: those run by the London Commodity Exchange, in the old Corn Exchange Building in Mark Lane, deal in cocoa, coffee, sugar, rubber, wool, soya meal and gas oil; while those on the London Metal Exchange, in Plantation House, deal in copper, lead, tin, zinc, nickel, aluminium and silver. The chapter ends by looking at the Baltic Mercantile and Shipping Exchange, which is chiefly a market for chartering ships (and now aircraft); at the London bullion dealers who deal in gold and silver and, jointly with the LME, run a futures market in gold; and at the hybrid between a money market and a futures market, financial futures.

The bulk of London's physical commodity trade is arranged not through organised markets but over the telephone or telex. For most commodities there is no market in a central meeting place, and where one does exist it may handle only a small part of the total trade. Usually the goods are shipped between third countries and never touch the City. In a few exotic commodities, such as furs and ivories, auctions are still held in London; the goods are imported, sold and then usually re-exported. Tea is also auctioned through a market which handles some 60 per cent of the tea drunk in Britain.

By contrast, all futures trading is carried on in organised markets. Representatives of the markets' member firms meet daily on a dealing floor, such as those in Mark Lane, Plantation House or the Baltic.

The purpose of a futures market is to provide traders and manufacturers with a way of insuring against a change in the market price of a commodity. A cocoa trader's job is to buy the quality of cocoa that the manufacturers are likely to want. A chocolate manufacturer's job is to make sure that he is producing the kind of chocolate that the public wants to buy. Both are specialists in judging this sort of risk. But neither wants to carry the additional risk of having to judge how fluctuations in the world market price of cocoa are likely to affect the value of their stocks.

There are two ways in which they can avoid having to take this price risk. Originally in London they used a forward contract. Whenever a trader or manufacturer bought stocks of cocoa which he intended to hold for, say, nine months, he also

194

arranged to sell a similar amount of the same cocoa for delivery at the same time.* If the price of the stocks of cocoa he was holding had dropped by the end of the nine months, any loss he made on the first transaction would be offset by the profit on the second. The trouble with a forward contract, though, was that when it matured the trader had actually to find specific goods to deliver to fulfil it.

So a refinement of the forward contract was developed, and became the basis for the present-day futures market. Its most important feature is that, instead of promising to deliver specific goods, it promises to deliver goods of a specific grade. Each futures market has one, or sometimes two, standard grades known as the market standard. In this, all contracts are written. So the trader promises to deliver a certain quantity of cocoa of a certain quality in nine months' time. By the end of the nine months he will have 'closed out' the contract. This means that he buys a similar quantity of the same standard cocoa on the futures market, to cancel his original transaction. A futures market, in other words, deals in promises to deliver and take delivery of a commodity – not principally in the commodity itself.

If the futures market is working efficiently, the trader can expect the price of the market standard to move roughly in line with the price of the cocoa he actually owns, if only because firms will take advantage of any differential by buying in one market if the price looks low and selling in another if the price looks high. Thus the two prices will keep fairly close together. So usually, when the time comes for him to close out his futures contract, the trader will find that any profit he may have made on it roughly cancels out any loss he has made on the value of his stocks.

If the market is working badly, prices on the futures market may fall by much less than the price of the physical commodity. In that event, the trader may choose not to close out his futures contract and actually fulfil his promise to deliver. A sign of an efficient futures market is one where a very small proportion of contracts runs to delivery.

It is not only merchants who find the futures markets useful as

*All the transactions described in this passage can naturally be made the other way round.

a way of insuring against price changes. They are also necessary to producers, exporters and manufacturers of raw materials, to metal scrap refiners and to anyone, in fact, who has to buy or sell stocks of raw or even semi-processed materials. As a commodity passes through the production and manufacturing process, it may be hedged several times on the futures market by several different firms.

A distinction is made on the commodity markets between the terms 'hedging' and 'speculating', even though both are frequently carried on by the same house. Put simply, the firm which enters a futures contract to insure a stock of goods against price fluctuation is hedging; the firm or individual who buys, say, cocoa in the hope that the price will rise is a speculator.

The amount of physical business varies from one futures market to another. On some of the soft commodity markets it may be as low as 1 per cent, while the average is only around 2 per cent. On the London Metal Exchange it tends to be higher, ranging up to 15–20 per cent on the copper market. Some market men, notably on the London Metal Exchange, believe that a high proportion of physical business ensures that the futures price reflects movements in the price of the physical commodity. Accordingly the LME has made strenuous efforts to increase its physical trade. Other market men more logically argue the opposite.

Quite apart from keeping prices of the futures market in line with those of the physical commodity, there is a further important reason why it has to be technically possible for a contract to result in physical delivery: it must, to comply with the Gaming Laws.

The soft commodity markets, the LME and LIFFE

In balance of payments terms, the commodity trade's contribution is much smaller than that of insurance or banking, and has hardly grown in real terms over the 1970s. In 1983 the Bank of England estimated that commodity trading earned £350 million, while merchanting of goods in general (trading in goods other than commodities) brought

196

in £275 million. Ten years earlier the figures were £110 million and £55 million.

The largest commodity futures markets in the world are not in London but in Chicago. These deal in everything from live cattle to pork bellies and propane gas, but they trade almost entirely in products produced in the United States for the US markets. They are still largely domestic markets, serving domestic consumers, though they are making great efforts to increase their international business. Indeed in one area, financial futures, they have had enormous international influence. They have in effect invented a new use for the futures market techniques: applying them to foreign exchange and interest rates.

The world's main international futures markets are in London and in New York. In some instances, such as cocoa, sugar and coffee, London has the dominant market, while in others, such as silver, New York has the edge. There has also been a trend for markets in individual commodities to flourish near the centres of production, such as the Sydney wool futures market, the Penang tin market, the Singapore rubber market and the Colombo and Calcutta tea markets.

Not all London's futures markets are equally successful. For a market to thrive, a whole range of complicated conditions has to be right. The standard and the currency in which the contract is denominated must be the ones most suitable for the raw materials which the main customers want to hedge. Prices must not be so dominated either by the existence of large stockpiles of the raw material or by international commodity agreements that manufacturers have no need to hedge their stocks. There must not be a widely used synthetic substitute to which manufacturers can easily switch if the price of the natural material rises sharply. There must be an important group of buyers and sellers of the commodity who want to use the market to protect the value of their stocks. The currency has to be right: traditionally London markets operated only in sterling, but the gas oil market was started in dollars, and the gold futures market switched the contract to dollars when a sterling contract failed to generate enough trading. And there must be opportunities for speculators. The experience of the individual London commodity markets shows how vital these conditions can be.

The most active soft commodity markets over the years have been cocoa, coffee and sugar. Cocoa is one of the most notoriously volatile of all commodity markets and so a place where a speculator can make the biggest profits or losses. Part of the reason for this volatility is that there has not yet been an effective world agreement to stabilise the price. The producers are at loggerheads with each other – in 1982, for example, the world's largest producer, the Ivory Coast, rejected agreements designed to hold down production. Since the boom of the late 1960s, the London cocoa market has taken the lead from New York and is substantially larger than the other two futures markets in Amsterdam and Paris. Cocoa in particular has benefited from a technical advantage which the London markets have over their New York rivals. On many of the New York markets there are strict limits on how far the price can move in a day. On the New York cocoa market trading has to stop for the day once the price has moved 1 cent a pound – or less than £10 a ton. In London, trading has to stop once the price moves £20 a ton – but only for half an hour. The staff who organise London's commodity markets argue that for a dealer or speculator who has to operate in a wildly fluctuating market, London is more attractive than New York.

Though New York dominates world coffee consumption, London has the only effective futures market. The New York coffee futures market is quieter. There are two other small futures markets, one in Amsterdam and one in Le Havre. Swings in coffee prices have been moderated by the International Coffee Organisation, which covers over 90 per cent of the world coffee trade. But prices still fluctuate enough to keep the London market reasonably active.

The sugar futures market in London has now overtaken the New York one. In the late 1950s the New York market was larger. But it ran into difficulties when Castro came to power, because its main standard was based on Cuban shipments. Despite the International Sugar Agreement, large fluctuations in sugar prices still take place. Not only does the price of sugar sold under the agreement move within a wide band, but a growing volume of sugar is produced by countries outside it altogether, notably the members of the EEC.

Of the other 'soft' commodity markets, wool in particular shows how important it is to have the right contract, denominated in the right currency. London was once the world's largest, but then shrank in size compared with the market in Sydney, Australia. Part of the reason for this is that wool has become largely a Pacific commodity, traded between Australia and Japan. The London market also found difficulty in finding a suitable standard, trying three different ones in the 1960s, none of which was successful. In 1978 it switched to New Zealand cross-bred wool, quoted in New Zealand cents, and linked with the traders there to run something close to a twenty-four hour market: while the trading floor is in London, wool is traded on the telephone in New Zealand, with London picking up trade during the time when New Zealand is asleep. Thanks in part to the way wool is regaining ground against synthetic fibres, the market has proved very successful.

Gas oil is another success story. The name itself is an indication why, for gas oil is the Continental expression for heating or diesel fuel, and the contract recognises Continental dominance of this trade. It is in US dollars, the international oil currency, but is for delivery in the Amsterdam, Rotterdam or Antwerp area. Trading started in 1981 and ran well ahead of expectations. This encouraged the market to launch a crude oil contract at the end of 1983.

Rubber, by contrast, is an example of relative stagnation. Unlike wool, where synthetics are being pushed back, or gas oil, for which there is no easy substitute, natural rubber is needed less and less by the market. The world's largest physical market is in Singapore, next door to Malaysia, the world's largest producer. But both London and Singapore have suffered from the switch to synthetics and the changes in tyre technology.

The last of the Mark Lane markets is in soya bean meal. This was started in 1979, but has failed to achieve a high level of trading, largely because soya meal is principally a US domestic commodity and trading is dominated by the Chicago market.

Other new futures markets in different commodities keep

199

sprouting. There have been successive attempts to start a soya oil market in 1967, 1978 and again in 1982, efforts which have been described as a triumph of hope over experience. But you never can tell how successful a market will be. In 1980 a potato futures market was started by the Baltic Exchange, and it confounded sceptics by operating at a level comfortably above that needed to ensure its survival.

London is also the centre for a number of auctions of physical stocks of 'soft' commodities, for example, there is tea – traded not in Mark Lane but in a building in Pudding Lane (where the Great Fire of London started). A tea auction is a much more leisurely affair than the hussle of, say, the cocoa market. The room is full of elderly men who have been in tea broking all their lives, like their fathers and grandfathers before them, who tell you sadly: 'Britons will drink anything now. They've lost their discrimination.' The London tea market's once pre-eminent position is now challenged by other markets in Pakistan, India and Ceylon, while turnover at both the Colombo and Calcutta auctions is now higher than that on the London market.

There are a handful of other auctions, for instance, occasionally in ivory and bristles. And auctions were once held in shellac, which was originally used to put the shine on top hats and which enjoyed a boom when it was used for 78 r.p.m. gramophone records. Auctions in jute have also stopped, though trade goes on, as does trade in sisal and that other well-known hemp, cannabis sativa, now dealt in Mincing Lane under a Dangerous Drugs licence.* There are trade associations for firms dealing in mica, almonds, Indian carpets and 'general produce' which includes such exotica as essential oils (aniseed, camphor, eucalyptus), gums, spices and beeswax.

The other main futures markets in London are the seven metal markets of the London Metal Exchange. These markets are much more closely linked than those in soft commodities – they are all run by the same bodies, the board of the LME and a management committee; and the metals are traded, one after another, in the same ring by the same firms. While the various

*Graham L. Rees, *Britain's Commodity Markets* (London, Elek Books, 1972).

soft commodity markets have separate memberships (though the same firm may belong to several), a member of the LME can deal in any metal dealt on the LME. The markets have a different ambience. While dealers on the floors of the soft commodity markets are usually fairly junior, senior members of LME firms come to ring sessions.

Of the seven metals – copper, tin, lead, zinc, silver, aluminium and nickel – it is the fortunes of copper which dominate the Exchange, though aluminium is now challenging it for leadership. The rise of the copper market dates from the mid-1960s when the attempts of the copper producers to control world prices of copper began to break down. Their efforts were finally abandoned in 1978 when Kennecott, the US's largest producer, abolished its controlled pricing system and based its prices on the quotes on the LME's equivalent in New York, Comex, or Commodities Exchange Inc. Most large brokerage firms have seats on both exchanges, and while Comex has a larger turnover, the LME is thought more influential in international terms.

In lead and zinc the New York markets have died – the US price of both metals is fixed by American producers. But elsewhere the price of lead and to a lesser extent of zinc is strongly influenced by the LME. In tin, the New York market is also very small. There is a larger market in Penang, in Malaysia, but it is a purely physical market, without hedging facilities.

In silver futures (and in gold), New York is ahead of London. The LME's silver contract was started in 1968 in response to demands, mainly from abroad, for a new market in London that would offer the same sort of trading facilities for silver as were available for other non-ferrous metals on the Exchange. The market has two rivals: the London bullion market (described below) and Comex, which probably has more influence on the world price than either of the London markets, and certainly has a far larger turnover.

The other two LME markets, in aluminium and nickel, are of more recent origin. Contracts in both metals were started on the LME in the late 1970s. Aluminium has become one of the most actively traded of all the markets.

On the LME, unlike the soft commodity markets, a relatively large proportion of physical business is carried out. This is actively encouraged by the Exchange, which is very proud of the fact that its contracts contain no *force majeure* clause (as do those of most metal producers) to provide an escape in case of strike or other obstacles to delivery. A purchase made on the LME is guaranteed to be delivered on the due date whatever happens. In the 1960s the LME took two steps to increase the volume of physical business. It opened a number of overseas delivery points, warehouses on the Continent. These allow someone in Hamburg who sells copper on the LME to deliver it straight to the LME warehouse in Hamburg instead of going all the way to London first. Secondly, the Exchange replaced the old copper contract, which was so broad that buyers could never be sure what grade of copper they would get. Since then, two separate contracts are now used, in higher grade cathodes, or wire bars, and in standard cathodes. But this has not been a complete solution.

The LME's influence on the prices of the metals it trades in shows how successful its efforts to encourage physical transactions have been. Although at most only 5 per cent of world trade in the metals it handles passes through the LME, its prices reflect changes in supply and demand at the margin. When there is the threat of a surplus, LME prices fall, but producers and manufacturers can always find a market through the LME. When there is a shortage, prices on the LME will rise, and attract sellers – and buyers who cannot find supplies at any other price anywhere else. Prices on the LME have become the basis for contracts between producers and manufacturers all over the world.

Useful though this volume of physical trade makes the LME as a barometer of supply and demand for metals, it has caused practical difficulties for the Exchange itself. As already argued, an efficient futures market is one where very few contracts run to delivery. In the LME copper market, delivery can represent a fifth of turnover. This mix of spot and futures business exacerbates the problem of finding a suitable standard. A standard general enough to be useful to hedging is too vague for a buyer hoping to take physical delivery. In a futures market it does not matter if several different grades of a metal can be delivered to fulfil a contract, but for a manufacturer who wants a certain quality of metal, it matters very much. Dealers on the LME cope with this problem through an informal arrangement whereby if one firm finds that the copper it has bought on the Exchange is of the wrong quality or will be delivered at an inconvenient point, it rings up another firm and arranges to swap that copper for a more appropriate brand, if necessary paying a premium on the deal. In other words a second, informal copper market has had to evolve to solve the problems which the mix of physical and futures business on the Exchange creates. Moreover, to work properly a futures market needs speculators, and the high proportion of contracts running to delivery on the LME tends to discourage them.

There is clearly an argument in favour of separating the futures and physical markets, but the LME has consistently resisted this. There is also an argument for having a longer-dated contract, as has Comex in New York. All LME contracts run only three months, while Comex contracts can run out to nearly two years and soft commodities in London are traded up to eighteen months ahead. London-based brokers can still quote metal prices for longer dates, but only either by carrying the risk themselves, or by hedging it in New York. There is a suspicion among those who find the London system inconvenient that the reason for it is the extra commission an LME firm collects each time a contract has to be renewed to extend the length of a hedge. But another more respectable reason is that metals, unlike soft commodities, are not subject to seasonable price fluctuations.

These then are the two traditional groups of commodity futures markets. But at the beginning of the 1980s they were joined by two hybrids, the London Gold Futures Market and the London International Financial Futures Exchange (LIFFE, pronounced 'life'). The first is a joint venture between the LME and the bullion market, the second a joint venture between the banks, stockbrokers, discount houses and the commodity brokers.

Both were set up in response to competition from North America. A gold futures market, with the extraordinary gyrations in the gold price at the end of the 1970s, suddenly became virtually essential for any industrial user of gold. London bullion firms normally dealt spot, but could quote forward on individual deals. But futures markets, able to quote up to two years forward, sprang up in Winnipeg, Chicago, New York, Singapore, Sydney and Hong Kong. Comex in New York became the world's largest futures market; London was left standing. In 1979 the LME and the bullion houses agreed to examine the possibility of setting up a market, which duly started in 1982 in Plantation House. But it chose the wrong contract – in sterling. This was a failure, so after a few months it switched to dollars, the natural currency for gold trading. Things improved, but London is still a long way behind New York.

LIFFE is also an attempt to catch up, but a more aggressive one. While the London commodity markets in the 1970s tried to get new commodity contracts off the ground, Chicago was pioneering a whole new concept in futures markets: in 1972, in currencies, and in 1975, in interest rates. The International Monetary Market of Chicago Mercantile Exchange took the techniques it had previously applied to cattle, pigs and pork bellies and applied them to the British pound, the Canadian dollar, the Deutschmark, and subsequently to US Treasury bills, whose price gave a proxy for US interest rates. It was followed by the Chicago Board of Trade and by Comex, and by 1982 financial futures accounted for some 20 per cent of all US futures turnover and was the fastest growing section of it.

Chicago was and is extremely important. London started by pooh-poohing the idea, but suddenly found that Chicago trading was moving exchange rates. Even the London discount houses, those most crusty of City institutions, found it convenient to deal in Chicago. London had to respond, and in 1982 opened LIFFE, grandly sited in the Royal Exchange immediately opposite the Bank of England. It started with just two contracts, in three-month eurodollars, and in sterling against the dollar. Within three months it had blossomed and was trading three-month sterling interest rates, twenty-year gilts, German marks, Japanese yen and Swiss francs.

Unlike the gold futures market, LIFFE got off to an

204

impressive start. It was helped partly, no doubt, by the natural demand for its services, but also by the strength and breadth of backing for it. The natural home for the eurodollar contract is London, for that is the key centre of that market, and the gilt contract also seems assured of success. Currencies, by contrast, have been less successful, and LIFFE is not sure why.

LIFFE's membership cuts right across the traditional specialised City boundaries. The big banks, British and foreign, are members, and they by habit are already dealing with discount houses. But stockbrokers and commodity brokers have for the first time found themselves dealing as equals with the banks. The jobbers, however, are restricted by Stock Exchange rules to taking orders only from fellow LIFFE members on the floor. This places them at a disadvantage compared with the other participants.

Still, LIFFE looks like being a success. It needs to be, for it is a big and expensive operation. Though it only employed at its start about 30 people, the total employment committed to it by its members was about 3,000. But its real interest for the City is perhaps the extent to which it encourages the breakdown of the rigid barriers between different types of organisation. In that way it may well prove a catalyst for City change.

Running the markets

Some 100 firms belong to the futures markets in soft commodities and to the LME. Though nearly two-thirds of these belong only to one market, many deal in several. A firm that has a seat on the LME may also be a member of some of the soft commodity markets. Thus Rudolf Wolff, as well as dealing in all metals on the LME, is also a full member of the coffee, cocoa, sugar, rubber, vegetable oil and gas oil markets. Generally, though, firms tend to stick either to soft commodities or to metals, while tea and rubber are mainly handled by firms which do little else.

Firms carry out a great range of activities, which fall basically into three groups: there are merchants, who trade in a physical commodity, hedging it in the futures market and carrying stocks for it themselves; there are brokers, who offer much the same service, but do not carry physical stocks; and there are commission houses, which generally transact no physical commodity trade, but deal in futures markets on behalf of clients. The large commission houses in London, like Bache and Co. or Merrill Lynch, are American, as Stock Exchange firms have been quick to point out, though there is one large commission house, G.W. Joynson, owned by an Australian consortium.

Each kind of firm may specialise in one commodity, or in several. A firm may be brokers in one commodity and merchants in another. Firms in recent years have tended to become bigger, either by amalgamation or by linking up with some other City institution. Merchanting, in particular, requires substantial capital resources. Some firms have moved into the production and processing of raw materials, as well as buying and selling: thus Czarnikow, probably the world's largest sugar broker, also has a spice manufacturing business. In the 1970s commodity houses spread into merchant banking and money broking. But by and large the most successful of the commodity merchants and brokers are those that have stuck to the business they know best.

All futures markets try to limit their membership to some extent. Membership of the soft commodity markets is usually divided into two main categories: floor members and associate members. The floor members are the commodity houses; the associate members, generally manufacturers, shippers and so on. Anyone who wants to deal on the market – even associate members – must do so through a floor member.

To become a member of one of the soft commodity markets, a firm usually has to buy its seat from an existing member. In most markets some firms own more than one seat, which they may be persuaded to part with. The cost is often a five-figure fee. The number of seats on all the markets is strictly limited and the market association tries to keep the number of floor members down.

The London Metal Exchange is even more exclusive than the soft commodity markets. New members have to be admitted by the board and the committee of the LME. They have to show £5 million of capital and reserves and also have to contribute

206

£500,000 to the LME's guarantee fund. In summer 1983, only 27 out of the LME's 36 seats were filled. The LME's justification for this is that it wants to make sure new arrivals are financially sound.

Technically, foreign firms are excluded from floor membership. This does not stop the American broker Merrill Lynch from buying cocoa for its clients, nor the German Metalgesellschaft from actually having a seat on the Metal Exchange, but both act through a British subsidiary whose board must have a certain proportion of British members. In 1983, though, well over half the LME members were controlled from abroad, with the largest single metal trader, Rudolf Wolff, owned by the Canadian mining company Noranda Mines. More xenophobic is the sugar market, on which no foreign firms are formally permitted to be floor members. This regulation dates from the First World War, when the sugar market lost all its German members. As they then dominated it, the sugar market nearly disappeared.

The alleged reason for limiting floor membership of both the LME and the soft commodity markets is that an open outcry market with too many members is chaos to run. On all the markets except the London rubber market trading is by 'open outcry'. Everyone shouts their bids at the tops of their voices across the floor and the noise is a rough indication of turnover. They are sometimes described as 'call' markets, because at specific times of day representatives of all the floor members or broking firms sit round in a ring making their bids, while (in the case of soft commodity markets) a chairman conducts business. While most dealing is done at other times, it is at these sessions that official prices are fixed.

The trouble with this argument for limiting membership is that a similar primitive system of trading is used on most of the world's smaller stock exchanges, exchanges which have a much greater volume of business and number of members than the London futures markets. Besides, if the reason for keeping membership down were really the limitations of the open outcry system, and not the fear of new competition, then the sensible solution would be to change the system. All the commodity markets already have telephone arbitrage dealings

207

with other commodity centres, while in the livelier markets 'late kerb trading' – after-hours dealing – is also conducted over the telephone after the market is closed. This could well be the way that the commodity markets develop. The foreign exchange and money markets of the City have proved that it is perfectly possible to run a market with a worldwide membership efficiently over the phone.

The market rules are laid down by the association which runs them. These set commission rates, and occasionally expel members who try to undercut them. They determine who is allowed to deal in what capacity, the number of seats in the market and the market's standard. The associations themselves are made up of representatives of the various commodity houses, and sometimes of producers and shippers as well. The seven markets of the London Metal Exchange are governed by the LME management committee. Separate associations cover physical trade and there are a few associations, such as the Tea Brokers' Association, the Timber Trade Federation and the Federation of Edible Nuts Association, for commodities which have no futures markets. There are a number of people who specialise in running these associations. Association secretaries may be responsible for running more than one market, and occasionally may launch a new one.

Contracts made on the soft commodity futures markets are registered and cleared through the International Commodities Clearing House (though the rubber market, ever eccentric, has its own Rubber Settlement House). The ICCH was owned by the finance company United Dominions Trust until 1981, when it was bought by a consortium of the clearing banks, plus Standard Chartered. Besides registering contracts, the ICCH guarantees that they will be carried out, thus protecting each party to a contract against default by the other. No such central clearing house exists on the London Metal Exchange.

It is the ICCH, too, which polices the deposit system on the soft commodity markets and on LIFFE. Whenever a floor member's client takes a speculative position in a market, the member must put up a deposit. The size of these deposits varies from one market to another, and is fixed in terms of the lot, or normal trading unit. Thus in cocoa it is £80 per 10-tonne lot, and in sugar £100 per 50-tonne lot. As a proportion of the value of a deal, this is very small. If the price moves against the speculator, his liabilities increase; so the floor member must put up additional 'margin' to maintain the deposit. The ICCH collects the deposit and margin from the broking house which handles the transaction. It is up to the broking house to decide what part of the margin it asks the client to pay himself, and how far it is prepared to carry the deposit lodged with the ICCH itself.

Because the LME has no central clearing house, it has no central body to guarantee the fulfilment of contracts – or to enforce the taking of margins. Indeed, the margin system exists only in the silver market, and without a central clearing house there is no ready way to make sure that all firms observe it. This is another reason why contracts on the LME run for a much shorter period than those in soft commodities. The longer a contract runs, the greater the chance of price fluctuations and the risk that a client will not be able to cover them.

The Baltic Mercantile and Shipping Exchange

The Baltic operates from a lofty Edwardian hall, lined with marble pillars, and almost as big as the floor of the Stock Exchange – though far more sparsely populated. At one end of the floor is the 'ring' – a sort of circular wooden fence – around which members gather to trade in grain futures. On the other side of the floor there has been since 1980 a market in potato futures. Potato futures have been a success, within a year the market becoming larger than either the US or the Amsterdam markets. Both markets are run by the London Grain and Feed Trade Association and clearing is through the International Commodities Clearing House. Elsewhere, there is a market in second-hand ships and aircraft. But the Baltic's main activity is providing a market for the chartering of tramp ship cargoes.

The bulk of the world's shipbroking may still go through London, but since the last war, the Baltic and its brokers have been finding life harder. First, less and less ship chartering is actually done on the floor of the Baltic. While before the war brokers would frequently spend the whole day on the Exchange, today they tend to use it increasingly simply as a place to swap market gossip. More and more broking is done by telex and telephone. Indeed many members involved in tanker chartering and in the Baltic's newest market, air chartering, rarely turn up at the Exchange at all. As a result, the floor is virtually unused (aside from the futures rings) except between noon and 2 p.m., when Baltic members meet for a chat, followed perhaps by lunch in the restaurant or coffee shop. Members who turn up only for lunch are nicknamed 'lunch members'.

While modern communications are taking business from the floor of the Exchange, changes in the organisation of world shipping are altering the work of a Baltic broker. The Exchange has suffered from the fact that the fastest growth in shipping has not been in tramp shipping but in containers, which are run by shipping lines, and in bulk carriers and tankers which are usually chartered by their owners directly, often before they are built, for many years ahead rather than for specific voyages. Ship-owners indeed can go directly to shipbrokers in the US or other centres for a cargo, or can find it directly without using a broker at all.

As a result, few brokers now depend entirely on competitive chartering of tramp shipping for a living. Commission rates in that field have been pared to 1.25 per cent. Most brokers rely for their bread and butter on monopoly charters, arranging all the shipping used by a large industrial firm processing raw materials. On such charters, commissions may range up to around a more rewarding 3 per cent. Brokers have also tended to diversify into other activities. Almost all the Baltic's brokers today are either subsidiaries of ship-owning firms or have ship-owning subsidiaries themselves.

As the Baltic is having to fight harder for its living, old restrictions on the membership of foreign firms have been partly relaxed. Women were allowed to become members only in 1974. But the Baltic's long-term future as an organised market in shipbroking is uncertain. An attempt to set up a similar exchange in New York died quickly, as

210

brokers found they could do business more quickly and efficiently over the phone.

But if the physical facilities of the Baltic are grossly underused, the firms that are members have in general been successful. The Baltic's invisible earnings have risen through the 1970s and 1980s, reaching £250 million in 1983, second only to Lloyd's, and way ahead of the Stock Exchange. Earnings have risen steadily despite the world shipping recession, and companies have self-evidently found it useful to keep up their Baltic membership: the number of individual members has stayed around 2,500 split among 750 companies.

The Baltic's shipbroking members claim it still has three uses. First, it gives brokers a central meeting place. Second, membership gives a broking firm a sort of seal of approval, useful for a company that deals on an international market and has to handle substantial sums of other people's money. And finally, some of the brokers who specialise in larger ships claim that it is easier to deal on the floor of the Baltic than over the phone. None of these arguments is sufficient to suggest that the London shipbroking market will not become, in a few years' time, almost completely a telephone market. Maybe that does not matter too much. If what the members need is merely a superior lunch club, the wheel will simply have gone full circle, and the Baltic will have returned to its coffee house origins.

The gold and silver bullion markets

The London gold market has always managed to shroud itself in a carefully cultivated aura of mystery. Much of its public glamour comes from the ritual of the twice-daily 'fixing', at which the price of gold is decided by the five gold bullion dealing firms. Men from Samuel Montagu, Johnson Matthey, Mocatta and Goldsmid and Sharps Pixley meet in the elegant offices of N.M. Rothschild. They sit with telephones beside them and little flags in front of them, which they raise to stop the price being fixed during tense conferences with their offices. Their decisions are flashed around the world, and gold prices from Bombay to Manila follow their lead.

This ceremony does sometimes acquire some genuine

excitement. For instance, when the gold price shot to over $800 an ounce in 1980 and people queued in Hatton Garden to sell their rings for melting, the fixing took well over an hour to reach a price instead of the usual five minutes. But most gold is bought and sold outside the fixing, on the telephone and telex, at prices which change constantly during the day. The unglamorous truth is that the London gold market has been through a difficult time. Until 1968 it was the world's largest gold market. It owed its pre-eminence to two things. First, it was through the London markets that the Bank of England, on behalf of the world's main central banks, operated the 'gold pool'. Through it, the market price of gold was kept within narrow limits on either side of $35 an ounce. Second, until 1968 London was the market on which South Africa, which produced 80 per cent of the non-communist world's gold, sold all its stocks. Since then, although neither centre produces turnover figures, Zurich for a while overtook London, with both South Africa and the second largest producer, the Soviet Union selling there. South Africa was upset by the closure of London for two weeks in 1968 and by a subsequent arms embargo imposed by the Labour government. Russia was understood to be unhappy about security at Heathrow, where the gold was flown in. Both have now to some extent switched back to London, and by the early 1980s London had regained much of the lost ground. This was partly thanks to the efforts of the Bank of England to encourage less developed countries to use its own vaults for storing gold; partly because the big US traders open dealings in London before moving to New York in the afternoon; and partly because Zurich acquired a reputation for overcharging clients. In physical trade in the metal, London is certainly larger than Zurich. In terms of market turnover, the two are probably level pegging. In terms of influence on prices, New York, with the futures market in Comex, is probably more important than either European centre.

As British citizens are not allowed to own gold bullion, the bulk of London's business is with international clients. Gold is bought by the bullion market itself only for immediate delivery.

The gold fixings are the only moments in the day when demand and supply from the world's main gold markets are matched up. But of the five London firms at the fixing, only two are continuously active in the gold market: Johnson Matthey, which has a large industrial demand, and Samuel Montagu.

Three of the firms that make up the gold market, Mocatta, Sharps Pixley and Montagu, also form the silver bullion market. Silver, unlike gold, can be bought forward as well as spot. The bullion market has been challenged by the LME's decision to deal in silver, although it claims that the LME has taken little business from it. When the LME silver market was under discussion, the bullion firms improved their contract and halved their commission rates. From the buyer's point of view the main difference is that with the LME he has – in theory – either to put up 10 per cent of the purchase price as margin or deposit one-tenth of his purchase with the dealing firm. The bullion market by contrast has no deposit requirement. This relaxed attitude sometimes proves expensive.

Every ten years or so one of the bullion houses loses a few millions because one of its clients fails to honour a contract: Johnson Matthey* lost £7 million to an unnamed client in 1970, Mocatta lost £2.5 million to a Saudi family in 1981.

But perhaps the most remarkable feature of the bullion trade, apart from its obsessive secrecy, is the way in which it transcends normal ideological barriers. For example, South Africa does not have any formal diplomatic relations with the Soviet Union, yet they cooperate closely on selling tactics. Gordon Waddell, an executive director of Anglo-American, the largest mining group in South Africa, and the former son-in-law of its chairman, Harry Oppenheimer, was spotted at the Bolshoi in the company of two Soviet officials. He was asked what he was doing there. "Oh," he replied, "I was just passing through."

The future of futures

For the commodity markets, the 1970s was something of a wasted decade. While commodity trading houses were

---

*The losses which struck Johnson Matthey in 1984 were on its banking side, rather than from bullion dealing.

frequently perfectly successful in their existing lines of business, London was not particularly skilful at establishing new futures contracts. It was not for want of trying. Contracts in cotton, fishmeal and vegetable oils were all attempted and failed. Gas oil, to be sure, was successful; potato futures managed to survive. But the real commercial need in the 1970s was for protection not against fluctuating commodity prices, but rather against fluctuating exchange rates and interest rates. Only a handful of companies were so dependent on commodity prices that they needed to hedge those, but just about every company which borrowed money or traded abroad had a theoretical requirement to hedge on exchange rates and interest rates during the volatile 1970s. It was only in the 1980s that London began to meet this need.

Looking ahead, it is not difficult to predict continued modest success for the 'conventional' futures markets, though these inevitably are affected by the general level of world economic activity. But the need to hedge, even given efforts by producers to stabilise prices, will not go away. It seems reasonable to expect new contracts to be established around the world alongside the present ones, possibly, for example, in strategic minerals. London will find the US markets much tougher competitors than they were fifteen years ago, but it should continue to be competitive itself.

The really exciting area, however, will probably be not in conventional commodity trading but in futures trading in interest rates, currencies or stock market indeces. These financial futures are where the potential growth lies, for unless there is a successful return to fixed exchange rates, currencies will continue to fluctuate and companies will need to hedge against that. And it seems virtually inconceivable that interest rates will not continue to swing about, and even if the movements are not as striking as in the early 1980s, firms will seek to hedge against them.

The hedgers will not only be commercial companies, for the financial futures markets have given the international investment institutions a completely new tool for their trade. It has become possible to hedge separately currency and interest-rate decisions, so that an investor who likes the

214

prospect for a currency, but feels that interest rates (and hence security prices) in that currency will move adversely, can still back his judgment on the currency while protecting himself against an adverse interest-rate movement. If there is an explosion of international securities dealing in the 1980s analagous to the explosion of international banking in the 1960s and 1970s, then the financial futures markets are bound to grow very rapidly too.

How far will London share this boom? It has some natural advantages in this type of futures trading: the fact that London's foreign exchange market is still the world's largest; that London's time zone is ahead of New York; the variety of foreign banking and investment institutions in London; the international orientation of London (and Edinburgh) financial institutions. And of course LIFFE has the active support of the authorities in the shape of the Bank of England. But if customer demand and institutional structure exists in London, how about the supply of speculators? Certainly private commodity speculation is small compared with the United States. Those firms anxious to encourage private speculation blame this difference on the refusal of the Stock Exchange Council to allow the same firm to carry on stockbroking and commodity broking. In America almost all the large firms do both.

Without speculation there is always the danger of too volatile a market with, say, everyone hedging against a rise in prices and nobody betting on a fall. But the attitude of much of the London commodity market is ambivalent towards speculation and particularly hostile towards private speculation. Indeed the London market, unlike the US ones, is not really organised to cope with the private speculator. The legal safeguards that exist in the US do not exist in London, and there have been a number of instances where individuals have lost large sums of money because of incompetence, even fraud, without the recourse that the same people would have had they placed money with a stockbroker in London, or any broker in the United States.

The commodity brokers, for their part, are worried about the possibility of private clients themselves defaulting on their contracts. This is a real possibility because of the way the deposit system works. The reason for having a deposit system is that the basic unit in which commodity contracts are written is a much larger trading unit than is typical in shares or bonds. For a comparatively small deposit the speculator risks an enormous loss, which he may not be able to stand. If he cannot, the broker has to pay. The risks on the LME, with its lack of a formal system of deposits or margins, are even greater than on the 'soft' markets.

As long as the commodity markets want to discourage the personal speculator, they can argue that a mixture of trust and small deposits is sufficient protection. But for the markets to grow, they may find they need more private money, and if private clients are to come in in large numbers, they (and the brokers) will need more protection. At the end of 1984 the commodity brokers were setting up the Association of Futures Brokers and Dealers to give private investors just this protection. Part of the problem is that London has few institutions which are prepared to take positions in markets as do the New York investment banks or the Japanese securities houses. The merchant banks have not got the funds, and the commercial banks would not dream of carrying out such an activity. That leaves the discount houses, which do trade in securities, but only in gilt-edged and in money market instruments, and the jobbers who only trade in gilts and shares. The only obvious professional speculator in these new financial futures markets would be the discount houses and they would hardly have the resources to do the job on a substantial scale.

There are other possibilities, like commodity funds (unit trusts dealing in commodities rather than shares), and possibly the pension funds and insurance companies. But curiously, in a nation of gamblers, the futures markets have never proved a preferred method of speculation, even if a lively market session sounds like the bookies' ring at a racecourse. A commodity trader will quote you a price on anything, but the official stance of the markets is to avoid any whiff of the gambling den.

NINE

The Bank of England

The paradoxical Old Lady

The Bank of England is the link between the City and the government. There is an inherent contradiction in its situation: it is the government's arm in the City, and the City's representative in the government – the gamekeeper and the poacher, the foreman and the shop steward. Understanding this paradox is crucial to understanding how the Bank works.

It began life as a private bank, backed by a group of City merchants and wealthy landowners, but with the special distinction that it was set up to raise money for the government. The first loan, of £1.2 million, was to finance William III's wars against France. Gradually the Bank accepted responsibility for the smooth working of the country's financial system and of the City's banking community. In 1946 its changed position was finally recognised when it was nationalised. Since then, it has continued to become more the servant of the government, less a part of the City.

The Bank's links with the City are emphasised by its location. The 'Old Lady of Threadneedle Street' stands right at the centre of the Square Mile, at the City's main crossroads. Cornhill, Lombard Street, Poultry and Threadneedle Street, all lined with clearing banks, merchant banks, discount houses and foreign banks, radiate from it. Outside, the Bank's tall, windowless walls, built by Sir John Soane in 1823–5, set in front of a 1930s Lutyens temple, give it the look of an elegant fortress. Inside, mosaic-floored corridors run round a square of laboriously cultivated grass. The doors are guarded by pink-coated 'gatekeepers' while fleets of messengers conduct visitors through the Bank's labyrinth of passages.

The Bank's contact with Whitehall is at many levels, mainly

with the Treasury, but also regularly with other government departments. It is from the Treasury, as the Bank of England Act of 1946 made clear, that the Bank's powers ultimately derive. The Treasury owns the Bank's shares and has formal authority over it. In any dispute between the Bank and the Treasury, the Chancellor of the Exchequer has the last word. Or as Montagu Norman, the Bank's best-known Governor, put it back in 1926: 'I look upon the Bank as having the unique right to offer advice and to press such advice even to the point of "nagging"; but always of course subject to the supreme authority of the government.'* This is important, for the Bank is often blamed for implementing government decisions. While the Bank must be held responsible for the technical expertise with which it performs any operation, the broad outlines of its public policy are determined by the Chancellor of the Exchequer.

The Bank carries out an enormous range of functions. First of all it is a bank. It is the government's banker, holding the accounts of the government departments. More important, it manages the government's finances, handling the note issue and raising government loans. And it gives the government advice on economic and monetary policy, which it also helps to put into force. It is the bankers' bank, holding accounts for the clearing banks, the discount houses and the accepting houses.

Next, it operates on behalf of the government in three financial markets. It intervenes in the foreign exchange market; and it operates in the bill market and gilt-edged market.

Finally, it controls the level of credit and it takes responsibility for the good order of the City. Most other central banks perform this under a legal banking code. Until 1979 the Bank of England was unique in that it did so largely under a set of voluntary agreements. Even now, though the 1979 Banking Act gives it formal powers, it still relies on its traditional authority to get its way.

Some of the roles clash or overlap with others. Thus the Bank's responsibility for raising funds for the government may

---

*Answer to Question 14,597, Minutes of Evidence, Royal Commission on Indian Currency and Finance, 1926.

make it difficult for the Bank also to enforce the monetary policy which the government wants to pursue. In controlling the banks, it may find it difficult to perform another function: that of channelling their views back to Whitehall. And in maintaining good order in the City, it may find it difficult to promote competition energetically among City institutions.

How the Bank is run

The Bank is not a branch of the Civil Service. It is a nationalised industry but with á number of special peculiarities. While the boards of other nationalised industries are appointed by a minister, that of the Bank, called the Court, is technically appointed by the Crown. In reality, directors are chosen by the Prime Minister with the advice of the Chancellor of the Exchequer. While in other nationalised industries directors' salaries are laid down by the minister, the directors of the Bank have the duty of deciding how much should be paid to the Bank's six full-time or 'executive' directors (including the Governor and the Deputy Governor). In 1983-4, the annual salary of the Governor, Robin Leigh-Pemberton, came to nearly £82,000 excluding pension contributions. Four of the part-time directors sit, together with the Governor, Deputy Governor and one of the full-time directors, on the Committee of Treasury which meets before the Court and helps to prepare the ground for it.

The post of Governor is one of the few that is directly in the hands of the Prime Minister, though it is taken with the advice of the Chancellor and must be reasonably acceptable to the City. Traditionally it has been a top merchant banker or occasionally a career Bank of England official. Thus Lord Cromer came from Barings, Lord Richardson from Schroders, while Lord O'Brien came up through the Bank. When Robin Leigh-Pemberton was appointed in July 1983, Margaret Thatcher broke with tradition by appointing the chairman of a clearing bank, NatWest. Depending on how you look at it, this was either a sensible and overdue recognition of the importance of the clearing banks *vis-à-vis* the merchant banks . . . or, as the *Financial Times* suggested, a political decision to appoint a Tory supporter with relatively little experience in international banking.

The Court is made up of the Governor, the Deputy Governor and sixteen directors. It meets once a week, on Thursday mornings. Today it is still made up predominantly of bankers, but industrialists and the odd trade unionist also serve on it. Only four of the directors, apart from the Governor and his deputy, work full-time. These six are the men who really run the Bank. The part-time directors are vaguely justified as 'contributing outside expertise'. They do attend Court meetings and sit on internal committees of the Bank, but they cannot take policy decisions, as these are made by the Governor with or without consultation with the Chancellor of the Exchequer. If the part-time directors are in the confidence of the full-time directors, they have to perform strenuous mental gymnastics to separate their private interests from their official duties. If they are not in the confidence of the full-time directors, they cannot comment effectively on the work of the Bank. In fact they are generally left in the dark. When Cecil King resigned his part-time directorship in May 1968, he described the part-time directors as 'dignified old gentlemen who turn up every Thursday and do whatever they are asked'.* The small body of full-time advisers employed by the Bank have far more influence. So do the heads of the more important departments of the Bank. Unlike the part-time directors, they have full access to the Bank's confidential information and in practice play a large part in formulating the Bank's policy.

The Bank is divided into five main departments. A glance at what they do gives some idea of the wide range of work the Bank carries out. Easily the most important is the policy and markets department, which has two of the four executive directors. This is the department that helps to frame and carry out the government's monetary policy. Within it is the economics division, which collects information and views on the British economy, information which forms the basis of policy advice to the Governor and to Whitehall. The department also takes in

*Interview with Nicholas Tomalin, *Sunday Times*, 12 May 1968.

the division responsible for the selling of government stock and controlling the money markets, the division that looks after the Bank's foreign exchange operations, and two that collect data on other countries and deal with international bodies like the IMF. The policy and markets department also handles financial statistics and the Bank's relations with the press.

A second department handles what are called the Bank's operations: its banking business (including business through its branches), its job as a registrar (it keeps a register of holders of all quoted government securities, of stocks of nationalised industries, and of some Commonwealth government and local authority securities), and the printing works in Loughton in Essex, which employs 1,500 of the Bank's 5,900 full-time staff printing all the new notes and destroying old ones. The head of the banking department, David Somerset, is the person whose signature appears on our banknotes.

There are two departments handling rather newer, but very important aspects of the Bank's work. One oversees industrial and financial supervision – everything from collecting an ailing company's bankers together to organise a rescue package, to advising the government on legislation for insider trading. The other supervises some 600 banks and licensed deposit-takers under the 1979 Banking Act.

Finally, there is the department that runs the Bank as a business, looking after its staffing, its business systems, its premises and its catering. There are, incidentally, five different grades of canteen in the Bank's two main City offices. Food for lunch guests in its small private dining rooms is rather ordinary, in contrast to dinner in the Governor's Bank flat in New Change, which is one of the best meals to be had in the City.

The Bank as a bank

The Bank of England is banker to three types of customer. It has a few private accounts, some commercial accounts left over from before nationalisation and some acquired since. Others are held by the Bank's own staff, who enjoy splendid cheque books but no overdrafts. Private accounts are kept on mainly because the Bank wants to give its staff experience in the techniques of commercial banking. Infinitely more important are the Bank's institutional customers, the government and the banks.

It was as the government's banker that the Bank of England began life. As the government's banker, the Bank handles the main accounts of all government departments. It considers this one of the essential roles of a central bank. However, handling these accounts is, from the Bank's point of view, neither a particularly profitable business nor an expanding one. The Bank has relatively few branches outside London and does not attempt to do the business of all government departments. It principally operates the government's central accounts.

It was out of this role as the government's banker that the Bank's task of advising the government on monetary policy originally arose. The Bank still tends to see this in terms of a banker advising a client. If it is the Treasury which usually decides the policy which the Bank implements, the Bank still has views of its own, as the Governor's speeches often reveal. Indeed, there are grounds for arguing that the Bank does not press its views upon the government often enough. Obviously the elected government should not be subject to the dictates of the central bank. But central banks invariably tend to see themselves as custodians of the purchasing power of their currency and as restraints on a spendthrift government. It is not hard to think of occasions since the war when the Bank of England could have acted as a counterweight to an electioneering government pursuing inflationary policies.

Above all, besides handling the government's accounts, the Bank also balances the government's books by borrowing for it. Spending which the government cannot cover from tax revenue has to be met by borrowing: and it is the Bank which handles the national debt.

A small part of the debt is covered by the note issue, though today this is determined not by the government's needs but by public demand. The British public dislikes handling used notes, and the 1,600 million new notes which the Bank issues each year is a high figure by international standards. Besides printing the notes, the Bank distributes them through its branches to the commercial banks, withdraws and destroys old ones and looks after about 60,000 claims a year to have mutilated notes replaced.

The vast bulk of the National Debt is held by the banks or by the public in Treasury bills or gilt-edged stock. Managing it is a formidable task. For Britain's National Debt is bigger, compared with national income, than that of any other major industrial country: in March 1982 British government stock stood at £81,534 million nominal value. Of this, £2,567 million was in index-linked securities and £2,256 million in the form of irredeemable stock, with the 3.5 per cent War Loan (launched originally at 5 per cent amidst a welter of jingoism in 1917) still the largest single issue at £1,909 million nominal value. Since it is nowadays unacceptable to issue irredeemable debt, the Bank has the never-ending task of paying off dated stock as it falls due – by issuing more debt, which in turn will have to be paid off over periods up to forty years ahead. If it were just a question of rolling over existing stock, it would be a massive task. But in most years the Bank has also to get rid of a staggering amount of new debt. The central government's own borrowing needs are usually increased by the need to raise money to finance investment by local authorities and nationalised industries. Not surprisingly, the Bank is constantly haunted by the fear that some day, perhaps because of a sudden collapse of confidence in the gilt-edged market, the public will refuse to hold long-term government debt. In such an eventuality it would still be able to raise money for the government by issuing Treasury bills. In the last resort the Bank could simply give the government a loan to enable it to pay its bills.

The Bank of England holds the accounts of some hundred foreign central banks, something that came in handy when the United States was negotiating the release of the Iranian hostages at the end of 1980. The Bank ran the crucial trust account set up by the Central Bank of Iran to cover claims against Iran – a demonstration that both a revolutionary and a capitalist country felt they could trust the Bank of England. The Bank also holds accounts for all the banks in London carrying out sterling business. They are required to place an amount equivalent to 0.5 per cent of their sterling deposits in a non-interest-bearing account with the Bank. The deposits – the bank's reserve requirements – give the Bank its income; it can lend this money out at interest and make a large profit on it. This 0.5 per cent is a minimum for all banks. The clearing banks in practice keep more funds on deposit with the Bank. This is because after the cheque clearing, their residual balances are settled by adjusting their accounts at the Bank and they are not allowed overdrafts.

Of the other banks' accounts, the balances tend to alter only in line with changes in their deposits. But the discount houses use their accounts the whole time, and they alone among the Bank's customers are allowed overdrafts. This is a part of their special privileges. As explained below, on days when the discount houses are short of funds, they can borrow from the Bank.

The Bank and the markets

The Bank of England is the government's arm in three key financial markets: the bill market, the gilt-edged market and the foreign exchange market. In the foreign exchange market the Bank's role is relatively straightforward; to manipulate the exchange rate of the pound by buying or selling sterling on the foreign exchange market.

In the bill and gilt-edged markets – the two markets in government debt – the Bank's role is more complicated. Its operations in these markets are the main way in which the government pursues its monetary policy – and tries to control the amount of money in the country. This means more than controlling the level of notes and coin in circulation. Definitions vary, but 'money supply' is usually taken to mean both notes and coin – and bank deposits, on the grounds that most people use a bank account just as if it were cash in their pocket. When people talk about broad definitions of money or narrow ones, they are referring to different ways of measuring bank deposits: narrow definitions would just mean counting current accounts, broader ones various types of interest-bearing account too. Britain's main narrow definition is called M1, and the main broad one, sterling M0. One of the main determinants of the level of bank deposits is the amount banks lend, because a loan from one bank usually ends up as a deposit with another. So if the Bank wants to control bank deposits it has to control the level of bank lending.

The other main determinant of the money supply is the way in which the government borrows. If the government borrows by printing banknotes, it is obviously increasing the money supply. If, however, it borrows by issuing long-term debt to the general public, then it is not. So the essence of market operations is to reduce the money supply by selling debt to the public (taking in money in exchange); or to increase it by buying debt from the public (paying for it with money). But by buying or selling debt in the market, the government also influences its price and hence the return on it.* As the government is competing with other borrowers, the rate at which it borrows affects all other interest rates.

The bill or discount market is the market in Treasury and commercial bills – three-month debt. What happens in it affects short-term interest rates including rates in the parallel sterling money markets (described in chapter 4) and, indirectly, bank overdraft rates. The Bank influences the bill market in two ways. First it can vary the amount of Treasury bills it issues to the market, through 'tender' every Friday. Second, and more important, it varies the conditions under which it 'helps' the discount market. Usually it helps by the 'back door', buying bills from the houses through the so-called 'special buyer' (Hugh Seccombe, the chairman of Seccombe, Marshall and Campion) set up by Montagu Norman specially for this purpose. But if it wants to push rates up sharply, it forces the houses 'into the Bank'. This means that it helps by lending straight to the houses at a penal rate. This was called 'Bank' rate until October 1972, when its name was changed to Minimum Lending Rate. It still exists but has not been published since August 1981 because the government has wanted to shift the responsibility for fixing interest rates onto the banks.

---

*Since the interest rate on debt is fixed, if its price rises, the return on it falls. Take £100 of government stock offering interest of 5 per cent: if its price drops to £80, the return on it will rise to 6.25 per cent (or £5 per £80).

Since August 1981, the Bank has divided money market rates into four bands, the first for money of up to one week's maturity, the second one week to one month, the third one to two months, and the fourth for money of two to three months' maturity. It aims by buying and selling bills to influence the relationship between interest rates in each band within a fairly narrow spread (see p.235). It agrees the spread with the Chancellor and his advisers in the Treasury, but it does not publish what the spread is, or when the range of rates is changed. That is left for the market to deduce from the Bank's actions. The aim is for the markets to determine rates – but at the level the autorities want them. So the money markets and the Bank are each day involved in an elaborate guessing game. The Bank calls it creating uncertainty; the market sometimes believes that it simply creates confusion.

What happens in the gilt-edged market influences long-term interest rates, such as the rate on industrial debentures. In 1985 the government still controls the supply of stock to the market through a private broker, the stockbroker Mullens and Co. Its senior partner, Nigel Althaus, is known as the government broker. The amount the government broker receives for his services is secret. Officially the fee is very small, and much of the business is done for no commission at all. But a number of government funds are tied to Mullens: if they want to buy, sell or switch holdings, they have to deal through Mullens. So Mullens is in fact rewarded by being given profitable government business that might otherwise have been given to other brokers. Just why the government broker should have to work at Mullens is one of those City mysteries. But he does. When, in 1982, the then government broker, Lord Cromwell, died after a riding accident and Mullens was unable to provide a suitable candidate, Nigel Althaus was chosen from rival brokers, Pember and Boyle. To take the job, he had to switch firms. In 1986, when the reform of the Stock Exchange trading system takes place, this peculiar system will end, and Althaus will transfer his office to the Bank itself.

When a new government stock is issued, it is promptly announced to be fully subscribed. In fact, any stock not taken up by the public on the market is immediately bought back by the issue department of the Bank. The issue then becomes a 'tap' stock. This means that it is sold off by the broker over subsequent weeks as there is a demand for it. The Bank usually tries to have at least two 'tap' stocks, one long-dated and one shorter-dated. The price at which the government broker is prepared to sell is generally known in the market, and it influences the whole structure of longer-term rates. Besides selling off new stocks, the government broker also buys in any issue which is approaching maturity so that by the time its redemption date arrives, the bulk should have been bought back. The aim is to smooth the trend of gilt prices.

There are a number of constraints on the Bank in its market operations. Thus in the bill market it also has to act as the lender of last resort: it must either buy bills from the discount houses if they present them – or lend against them. It can, however, make this expensive. The Bank faces more serious handicaps in the gilt market. It wants first to smooth out any violent fluctuations in the price of gilt-edged and thus make it easier for the Bank to float new issues and redeem existing ones; and secondly, as mentioned, it wants to influence the level of the country's money supply. Until the late 1960s, the first aim was the dominant one. Then came Britain's slow recovery from the 1967 devaluation, a recovery which in the eyes of the visiting International Monetary Fund mission and of some Treasury officials was hindered by the rapid growth of the money supply. The Bank came under attack for being too ready to buy securities in the gilt-edged market to support sagging prices at a time when the public was generally unwilling to hold government debt. Its policy, however necessary to cope with rising government borrowing, was behind expansion in the money supply, and in 1971 the Bank announced that in future it would not necessarily support the longer-term gilt market.

In the early 1970s, this clash of interests temporarily faded into the background with the return of public willingness to hold government debt. But it did not disappear completely. As the Governor of the Bank told the Select Committee on Nationalised Industries in 1969 (Question 735), 'We have found recently and I think will continue to find in the future that it is often difficult to reconcile the pedestrian day-to-day desire for an orderly gilt-edged market and the overall policy desire to let us restrain the money supply.' In 1972–3, this problem re-emerged. With a massive government deficit and political pressure to keep interest rates down, the Bank lost control of the money supply.

This experience exacerbated the runaway inflation of 1974–5, and created the conditions for the fringe banking crisis. Then came the international collapse of confidence in sterling in 1976, when Britain had once again to borrow from the IMF. The Labour government had begun in July 1976 to publish formal targets for the growth of money supply. In the wake of the IMF loan, monetary policy received increasing emphasis.

The record of money supply targets in Britain has been mixed: they did to some extent help to keep monetary objectives at the front of the government's mind, but they were frequently missed, arguably because they were set by both Labour and Tory governments at unrealistically low levels. In the view of the Bank, the principal reason for the difficulty it had in meeting monetary targets was the excessive borrowing made by successive governments to finance their budget deficit, and the reluctance of politicians to see interest rates rise high enough to cut back private sector borrowing.

This underlines the problem that the Bank faces in all its market operations: it cannot simultaneously control both the amount of debt it sells and the price at which it sells it; nor both the money supply and the level of interest rates at the same time.

In the foreign exchange market, unlike the other two markets, the Bank operates through its own team of foreign exchange dealers. Technically it is managing the 'Exchange Equalisation Account', in which the country's gold and foreign currency reserves are held. This involves the Bank in buying and selling sterling for foreign currencies (and usually for dollars, the world's key currency), in order to stabilise the sterling exchange rate. For the first quarter century after the end of the Second World War, exchange rates were fixed by international agreement. That meant the task of the central bank was to maintain the international value of the currency

228

within specified limits. In a sense it was a straightforward job – at least its aims were clear. The amount of foreign currency the Bank bought or sold was determined by the need to maintain the exchange rate. Only if sterling were at its 'ceiling' and the government were unwilling to let the Bank hold more foreign currency, or if it were at its 'floor' and the authorities had no more foreign currency to sell and were unable to borrow more from other countries, would the Bank's general priority be overridden. In the first case the government's obvious course would be to allow a revaluation of the currency; in the second, to devalue.

The last grand attempt to fix exchange rates, the Smithsonian Agreement of December 1971, failed after six months. Since then, currencies have floated, though since 1979 all the EEC currencies except sterling have found themselves together in a collective bloc within the European Monetary System which floats against other currencies.

From the point of view of the Treasury, which ultimately determines exchange-rate policy, and the Bank, which has to try to carry it out, floating rates appear to create more freedom. The authorities can decide how far to try to influence the exchange rate by intervening. But this freedom is more apparent than real. The Bank would certainly prefer a stable exchange rate. But it was repeatedly demonstrated in the 1970s that the resources of the world banking system could easily overwhelm even a determined central bank. Central bank reserves were insufficiently large to resist pressure for a devaluation, while the amount of currency needed to be bought to resist a revaluation would have almost equally unhappy effects, by making it impossible for the central bank to meet its domestic monetary targets.*

The need to maintain international confidence in the currency gives the Bank an authority independent of the Treasury or indeed of the government of the day. One lesson of

---

*If a central bank takes in foreign currency as part of its exchange-rate policy, it has to issue domestic currency, or borrow it to pay for the foreign currency it has bought. The effect is similar to its own government trying to borrow more: such borrowing tends to increase the money supply.

the successive sterling crises of the 1960s and 1970s was that they provided a weapon which the Bank could use to get a government to adopt more restrictive policies than it would have chosen on domestic grounds alone.

The Bank's involvement in the financial markets has a profound effect on its attitudes to government policy. It is the fact that it has to sell public debt that makes it so concerned with the level of government spending; the fact that it has to try to keep the gilt market happy that makes it so suspicious of anything – like published monetary targets – that forces it to sell a specific amount of debt at a particular time. And it is the fact that its intervention on the exchange is the first line of defence for sterling that makes it particularly anxious about any government policy that might reduce foreign bankers' confidence in Britain.

On the face of it, the Bank's record in financial markets is poor. It has since the war presided over two formal devaluations of sterling and a period in 1976 when the pound ran into a further serious crisis of confidence. It has lost control of the money supply – or seriously overshot monetary targets – on at least three occasions. And in the market where it has had an apparent success – in selling government stock – it has been bolstered by the fact that government-guaranteed debt inevitably has greater attractions than debt issued by corporations, and that the government does not seem to care what interest rate it pays on its money.

But the Bank is frequently blamed when it is simply carrying out instructions from the government. The cabinet is ultimately responsible for Bank policy. The only legitimate grounds for criticising the Bank is over the quality of advice it gives the cabinet and the technical competence with which it carries out cabinet policy.

On the first there are plenty of grumbles, both in private and (after they have retired) in public from Treasury ministers. On the second, too, there is no shortage of complaints from people involved in City markets. But the Bank's interests are and should be slightly different from those of the Treasury: it has both a longer time horizon and a greater concern with the value of the currency than other measures of economic performance.

230

And its interests are frequently and obviously in conflict with people and organisations involved in City markets. The markets' principal concern must be to make profits, the Bank's to maintain order and to hold down cost to the taxpayer of paying interest on government debt. Yet both activities are liable to reduce City profits.

Perhaps it is only proper that the Bank should be unloved. But central bankers are human and occasionally they can be excused for feeling sore about this.

Monetary control

The Bank of England polices large parts of the City, and in particular the banking community. Long before nationalisation in 1946, the Bank's dominant position and its emergence as lender of last resort had led it gradually to assume responsibility for seeing that the other banks ran their affairs in a safe and stable way.

As the government came to pursue a more active part in managing the economy, so the Bank's job altered. Today it still maintains its role as guardian of good order in the City. But it has also acquired the task of inducing the banks to follow government policy, policy which often conflicts with their commercial interests. Thus the Bank controls bank lending for the government and until 1979 enforced its policy of exchange control.

Not only has the Bank's work changed; the basis of its power has altered. The Bank's responsibility for the City's good order had its origins in the City's long tradition of self-policing. With nationalisation, the Bank's authority acquired a semi-legal basis. In 1979, with the passing of the Banking Act, the Bank finally gained both a formal responsibility to order the banking system, and legislative powers to enable it to do so. Since this development has taken nearly three hundred years, it is hardly surprising that it should not as yet have substantially changed the way in which the Bank's authority is exercised. The Bank still relies, with varying degrees of success, on personal contact to cajole and persuade the banks into doing what it wants. For though anyone taking deposits from the public is required to

231

register with the Bank of England to be duly divided into 'real' banks and what are called 'licensed deposit takers', the sanction that the Bank has – refusing a licence – is really only relevant to fringe institutions. The principal reason why our banking regulations were made formal was to bring under the jurisdiction of the Bank the host of small deposit-takers and near banks that had hitherto been supervised inadequately by the Department of Trade. The Bank bases its decision both on the quality of management and the financial practices of the bank concerned. The Banking Act gives a very large degree of discretion to the Bank in granting licences (though if a bank does not like the Bank's decision, it can appeal to the Chancellor). But it would be unthinkable for the Bank to revoke a licence of one of the clearing banks or acceptance houses.

Until 1979 the Bank also operated exchange control, carried out through the banks in London authorised to deal in foreign exchange. There it had a formal policing task which it was required to carry out by the government. The effect of this was to give the Bank a further lever on City banks. The Bank never liked exchange control, but when that was dismantled it lost one form of authority over the City. It will only gradually become clear to what extent that authority has been replaced by the powers under the Banking Act.

Adjusting the level of bank lending is one part of the mechanism by which the Bank controls the money supply, the other part being its management of the National Debt. In 1971 and again in 1981 the system of credit control was completely overhauled. But in order to understand the present system (and to see where the previous ones went wrong), it is worth going back briefly to the pre-1971 system from which it has evolved.

Before 1971 the clearing banks had to maintain two ratios linking their assets to certain types of debt controlled by the Bank. For every £100 they took over the counter they had to hold £8 either in cash or in their non-interest-bearing accounts with the Bank of England. This 8 per cent ratio was called the cash ratio. The next £20 they had to hold as liquid assets – assets they could turn into cash within a day or so. The three most important of these were money with the discount

232

houses, Treasury bills and eligible bank bills.* This 28 per cent ratio (i.e. £8 plus £20) was called the liquidity ratio. The rest of the bank's deposits (i.e. £72) were in theory available to be lent to customers, but in practice banks held £15 to £20 of them in the form of investments, mostly short-dated gilts. Thus only about £50 to £55 out of each £100 taken in by the banks were in fact re-lent.

Before the Second World War, the cash ratio was the Bank's main instrument of control. But by the 1950s emphasis had shifted to the liquidity ratio. When the Bank wanted to squeeze credit, it reduced the number of Treasury bills on offer and so squeezed the volume of bank lending.

That, at any rate, was what happened in theory, as the famous 1959 report of the Radcliffe Committee on the Working of the Monetary System described it. But Radcliffe was over-optimistic. Not only were the links in the system it described in practice more elastic than the Committee realised, but the only way that the Bank could cut down the supply of Treasury bills, if the demands of government finance were unchanged, was to issue more long-term debt. To issue more long-term debt might be to risk a steep drop in price. And for much of the 1960s, the Bank's fear was that a sudden drop in the price might leave the gilt-edged market too shaken to buy securities, and the Bank unable to service the National Debt. Accordingly, its ability to organise a credit squeeze depended on the government. If the government needed money, it could not organise a squeeze; if the government did not, it could.

There was one other weapon in the Bank's armoury: calling for special deposits from the banks, which required the banks to lend money to the Bank of England rather than to their customers. It did this from time to time. But at the end of the 1960s it found that the only way it could hold down bank lending was simply to tell the banks not to lend more. It imposed ceilings on bank lending.

These worked for a while, but had other damaging effects on City competition. It was to get away from this device that the whole system of credit control was redrawn in 1971 and

*See chapter 4 for a description of these types of assets.

published in a Bank paper called *Competition and Credit Control*. Two years after it had been published, Britain went through the worst explosion in monetary growth it had ever experienced in peacetime, and saw a large number of its smaller banks collapse ... leading to the observation that the paper had ensured neither competition nor credit control.

That is unfair. The post-1971 system was not that different from its predecessor. Under it, the ratio upon which the Bank operated was changed: the 28 per cent liquidity ratio was replaced by a reserve ratio of 12.5 per cent, and it was applied to all banks doing sterling business. The range of assets that a bank could count towards its reserve ratio was a little wider than those that could count towards the liquidity ratio: as well as cash with the Bank, call money with the discount market, Treasury bills and eligible bank bills, they could also count short-term gilts. But the new system should have got rid of most of the disadvantages of the old, provided the authorities were prepared to restrict the supply of Treasury bills and to let interest rates rise to choke off credit demand.

A more flexible attitude to interest rates was certainly intended. The old Bank rate became Minimum Lending Rate, and was fixed by a formula related to Treasury bill rate rather than administrative decision. The idea was to allow the markets, rather than the government, to set interest rates.

Yet the 1970s turned out to be an almost exact rerun of the 1960s: a retreat from the idea of giving market forces their head. By 1973 the Heath government had brought in a ceiling on personal bank deposit rates to try to protect the building societies. The two Labour governments between 1974 and 1979 used a string of devices to curb the growth of bank lending, including a form of tax on any deposits a bank attracted over and above a certain amount, the so-called supplementary special deposit scheme. Provided a bank's deposits were held down, the reserve ratio system ensured that its lending would also be held down. But this too failed, largely because companies were able to increase their borrowing by issuing more bills. Perhaps most significant of all, the idea that Minimum Lending Rate could be fixed by a formula was abandoned.

234

The achievement of the Labour governments, though, was to establish the concept of published monetary targets, even if the incoming Conservative government in 1979 was to garner much of the opprobrium for this particular device. At least monetary policy had a yardstick against which its effects could be measured, even if money supply growth could not be contained within its appointed range.

It was the Conservatives' failure to hit money supply targets that led to yet another redrawing of monetary controls in 1981. This newest system recognises that in practice there is no way the Bank can have real leverage on the banks, and instead assumes that the only way of controlling bank lending is to vary its price.

It has two main new features. First, the reserve ratio has been abandoned and credit is controlled only by cost. The banks have to hold at least 0.5 per cent of their sterling liabilities in the form of a non-interest-bearing account with the Bank. But this is to give the Bank its income – it can lend money out at a profit and accordingly pay for its various operations. It is not a fulcrum upon which the Bank can operate. Second, Minimum Lending Rate is no longer posted (though it has been kept in reserve in case the Bank feels it needs to give an unequivocal interest-rate signal to the market). Instead, the Bank aims to hold very short-term money with maturity of less than one month inside an unpublished band of interest rates. It does this by its intervention policy on the bill market, buying and selling bills to and from the discount market to feed money into the banking system, or to mop up surpluses as they arrive. This is why the market has to guess from the Bank's intervention rate just where the Bank wants short-term interest rates to go.

In abandoning the technique used by other central banks to control the banking system – some form of reserve ratio – is the Bank of England being foolhardy, or just realistic? As in 1971, the authorities are arguing that there is no point in trying to control the volume of money except by price. If the government puts controls on the banking system, the result may be merely to encourage banking business to be carried out by other intermediaries outside the controls, or indeed overseas. This is precisely what has happened in two countries that have had

235

relatively strict reserve requirements on their banks – the United States and Germany.

There are two very different criticisms of the Bank's new system. There is the argument that quantitative controls on bank lending can be, at least temporarily, an effective way of taking some of the load off interest rates as a means of curbing the growth of bank lending. And there is the contrasting view that the present system gives the Bank (and the Treasury) too much freedom in setting rates. People who argue this would prefer a more mechanical system; they usually believe that the Bank should control the one measure of money that it absolutely can control – its own deposits from the banking system – and that by using these, the country's 'monetary base', as the target measure of money supply, it could make sure that its monetary objectives were met. To keep this base growing at a steady rate might mean large swings in short-term interest rates as banks adjusted their total deposits to a certain specified ratio of the deposits with the central bank. But advocates of monetary base control believe this would be beneficial, for it would encourage both borrowers and lenders to lengthen the maturity of their loans and deposits.

The one thing that critics of the Bank and its supporters have in common is that all are agreed that there is not much that a central bank can do about long-term interest rates. That is a function of present inflation and expectations about its long-term trend.

Policing the City

The Bank's control over the banking community goes beyond determining the level of interest rates and the growth of the money supply. It has a general responsibility for the good order of the banking system. This is exercised through constant contact with the banking community at many levels. This contact allows the Bank both to tell the banks what it wants them to do, and to discover what the banks are thinking and what is going on elsewhere in the financial community.

All banks and licensed deposit-takers have to report to the Bank. This is a requirement under the 1979 Banking Act.

236

Before that, the Bank reporting system was less formal, with core City institutions like the clearing banks or acceptance houses reporting frequently, but small out-of-town banks reporting only once a year, and to the Department of Trade rather than to the Bank. The Bank relied partly on a variety of different legal powers, of which the most important was exchange control, to control City institutions, and partly on the intangible authority it derived from its role as lender of last resort to the banking system. The effect was that the further you got away from the money markets, the more diffuse its powers became.

The Bank was able, when a discount house got itself into trouble, to arrange for a more successful competitor to take it over. It was able to see that accepting houses were properly run; or if it saw trouble coming, to arrange for new management to be put in place. It had a practical way of making sure that foreign banks setting up branches in London knew the ropes: it would insist that an experienced (and recently retired) clearing banker was taken on before it would give permission for the branch to open its doors. Yet it had no control at all over the so-called section 123 banks, that is, banks licensed under section 123 of the 1948 Companies Act. These were licensed to take sterling deposits, but not authorised to trade in foreign exchange, which would have brought them under the Bank's wing.

The result was disaster. Between December 1973, when London and County Securities collapsed, and September 1974, no less than twenty-six secondary banks were rescued by the 'lifeboat'. This was the Bank of England's rescue scheme where the clearing banks borrowed money and then lent it on to the fringe banks. It was still in action in 1984, with one final passenger, First National Finance Corporation.

With hindsight, it is clear that the core of the problem was that a combination of over-enthusiasm and dishonesty meant the normal rules of banking were not applied by the newcomers. The Bank had no authority to look at the accounts of banks that did not report to it, so it did not know what was going on.

Since then, a formal method of control has been superimposed on the old, informal one. Under the 1979

237

Banking Act all institutions wanting to carry out deposit-taking business in Britain are required to register with the Bank. These institutions are then divided into two groups: full banks which roughly approximate to the old 'authorised' bank status, and licensed deposit-takers which roughly approximate to the old finance houses and the 123 banks. Only the first group are allowed to use the word 'bank' or 'banking' unless they happen to be using a name registered abroad. The first challenge to this particular aspect of the new rules came from the People's Bank of Bradford, which was deemed not to carry out a sufficiently broad banking business to call itself that. It tried to get the decision reversed by appealing to the Treasury. It failed, and is now the People's Trust.

The first failure, or near failure, under the new system came in 1984 when the Bank itself was forced to take over the banking side of bullion dealers Johnson Matthey to save it from collapse. The Bank's supervision department had failed to pick up the weakness of the bank's loan portfolio, and even to warn the Bank of the scale of its problems when it took it over. The government and the Bank set up an inquiry to try to determine what went wrong.

Even under the new system, the Bank still prefers to try to use informal channels where possible to enforce its wishes. Though all banks and deposit-takers report their figures to the Bank, the closer the institution is to the Bank in terms of its banking and money market operations, the more the Bank will know about its activities.

Bankers still tend to talk to the Bank's supervision division to sound out its view about less routine business. The special buyer in the discount market and the government broker in the gilt-edged also keep the discount houses, banks and stock market in touch with the Bank's views.

Interestingly, though, banks increasingly feel that they get a less clear view than they used to of the Bank's intentions both in the money market and the gilt market. Even before the change in monetary control in 1981, which was intended to keep the City guessing about the authorities' intentions over interest rates, the banks found that gilt market tactics were, as they would put it, 'played very close to the chest'.

238

The heads of the clearing banks have a formal meeting with the Governor twice a year. These meetings the clearing banks find less useful, partly because they have become steadily less consultative and more platforms for the Governor to lecture the banks, and partly because the increase in competition among the banks puts a restraint on joint discussions.

The Bank likes and encourages the formation of City groups like the Committee of London Clearing Bankers. It means that there is one forum where it can put its views, one spokesman to deal with and fewer letters to write. The merchant banks talk to the Bank formally through the Accepting Houses Committee, whose chairman has access to the Governor whenever he wants. The American banks' organisation, the American Bankers in London Association, was set up at the behest of the Bank of England to give the Bank a body to talk to. But the heads of all London banks can – and do – easily call on the Governor to discuss any major policy issue. 'The great thing about the Governor,' in the words of one of the older and more establishment merchant bankers, 'is that he is infinitely available.'

Why do the banks go to see the Bank? Usually it is either to find out whether what the bank wants to do is acceptable to the Bank, or to tell the Bank of some new move. A bank doing a large operation in foreign exchange or corporate finance for a client might ring the Bank and ask, without mentioning names, what the Bank's reaction to such an operation would be. A bank moving its headquarters would tell the Bank in advance, largely as a matter of courtesy. And a foreign bank setting up a branch in London would come to the Bank for its licence under the Banking Act.

When an established bank wants to embark on an entirely new venture, moving into a new line of business or linking with another bank, communication is more delicate. A clearing or top merchant bank might feel strong enough to chance telling the Bank at the last moment, but only if it judged that the Bank would not regard this as too serious an act of defiance. An American bank, conscious – and from time to time reminded by the Bank – of its dependence on the Bank's goodwill for its place in the City, would be more cautious.

239

If the banks do not ask the Bank what they can do in advance, the Bank sooner or later tells them. This is how it has in the past controlled the banks' lending. It keeps a particularly tight hand on mergers and takeovers. It dropped a clear hint to the discount house Gerrard and Reid that it would like to see it take over the failing business of the National Discount Company; and it gave a firm warning to Sir Kenneth Keith, when head of the merchant bankers Hill Samuel, that it would not like to see him link up with a clearing bank. And it is widely believed to have tried to orchestrate the abortive takeover of the Royal Bank of Scotland Group by the London overseas bank Standard Chartered, with embarrassing consequences, as we shall see.

The Bank's power is exercised in what is arguably a highly arbitrary way. The City is made aware of its general prejudices, and in general understands that a nod from the Bank is as good as an order. If a bank is recalcitrant, the Bank's policy is first to talk to it. But the Bank's hints and suggestions are in the last resort backed by a combination of the Banking Act and commercial sanctions. Thus while the discount houses are dependent on the Bank for their livelihood, the banks are also vulnerable to commercial pressure. Those that issue commercial bills could find that the Bank removed their name from its list of banks whose paper is eligible for rediscount. Ultimately it now has the power to withdraw a banking licence. But the Bank would not be free to impose legal sanctions without being prepared to justify such an action. The advantage of its old form of control, resting as it did as much on the Bank's position as banker to the other banks as on legal powers, was that the Bank's decisions would not in general be challenged and need not be justified.

The system has considerable advantages. At its best it gives the Bank a sensitive means of guiding the City's development: of encouraging new lines of business, of seeing that weak institutions are given sound management, of enabling the City to get on with the business of making money untrammelled by unnecessary formal regulations.

But there are also dangers. For a start, the informality of communications results in misunderstandings. The most remarkable examples of this have been over the Bank's policy on clearing-bank mergers. After the report of the Colwyn Committee in 1918 discouraged clearing-bank mergers, an informal agreement was reached that no more would occur without the agreement of the Treasury. Not until 1968 did any merger among the Big Five take place. This followed a hint dropped in the 1967 Prices and Incomes Board report on bank charges, indicating that the authorities would look favourably on further mergers. Immediately there was a scramble to merge, a scramble which was ultimately stopped by the Monopolies Commission. Not only had the Bank and the clearing banks managed to misunderstand each other. The informality of the Bank's controls on mergers allowed it to avoid thinking through what its real policy should be. As a result, it suffered the indignity of seeing such policy as it had reversed by the Monopolies Commission.

A somewhat similar confusion existed over the Bank's 'rules' on links between the accepting houses and the clearing or foreign banks. What these rules were was never made clear until the Bank announced, in autumn 1972, that they were being changed. With the announcement, it was apparent that the rules had not always been observed – or even understood – in the City. UK clearing banks, the Bank proclaimed, would henceforth be allowed (in cases where the Bank approved) to take more than a 25 per cent stake in accepting houses. EEC banks, though not other foreign banks, would be allowed to buy more than 15 per cent of a merchant or overseas bank. Yet already Midland Bank had a 35 per cent stake in Montagu Trust (it eventually took full control) and First National City Bank owned 40 per cent of National and Grindlays.

But perhaps the best example of the confusion which the informality of the Bank's control can cause – in the Bank as much as in the financial community – came in 1981 when Standard Chartered Bank tried to take over the Royal Bank of Scotland Group. It duly put in its bid, with the blessing of the Bank. The Hongkong and Shanghai Banking Corporation decided to put in a rival bid for half as much money again. It told the Bank, the Bank said don't, and it ploughed on regardless.

The Governor was furious, not just with Hongkong Bank,

but with Hambros, who organised its bid. Yet there was nothing the Bank could do, as it had no formal powers to stop the bid. Indeed there was a genuine confusion: the Bank pointed to its 1972 guidelines, saying that Hongkong had broken these, while Hongkong argued that these only applied to an accepting house being taken over by a clearing or foreign bank, and not to a clearing bank being taken over by a bank registered outside the UK. (Hongkong Bank is registered in a British crown colony, not Britain itself, though it did move its headquarters to London during the last war.)

Ultimately both bids were stopped by the Monopolies Commission on the ground that it would damage Scottish interests were control of the group to pass out of Scotland. This decision saved the Bank's face. Had the two rival groups been allowed to fight it out, Hongkong Bank – the larger and financially stronger – would probably have won, and the Bank would have been powerless to enforce its wishes. As it was, the Bank was shown to have no effective sanction against a large commercial bank that chose to ignore it. And it was shown that decisions over the ownership of a large British bank rested not with the Bank but with the Monopolies Commission.

If the informal system is unsatisfactory, is it actually damaging? There is some evidence that it may have discouraged innovation: banks have not introduced services because of a fear, real or pretended, that the Bank would not like it. Arguably, the banks delayed entry into a number of new areas for this reason: term loans in the early 1960s, personal loans in the late 1960s, mortgages in the late 1970s, paying interest on current accounts in the early 1980s.

If the Hongkong experience has any lasting value, it may be that banks should not allow the disapproval of the Bank to stop them behaving in what they see to be their customers' and shareholders' best interests.

The question that is impossible to answer until it has had more time to settle down is whether the blend of formal powers under the 1979 Banking Act and the tradition of informal control will together produce a satisfactory method of control. The Johnson Matthey episode suggests controls may need to become more formal still.

Informality has its advantages: the alternative, banks argue, would be the American situation where they have to follow a detailed code, and which US banks came to London to avoid. As far as international business is concerned, those legal regulations have undoubtedly been more inhibiting than the informal mode of conduct of the Bank. The dilemma is a familiar one in the City. An infinite variety of complex situations has to be controlled. Each requires a rapid ruling, and many involve vast amounts of money. The ideal form of regulation is that exercised by a body acting on the basis of the broadest possible, publicly stated guidelines, and one capable of delivering instant and authoritative interpretations of them. If the guidelines are vague, it will be far harder to find loopholes in them. If the interpretations are delivered rapidly, it will be easier to act quickly. If the judgment is authoritative, there will be no danger of finding it rescinded after it has been acted on and large sums have been committed.

Thanks to the Banking Act, the Bank's job of regulation has become more precise. It is also establishing a set of prudential controls on bank liquidity and capital adequacy, and should in theory, at least, have a sophisticated and flexible way of ordering banking business.

But the more explicit its regulations become, the more explicit too will become the conflict between its roles as policeman in the City and as spokesman. In the late 1950s there was a tendency, especially among the clearing banks but also among other parts of the banking community, to regard the Bank as the City's ally against Whitehall. But in the course of the 1960s the clearing banks in particular found that they had to move into new areas of business – hire-purchase, money market activities and merchant banking – in order to expand. The Bank did not wholeheartedly approve. At the same time, the Bank was persuading the banks, and again particularly the clearers, to accept increasing restrictions on their lending. Relations between the Bank and the banks became more distant.

There are many times when the blurring of the Bank's role is extremely useful to it. For example, it was the fact that the Bank was the City's spokesman to government which made its

243

support essential to Lloyd's in its efforts to get the Lloyd's Bill through Parliament. But this in turn gave the Bank a natural authority over Lloyd's which allowed it to step in and appoint Ian Hay Davison in a role of (effectively) the Bank's creation, as chief executive. Then again, in the case of the Stock Exchange's case with the Office of Fair Trading it was the fact that the Bank had been lobbying the government to have the case called off which made it the natural body to oversee the reforms which the Stock Exchange eventually agreed to undertake.

Both the reforms at Lloyd's and the changes at the Stock Exchange take the Bank forward explicitly into new areas of control where its authority has, up to now, only been implicit. In both cases, the Bank's control is much looser than it is in the banking system, where it enjoys the ultimate weapon of controlling credit. But since 1983, the Bank has the formal power of approving lay members to both the Council of Lloyd's and the Council of the Stock Exchange; it has the task of monitoring changes in the way the Stock Exchange works jointly with the Department of Trade; and it effectively has acquired the power of veto over future chief executives of Lloyd's. There remains only one major area of the City where the Bank has no formal involvement: the commodities markets. Not surprisingly, in 1984, these markets were one of the Bank's new preoccupations.

TEN

Where the City goes now

Parasite or paragon?

A large number of people in Britain see the City as a parasitical growth on the economy. It is inhabited by rich, arrogant young men and cigar-smoking tycoons, interested only in making money for themselves. They have no sense of responsibility for the national good, no ideas and no morals. They make vast fortunes from share speculation, property speculation and commodity speculation, activities which are no more than legalised gambling and require neither intelligence nor effort. They loathe the working classes and the welfare state, and they pay the Conservatives millions of pounds to try to keep any other party out of power.

Now to the City, much of this sounds absurd. Many of the criticisms aimed at the City are really criticisms of industrial directors. The two are easily confused in the popular mind. The City itself, its defenders argue, has been reborn as the leading international financial centre despite years of stagnation in the British economy. It not only helps to keep the balance of payments out of the red, it also provides new and well-paid employment, and it offers the rest of the country the best banking system and capital market in the world. If only British industry were as good as the City, we would not have the economic problems we do.

Yet there remains a great deal of truth in the standard left-wing perception of the City. It tends to focus excessively on the City's morality – although it is possible to argue, especially in the light of the fringe bank crisis and of events at Lloyd's, that there are parts of the City where public moral standards have been every bit as bad as the left would paint them. There is also a great deal of truth in the view that the world's major financial centre serves its British clients worse than its overseas customers. Indeed, when we wrote the first edition of this book, in 1971, we regarded this charge as the most severe criticism of the City.

That is no longer the case. There are other weaknesses which seem to us now more disturbing. The City has gone some way towards improving the quality of services which domestic customers – individuals and companies – receive, though the impetus for change has come from the fringe.

The financial services available to personal customers in Britain are probably no worse than in most other industrial countries. Yet in the international financial capital of the world, banks are not open when ordinary people want to use them. Such improvements in personal banking services as have come about – cash dispensers, high-interest deposit accounts – have happened largely because the banks were frightened by the inroads made by the building societies into their personal deposits. Traditional life assurance companies took a long time to accept unit-linked policies. They began to offer them only when alarmed by the success of an outsider called Mark Weinberg. There is still no way in which private customers can readily buy shares. British stockbrokers have no retail offices, so investors are herded instead into buying in unit trusts. In time, no doubt, American stockbrokers will find some way of selling shares directly to British savers, and then British firms will become more interested in personal business.

The improvement in services to industry has gone further. The banks have developed medium-term lending for large companies; the financial futures market allows companies to hedge currency positions in a way they could not do before; the Stock Exchange has developed a cheap and efficient way for small companies to raise money. Here again, though, in every case the impetus has come from outside. It was the US banks which first began to pinch customers from the clearing banks by offering them medium-term loans. It was Chicago which invented financial futures. And it was the success of small British securities firms which were not members of the Stock Exchange which frightened the Exchange into setting up the unlisted securities market (after the entire City establishment had assured the Wilson Committee that there was no important gap in sources of funds for small firms).

246

This reluctance to innovate sits curiously beside the City's passion for a good gamble. The reason is, perhaps, that there are really two Cities. There are the big battalions – the clearing banks, large insurance companies and life funds, and the Bank of England. All are cautious, corporate, conservative. Then there is the heartland – the cottage industries which give the City life its peculiar flavour. These are the merchant banks, the stockbrokers and jobbers, the Lloyd's underwriters and brokers, the commodity firms and – *par excellence* – the money brokers. They have a quality which is hard to pin down, but which anyone who has worked in the City will recognise. It is anti-intellectual, it is clubby; a combination of considerable dealing skills with a casual, even cavalier attitude to risk and a pride in amateurishness. Everything is a gamble, for finance is such a boring pursuit that the only way to make it bearable is to treat it as a game.

The gambling instinct and even the amateurishness are part of the City's strength. They may be qualities alien to the Puritanism of the left and to the plodding caution of British industrial companies, but they have won the City its international business. If it has to put together a billion-dollar eurocurrency loan, or reinsure a string of communications satellites, or mastermind an international merger, the City does it dazzlingly well. In each case, someone else has done the dull solid work of running the day-to-day financial business of the companies involved.

But the clubbiness has become a source of weakness. It has lulled some parts of the City into a sense of isolation – not just from the moral code of the business world at large, but from the forces of change and competition which have been gathering strength in the late 1970s and early 1980s. The prosperity of many City institutions has been based, in effect, on the exploitation of a protected market. And this now seems to us the most serious weakness of the City as it enters the late 1980s.

Behind closed doors

Most people in the City would be appalled at the suggestion that they make their money by exploiting a protected market. In their

247

day-to-day work most of them would feel that they were competing vigorously against each other. But in fact on the domestic side of their business, though not in the international, they operate in a highly cosseted environment. They compete against each other, to be sure. But outsiders are effectively kept out.

In some cases the protection has its roots in the essential structure of a particular financial service. Thus the principal reason why the big four clearing banks are the same banks, allowing for a couple of mergers, as ran the banking system in the 1930s, is that the size of their branch networks makes it virtually impossible for an outsider to break into retail banking. It is no coincidence that retail banking offers such wide margins: branch banking is much more profitable than corporate banking, where other banks, in particular the Americans, can compete. The clearing banks have reinforced the protection of high entry costs by using their monopoly over cheque clearing to exclude foreign banks and building societies.

The principal innovations in personal banking have tended to come not from the big four, but from the smaller banks like Bank of Scotland, from merchant banks, or unit trust groups, or from building societies. It is no coincidence that the building societies offer a much more imaginative range of savings packages than the banks. Competition is keener because there are many more large building societies than there are large banks. The clearing banks' grip on their market is a wasting one.

In other cases the protection is deliberately fostered by the Bank of England. Thus entry to foreign exchange and currency deposit broking is restricted. Discount houses cannot be taken over without the approval of the Bank. The role of government broker is automatically fulfilled by one firm of stockbrokers, Mullens, which has a complete monopoly over this business until the changes planned for 1986. Bids for new issues of government stock at the 'tap' have to be made through two jobbing firms. And the Bank firmly stops large industrial companies from issuing certificates of deposit in their own names. That privilege is reserved to licensed deposit-takers – all financial companies.

Some of these restrictions are understandable. The Bank of England's restraints on outsiders are intended to confine the market to those whom the Bank can trust – or 'manage'. For instance, until the Bank stepped in to control the participants in the foreign exchange market in the 1930s, it was notoriously full of sharks. But understandable is not the same as justifiable. Blanket restrictions on competitiveness are easier for a bureaucracy to operate than a set of flexible rules which would allow new entrants of good quality but keep out the dishonest or incompetent. And it is easier for a central bank to extract compliant behaviour from a small group of firms which owe part of their livelihood to its patronage than from a large market over whose members it may have less influence.

In some cases the protection has been maintained by a trade association without the need for explicit Bank support. The Stock Exchange's monopoly of British company and government stock trading is one good example. Anyone is allowed to trade securities, but the Stock Exchange has managed to control virtually all the business in UK equities and gilts. This is largely because of the natural advantages of size, but also partly because the market is cosseted by the authorities: the ability of the jobbers to trade in equities without paying stamp duty gives them a unique advantage which helps to keep foreign traders out.

The tax regime within which the City operates is remarkably benign: in a host of different ways, the British tax system is designed to underwrite the existing financial institutions. For example, special concessions to Lloyd's insurance market enable individuals to build up assets deferring part of their tax liability. People can build up savings through pension contributions on far better terms than they could if they invested themselves.

The protection with which the City is surrounded is now beginning to break down. It is being undermined from three directions – by changes in technology; by the breaking down of barriers between different types of financial institution; and by a change in government policy towards monopolies.

Technological innovations are beginning to cut the entry costs to types of financial business which have up to now needed branch networks. A merchant bank wanting to attract personal deposits no longer has to gather these through branches: it can offer an interest-bearing current account, sell the service through newspaper advertisements and operate it with a single computer centre with which customers deal by post. Building societies are learning this trick too, relying heavily on advertising their savings packages, rather than extending their branch networks, as a means of attracting new business. The Nottingham is pioneering a system where customers can carry out all their financial transactions via the television-based Prestel system. As financial transactions become more automated, and shared cash dispenser networks are established, the clearing banks will gradually lose the hold they still have over personal banking and, by the same token, the large building societies will suffer too.

Technology will also help to break down barriers between different types of financial institution. In the United States, the money market funds run by the big securities houses like Merrill Lynch have attracted deposits away from the banks. Here we have a life assurance group, Allied Hambro, offering a banking and financial advice service. It is able to do this because computers can handle the paperwork far more cheaply than would have been possible a few years ago.

The impact of technology is still in its infancy. More important so far has been the breakdown of barriers between different types of financial institution which happens when those which already have big selling networks look around for other ways to use their outlets. There have been three main examples. First, the clearing banks have been looking for other uses for their branch networks, and have begun to offer unit trusts and insurance broking side by side with their more traditional services such as acting as trustees or drawing up wills. Second, the direct-sales life assurance companies have been looking for ways to use their door-to-door (or telephone) sales staff to sell products other than life assurance. Third, the main unit trust groups – which sell through a computer-based mailing list – are trying to sell their customers other items, such as banking and insurance.

This move towards financial supermarkets would

undoubtedly have taken place earlier had it not been for the secondary banking crash. Many new and rapidly growing financial institutions were caught up in the crash, which meant that many of the innovators did not survive. Those new companies which were boldest in their efforts to cross the barriers which divided financial institutions in the early 1970s were the ones which went most frequently to the wall.

Because the failure of the fringe banks has made both the authorities and the mainstream financial institutions nervous of dramatic rearrangements in the City, it is hard to be sure how far the move towards the development of financial supermarkets will go. But one change is a virtual certainty. Until the early 1980s, it has been mainly the banks, the unit trusts and the life assurance companies which have been invading each other's territory. The item most conspicuously missing on their shelves has been the equity share. There is no easy way (except through a bank which rings up a stockbroker who rings up a jobber) for the ordinary person to buy shares in the High Street.

This will undoubtedly change as the rules restricting competition with stockbrokers and jobbers are changed. We are probably not far from the day when banks, and even insurance companies, own stockbrokers and sell equities directly to the public. The most dramatic collapse of a barrier to competition in the City has come about with the changes extracted from the Stock Exchange by the government in return for stopping the court case brought by the Office of Fair Trading against the Exchange's rule book. This collapse has occurred not because of technology or new sales outlets, but because of pressure from foreign competition. And it is to the very different atmosphere of the City's international activities that the next section turns.

The global market

In most areas of international business, London is competing for activities which could, in theory at least, be located almost anywhere in the world. On the world's financial markets, there is always room for a new competitor. Chicago, which has long dominated US commodity trade, was unknown as an international centre until it started its markets in financial futures. Now what happens on the Chicago currency futures market has an important influence on what happens on the world foreign exchanges.

Increasingly, financial markets operate round the clock. In some – such as foreign exchange – there is a true twenty-four-hour market. In others, like US domestic securities, there is one big market on Wall Street, while other centres merely dabble.

Most of the institutions involved in international financial markets have world-wide operations – a headquarters in New York, perhaps with branches in Frankfurt, Tokyo, Brussels, perhaps Singapore, and London. Within limits, they can shift business from one centre to another. Naturally, business tends to be concentrated near the customer: thus Tokyo dominates trading in Japanese securities.

The City's geographical location has become an important advantage: it is close enough to Hong Kong and Singapore to open trading just before those Asian markets close – and yet an hour closer to New York than any rival European centre. The English language is an unquestionable advantage, as is the tradition of dealing, based on London's long history as a commercial and trading centre. Then there is the fact that it is an easier place to live (particularly for Americans and Japanese) than Continental centres such as Brussels or Frankfurt. Europe probably has room for only one major international financial centre, and London has been lucky enough to get there first.

London still has the most important single concentration of international financial markets in the world. To keep its edge will take more than luck and the English language. World financial markets are changing with extraordinary speed. London's main rivals, New York and Tokyo, are also each passing through a transformation – and have the advantage of a much larger domestic pool of savings and national economy to service. London has to find a way of turning its disadvantage – the dwindling relative size of the British economy – into an advantage by being more internationally-minded than its rivals. If at the same time it can continue to improve the service it offers to its British customers, then in the long run the whole economy will gain.

252

Index

Index

255

257

259

For Product Safety Concerns and Information please contact our EU
representative GPSR@taylorandfrancis.com Taylor & Francis Verlag GmbH,
Kaufingerstraße 24, 80331 München, Germany

Printed and bound by CPI Group (UK) Ltd, Croydon, CR0 4YY
01/05/2025
01858346-0001